A HISTORY OF
POCKLINGTON SCHOOL

The School about 1930

A HISTORY OF POCKLINGTON SCHOOL

EAST YORKSHIRE

1514–1980

By
P. C. SANDS, M.A. and C. M. HAWORTH, M.A.
1514–1950

AND
J. H. EGGLESHAW, M.A.
1950–1980

Highgate Publications (Beverley) Ltd
1988

iv

ISBN 0 948929 10 3

Published by Highgate Publications (Beverley) Ltd.
24 Wylies Road, Beverley, HU17 7AP
Telephone (0482) 866826

Printed and Typeset in 10 on 11pt Plantin by
B.A. Press, 2-4 Newbegin, Lairgate, Beverley, HU17 8EG
Telephone (0482) 882232

CONTENTS

ILLUSTRATIONS

PREFACE TO THE SECOND EDITION (1988)

When the Governors resolved that a second edition of this history be published, to include all developments up to the retirement of G. L. Willatt in 1980, they also decided that it would be appropriate as well as convenient to reprint the Sands-Haworth text of 1950 unaltered. The new section, written by J. H. Eggleshaw, second master 1939-1976, begins on page 157 with a preface of its own.

viii

PREFACE TO THE FIRST EDITION (1950)

This book is offered to the British public in general and to the boys, old boys, masters and friends of Pocklington School in particular. These will naturally welcome it with curiosity, and also, we hope, read it with industry and, possibly, pleasure. To the general public its appeal may lie in this fact, that its tale is about the bequest of a small piece of property, and that the legal sense of the Englishman, his sense of the value of property and the sanctity of a will and testament, is so strongly developed that in spite of all mismanagement and threats to alter its course the purpose of this bequest is still being carried out after more than four centuries, and the property's value is more than intact; for the motto of the law, as that of the bulldog, is, 'What I have, I hold.'

A wider appeal may also arise from this circumstance, that the School is one of a class very much discussed of late; one of a class that has been a keystone in English education for some centuries, governed in the spirit of William of Wykeham's motto, 'Manners makyth man', and of that other motto adopted by Cranleigh, *'Ex cultu robur'* — 'from culture comes strength'. The recent Education Act has sadly reduced the number of schools in this grade.

While we tried to keep the book readable for other people, we hoped not to offend old boys in omitting many names, lists, and minute details which would be tedious to other readers.

We wish to thank those who have helped our researches, especially the Master and the President of St. John's College, Cambridge and Mr. F.P. White and Dr. G.E. Daniel, Fellows of the same, the Editors of St. John's *Eagle Magazine,* and the old boys who have replied to queries at some length, in particular G.F.D. Pearson, whose laborious scrutiny of past records was the basis of our chapter on games and athletics.

Above all, we owe a debt to the late A.F. Leach's essay on 'The Foundation and Re-foundation of Pocklington Grammar School' published in Volume V of the *Transactions of the East Riding Antiquarian Society*, 1897.

While the authors are jointly responsible for the whole book, C.M. Haworth contributed chapters 1 and 3 to 11, P.C. Sands chapters 2 and 12 to 26.

C.M.H.
P.C.S.

CHAPTER 1

A GRAMMAR SCHOOL:
'VIRTUTE ET VERITATE'

By one of those curious revolutions of fortune which prompt the historian
to make the rash claim that history repeats itself, the grammar schools of
England have been placed by the twentieth-century Education Acts in a
position they have not held since Tudor and Stuart times. Trevelyan in his
Social History of England stresses the importance of the grammar schools in
the fifteenth and sixteenth centuries, going so far as to say that they were
'the cause of the English Reformation', and again that in the Elizabethan age
the typical unit of education was the grammar school, but in the eighteenth
and nineteenth centuries the units of education were 'the Charity School,
the Village School and the great Public School, where the classes were
educated in rigorous segregation'.

Class distinctions were as evident in Elizabethan England as they are in
fact now, though the impulse to conceal them was not strong. They were
accepted in a commonsense way and the gentleman's son and the labourer's
boy — if he was clever enough — had to share their Latin lessons as they
shared the all too frequent floggings dispensed by the master and the usher
of their grammar school. As this kind of schooling proved a source of
strength and vitality in that glorious age, so it may be hoped that grammar
schools in the second half of the twentieth century will bear as rich a crop for
England. It is hard to distinguish cause and effect in history, so many forces
have interplay with each other, social, economic, political and religious; it
is only possible to observe that, as England passed from the age of
Shakespeare to that of the Hanovers and Queen Victoria, the grammar
schools steadily lost ground and were replaced by types of school which by
their very nature failed to preserve that invigorating sense of national unity
which was England's heritage.

This lesson in human relationship, call it democracy or what you will,
civilisation perhaps, has been taught again in this country by one world war
and reinforced by another. The twentieth-century grammar school,
whether wholly or partly independent, or entirely under the control of a
local education authority, meets in some degree the essential requirement
that the most intelligent boys of the country should be given together,

regardless of class, the best possible education, to fit them to fill the many professions crying out for men of ability and integrity.

The particular history of one such school, Pocklington School, founded in 1514 in close connection with one of Cambridge's greatest colleges, St. John's, forms the subject of this book; and it illustrates well enough the history of our country grammar schools generally. It was a guild foundation, which escaped the clutches of Edward VI's ministers through the generosity of a private citizen. It flourished, with occasional lapses through the fault of individual masters, exceedingly well until towards the end of the seventeenth century, then passed through a century and a half of unimportance, sending only a thin stream of boys to Cambridge, and educating a mere handful compared to the numbers in its early days. Resuscitated in the nineteenth century by the vigorous personality of Gruggen, it was criticized by Queen Victoria's Commissioners for 'partaking too much of the nature of a private school'. This headmaster did a great deal for the School and his work is remembered with gratitude today: none the less the criticism goes right to the mark. From 1914 onwards, under an equally energetic headmaster[1] with a very clear notion both of the social trends of his own time and of the original intention of the Founder, the School returned to its former position. Now, at Pocklington School, boys from all sorts of homes, from Pocklington, from the East Riding, from Yorkshire, and from further afield, work and play together as they did in the past. A fair proportion of them still go on to the universities, in particular to St. John's College — best of nurse-mothers — at Cambridge. Others leave school earlier, too early sometimes, but they fill positions of importance in the service of the community with confidence and ability. Times have changed and Latin has long since ceased to be the only study; but the change is less sweeping than it might seem, for what the modern Pocklington boy learns is still in a sense grammar, the elements of learning. Under the new system, technical schools aim at combining this grammar with something more directly connected with the needs of a machine age. The secondary modern schools are trying in a new and experimental way to combine it with something different, perhaps hoping to recover that precious something which was lost when the apprentice system largely died out in England. They each have their special aims, and the aim of the grammar school is well enough expressed in the words of our second founder, Thomas Dowman, 'the education and bringing up of youth in virtue and learning'.

---

[1]P.C. Sands, headmaster 1914-44. The responsibility for what is written in this and all the earlier chapters except *the next* one is mainly mine. — C.M.H.

CHAPTER 2

POCKLINGTON

The School is not so famous that a brief description of the town and countryside itself will be out of place here; and it may, perhaps, bring back pleasant memories to those who knew the place well. Pocklington, mentioned in Domesday Book, is still a village to strangers, but is always called 'town' by its residents, its population being about 3,000. Lying at the foot of the Wolds, it is somewhat sheltered and enjoys a really excellent climate, dry, but not too dry, less subject to mists and fogs than Hull to the east, and free from the 'mugginess' of York in its river bed to the west.

The lower spur of the wold immediately at the back of the town, called Chapel Hill, though it looks low enough under the main wold behind it, commands a fine view of the plain even beyond York Minster, thirteen miles away. Incidentally, it provides good slopes for sledging in winter and compensates the boys for the loss of their playing-fields under frost and snow. The Wolds themselves stretch northwards to Garrowby, and south-eastwards through Warter with its lovely park and Priory to Londesborough and Middleton.

A little stream meanders through Pocklington, partly under cover, and finally emerges in front of the School to curl away by Thirsk's Mill to Canal Head. The saving feature of the town, as of many English hamlets, is the Church tower rising on its fringe, once the scene of a fatal experiment of a 'flying-man' who launched himself from its height but perished through faulty apparatus. To the north of the School are the notable carrot lands. Century after century has seen carrots 'pied' or clamped in the light-soiled acres of this district, which must have contributed considerably to the prosperity of the little town. In the School's 'Vellum Book' or old register, whose entries start in 1650, there is an entry describing the carrot lands owned by the School and their rental. Carrot weeders till recently gathered near the School in the early morning for their exposed ride on the rully to the farms, and two or three places may be seen on the becks that flow through Barmby and Pocklington where the carrots were washed, weighed and bagged. The light soil in which they grow can at times be a nuisance. A gale in the wrong direction will distribute it in a fine layer all over the town as in a dust storm, while larger deposits block the roads and have to be cleared like snow. The same gales at the wrong time of the year sweep the soil from the young carrot seedlings, leaving them high and dry, so that the field has to be re-sown at a loss to the growers.

'Town-leave' was formerly confined to half-holidays and was sorely missed when any epidemic was rife and put the boys in quarantine. For, however strange it may seem to one who knows the limitations of the place, sauntering through the streets to buy sixpennyworth of sweets has attractions for boarders, even in shops that enjoy the very limited patronage of the Wolds. Walks further afield take one near the pheasant preserves of Kilnwick and the wold estates, where hares are abundant, and pheasants are said to be preserved in a new sense — in cans for export to the States. Warter, with its once lovely beeches, now unhappily decimated, and its little colourful lake at the far end, was too distant for the saunters of the boarders. So is the favourite haunt called Millington Springs, a curious defile winding for two or three miles between high wolds, resort of picnickers in motors on Bank Holidays, and like many another pocket in the Wolds, Kirby Underdale for instance, offering a charm unsuspected while traversing the rather bald expanses between Pocklington and Driffield. Bishop Wilton again, with its stream dividing the village street or valley, nestling under hills that rise up to Garrowby and offering a magnificent view of the vale of York, never fails to give delight to visitors. Nearer to Pocklington is the attractive approach to Millington through Kilnwick Park, down a valley road with the wold on one's right and the prospect of the village a mile ahead. But boys, after their week of strenuous games, rarely walk. Like King Charles II, they saunter to satisfy the regulations of the Sunday walk and to pass the time till they may return to small cricket or a book in the shade, or, best of all, swimming and sunbathing in the bath. Whit Monday, however, used to be an exception. In the twenties, when motors were few, the headmaster instituted a whole day's hiking holiday, which most of the boarders made shift to spend on foot or a hired bicycle, taking with them a picnic lunch and tea, and returned sunbaked and pleasantly tired to a bathe and bed. The demand for bicycles taxed the resources of the local shops, whose enterprise hastily produced assembled parts of disused machines for this special occasion. One boy would return with a tale of thirteen punctures, another minus a brake. Two boys would share one bicycle on occasion, the smaller riding across the handlebars. But no disasters happened, and the convoy of parents' cars that at last replaced the old bicycles has removed the thrill that some hikers felt of a whole day in the countryside at its best in May, roaming off the beaten track with a well-stocked picnic bag and no cares, in the middle of term.

The railway line dividing the School from the town tended to promote a certain detachment in outlook also and sever their interests, especially when the Pocklington Literary Society, whose lectures the boys attended, lost its hall to the cinema industry, and the School started to engage its own lecturers. But of late the increase in the number of day-boys has naturally strengthened the interest of the residents in the School, being *alumni* themselves or having had sons educated there. Gone are the days when the young townees threw epithets and missiles at the so-called 'Grammar Ducks'. Relations of town and School are more and more closely woven. If the notorious caution and understatement of East Riding folk allowed them, the townsfolk would probably confess to some pride in the old Grammar School. This history shows them from the beginning to have been jealous of the educational advantages it offered their sons, but the tradespeople naturally regarded it also as a possible source of profitable business, and to the rest its doings have always provided a favourite topic of gossip and criticism. On reflection they would perhaps admit the benefit to the district, both social and cultural, which enriches the community, when a staff of educated men and their wives and families share the life of a small market town, fourteen miles from the nearest city. The presence of the School is notably felt in the morning services of the parish church and during holidays the boys are much missed. School matches provide interest on shop-closing days, and the Commemoration is a great occasion for town as well as school.

CHAPTER 3

THE FOUNDATION: JOHN DOWMAN

On 24 May, 1514, Henry VIII granted John Dowman licence to found a guild in the parish church of Pocklington. It was to contain a grammar school. The Dowmans had been for some time, apparently, lords of the very ancient manor of Pocklington, which is mentioned in the Domesday Book and existed in Saxon times. It consisted of lands and property in Pocklington, Millington and adjacent villages. John Dowman, our Founder, was doubtless born at Pocklington; he became a lawyer and a churchman of some eminence. After holding in succession a number of livings in the south of England, he was appointed Prebend, first of Sarum, then of St.Paul's, and finally, in 1509, of Lichfield Cathedral. In 1507 he was appointed Archdeacon of Suffolk. Meanwhile, in 1488 and 1494, he was made Bachelor of Canon and Doctor of Civil Law (*utriusque iuris*) by Cambridge University, although it is not certain that he was ever a member of the University. He is said to have been Auditor of Causes under Cardinal Wolsey. Bequests in his will to numerous churches in Surrey suggest that his services as an ecclesiastical lawyer were well rewarded by the gift of a number of benefices which he held simultaneously, a frequent abuse at that time.

It is not surprising that a man of his position should have sought to leave a permanent memorial of himself by founding a school in his native town. Many eminent men, such as Bishop Fisher and John Colet, were vigorously and with open generosity promoting the cause of better education in England. Most towns of importance boasted a school by this time. In Yorkshire, certainly, there were more than a few; among them the very ancient school at York, where Alcuin's master, Archbishop Egbert, was teaching in the early eighth century, and Beverley School, so old that its records were being consulted in 1304 to settle a dispute about 'a very ancient custom'. But these old schools were ecclesiastical, for medieval England had entrusted its education to the Church. The need for choristers and clerks able to recite, if not to understand, the Latin liturgy, made it a duty for the Church to educate sufficient boys in the science of Latin grammar. Throughout Europe the Church had been the preserver of real learning and scholarship in the Dark Ages. The great pagan writers, Virgil and Cicero, were used, not without trepidation, as the whetstone on which the wits of future theologians might best be sharpened. There had always been a conflict between secular and religious learning. It so often happened that the wits which had been sharpened for theology were more inclined to stick to the pagan grindstone through a happy lifetime. By the eleventh century the rift was open. From this time secular learning was accepted at its own value; but the Church maintained its hold on the schools, although in the eighth century Alcuin and his successors had abandoned the schoolroom for the pulpit, forsaking Latin grammar for theology. By the thirteenth century schools were founded which were secular both in their purpose and in their government. To provide lay governors for such a school, in default of any precedent for creating a special governing body, the roundabout procedure of founding a guild was discovered. The guilds, though they were served by one or more chaplains, and were established in a parish church or a cathedral and were of avowedly religious intent, were yet secular in so far as their members and officers were all laymen. Apart from containing a grammar school, as so many of them did, their purpose was, firstly, to insure their members sick pay, a decent Christian burial and sufficient prayers for their souls when departed this life; and, secondly, to perform various charitable duties in the parish. For this reason it was consistent for a high officer of the Church, like John Dowman, to found his Free Grammar School within a guild. The guild was in one sense a religious body — hence the specific term 'religious guild' — though in another a secular society more anxious to promote the increase of learning than the 'increase of clerks'.

These 'Free Grammar Schools' were so called because they gave free tuition; needless to say, that tuition was in Latin, properly called the science of grammar. Though schools may have varied in their practice, it is probable that boys would at least know how to read and write before being taken into a grammar school. To judge by Roger Ascham's remarks in his *Scholemaster* a high standard was achieved. Other fees such as entrance, fire, board, cock-fighting and birch fees were likely to be charged.

The foundation and re-foundation of the School are reasonably well documented. The date of the licence, granted by Letters Patent under the Great Seal, is 24 May, 1514, and it is reasonable to think that the schoolmaster was appointed soon after. There is, in fact, some evidence to suggest that the Guild was already in existence, perhaps in the form of a Lady Guild in the parish church. But the Guild, as already said, was now responsible for appointing a schoolmaster. Land and new buildings for Guild and School were made available in 1522 (see Chapter 25). In the deed of 1 December, 1525, granting lands to St. John's College, Cambridge, to provide scholarships for boys from Pocklington School, Dowman refers to 'my school, lately erected at Pocklington'. Pocklington, as a place of some importance, now had its grammar school like York, Beverley, Howden. Hemingborough and Hull. Though John Dowman, as far as we can make out, never completed the formal transfer of the property mentioned in the licence to the Guild, he is rightly to be considered founder of a school whose only endowments were those which he arranged to give the Guild; nor did he feel it improper to describe it in a legal document as 'my school at Pocklington'.

The original patent still exists, setting forth in Latin the details of the Guild's intended constitution. It was to be a full corporation called the 'Fraternity or Guild of the Name of Jesus and the Blessed Virgin Mary and Saint Nicholas founded in the parish church of Pocklington in the County of York by John Dowman Doctor of Laws'. It was to have a master and two wardens with brethren and sisters; any subject of the King was to be granted admission. The School is first mentioned quite casually, as though it were to be taken for granted. Below we find that the Guild was to be allowed to hold lands to the yearly value of £13 6s. 8d to 'find from time to time one man fitted, and sufficiently learned in grammar, to instruct and educate all and singular scholars who resort (confluentes) to the town of Pocklington for the aforesaid purpose of receiving education according to the ordinances and statutes to be made by the said John Dowman in this matter'. (Dowman then did not intend his benefaction to be confined to the boys of Pocklington.) 'And to perform and fulfil other works of piety according to the sane discretion of the said Master and wardens...' These works would be the giving of alms to the poor and the saying of masses for the soul of Dowman and others. The rest of the deed is taken up with such items as a dispensation from the various requirements of the Statute of Mortmain. The School seems definitely to be the most important item.

The statutes which Dowman was empowered to make for the Guild and School have been lost. We shall later see (page 11) that one of them was a provision that the schoolmaster was to be appointed, and, if necessary, removed, by the Guild with the advice of St. John's College, Cambridge. This is the first connection between the School and St. John's College, which had itself only very recently been founded. The only certain record of the Guild which remains to us is the seal, which as a corporation it was specially entitled to possess. It is a comparatively rare specimen and, according to Leach, typical of the rather too 'crowded' pre-Reformation seals.

Seal of Pocklington School

Leach describes the seal in these words:

It gives us the boy Jesus, ... a chubby, naked urchin, with his monogram, Ihs, stamped upon his stomach, and the whole seal powdered with the same monogram, for the dedication to the 'Name of Jesus'. The Virgin Mary crowned, with the Infant Jesus in her arms, appears for the dedication to the Virgin. The place of honour is reserved for Bishop Nicholas (of Myra), the patron Saint of schoolboys, with a delightful representation of him in full pontificals by a tub, in which two boys are standing, while a third is putting one leg over the side in order to get out. This refers to the well-known story of Nicholas having arrived in the nick of time to save the boys. They were on their way to school at Athens, and had been murdered at an inn at Myra by the inn-keeper for their money and clothes, then cut up and put into the pickle-tub, where they were scented out by the Bishop in consequence of a dream, resuscitated, and sent on, not, perhaps, 'unwillingly to school'.

Below these figures is the excellent founder kneeling at a desk praying. The seal is round and bears the legend, *'Sigillum commune fraternitatis nominis Jesu, Beatae Mariae et Sancti Nicholai de Poklington'*, in an abbreviated form.

St. John's College was founded in 1511 by Bishop Fisher, acting as executor to the Lady Margaret, mother of Henry VII, and previously foundress of Christ's College. The executors lodged for a time with Dr. Dowman,[1] possibly seeking his legal advice, and so he became interested in the College at the time of its foundation. Of this he gave several subsequent proofs. First, there was his statute obliging the Guild officers to consult the College about the appointment of a schoolmaster. Then, in 1525, he made

---

[1] *Memoir of Margaret, Countess of Richmond and Derby*, C. H. Cooper, Cambridge, 1874, p.191. The authors are indebted for this note to Mr. Allen Foxley, a distinguished Old Boy and the architect of the present School Hall.

two notable benefactions to the College, founding nine sizarships in September and five scholarships for Pocklington boys in December. A chantry foundation in St. Paul's Cathedral of about the same date was also to be served by two priests from the College. Finally, in his will of the next year he left his books of divinity to the College library.

As prebend of St. Paul's he must have been interested in the foundation of the new St. Paul's School by John Colet. We must conclude that he was a man of importance in those days of renewed interest in learning. His death, in 1526, saved him from the embarrassment of choosing between his conscience and his career, when Henry VIII broke away from the authority of Rome in the endeavour to gain an heir to ensure the Tudor succession. His age is not known, but as he held a living in 1475 he must have been over seventy when he died.

The foundation of his nine sizarships does not immediately concern the history of the School, because the sizarships were open to all. Sufficient to say that he gave the College £140 to pay for 'nine proper sizars'. The date is 1 September, 1525. The sizarships still awarded by the College, though no longer exactly nine in number, are still called Dowman sizarships. The endowment is merged in general College finances.

The deed granting the five scholarships, later converted to four Dolman exhibitions, or a copy of it, is still in existence and is dated 1 December, 1525. It is of enough interest to demand at least a summary. The main clauses are:

1.   Grant to the College of lands in Yorkshire and Derbyshire, recently acquired by Dowman and worth £15 a year, 'for the exaltation of Holy Mother Church and for the increase of clerks in the University of Cambridge'.
2.   The College to incorporate statutes for Dowman's five scholars with those already existing for the foundation scholars.
3.   The five scholars to be appointed during his life by Dowman, and after his death by the officers of the Guild, within two weeks notice of a vacancy : in default by the Dean of York : in default by the Chancellor;
4.   to be admitted in the same way as the other scholars;
5.   to have the same emoluments as the other scholars.
6.   The qualifications for these Dolman scholars were to be: 'that they must be born in Yorkshire…; and that those scholars especially should be elected and taken who were of his name and kin, whatever the country of their birth or wheresoever they were born, if such could anywhere be found sufficient for the purpose. Otherwise (alioquin) such scholars were always to be chosen as were instructed and brought up in his Grammar School at Pocklington, in whatsoever country they were born, yet especially any who were born there where the aforesaid holdings and possessions lay (i.e. the lands in Yorks and Derby) and were cleverer at their studies (habiliores ad hoc) and in other ways more outstanding; but that they must not be taken from elsewhere than from his School aforesaid in the aforesaid form and manner and without exception from those who were simply the best grammarians and those who were more excellent and outstanding in character.'

The puzzle is how to put the qualifications in their correct order of preference. Each clause seems to contradict its predecessor. The Act of 1551 refers simply to 'five scholars that had been brought up in the Grammar School'. Leach points out that this established education at the School as the first and essential qualification. But that first preference may have been intended for the founder's kin is suggested by the fact that several Dowmans born in Leicestershire and Hertfordshire won the scholarships before 1630, though there is no evidence that they went to school in Pocklington.

7. The scholars to take the usual oaths on admission with four differences:
They had (a) to be called Scholars of Mr. John Dowman, LL.D., Archdeacon of Suffolk;
(b) at Mass, devoutly and clearly to say the psalm 'De Profundis', or, if priests, a special collect, for the soul of John Dowman, his parents, friends and benefactors;
(c) to make special recommendation of those souls in their sermons (i.e. in the Bidding Prayer);
and (d) to give notice of a vacancy to the Guild within six weeks.
8. Since the learning and character of the Master and scholars cannot be ascertained clearly enough from the members of the Guild, 'whenever the Master of the College, or a Fellow by him appointed, approaches Pocklington, he must go to the town, salute the Master, or if absent have him fetched, and diligently examine him. And if he find him at fault in his learning or unsuitable, must have him removed....' So that Dowman cannot be blamed if the scholars are found wanting.
9. Dowman had added what he had already put in the statutes of the Guild and School, namely that the Master must be appointed by the Guild with the advice of the College.
10. Gift to relapse to Christ's College (also founded by the Countess of Richmond), if St. John's default.
11. Bond by St. John's College to Dean and Chapter of York, to pay a penalty of £5 for every month in which no scholar is elected when he ought to be.
12. A witness clause with the College, the Founder, the Guild and Christ's College as attestors.

This deed served to cement the connection between School and College. Boys have gone up from Pocklington to St. John's as Dowman Scholars (or, since 1859, as Dolman Exhibitioners) from that day to this. It will also be noticed that the College was made responsible for the standard of scholarship attained by the boys whom it was obliged to accept from the Guild.

The next document is Dowman's will, made on 8 November, and proved at Canterbury on 6 December, 1526. It is chiefly interesting for its omissions. The School was not mentioned at all. The College got only his divinity books. His many parishes received small bequests with instructions to pray for his soul and to give ale and cheese to the poor. Forty shillings were set aside for the release of those imprisoned for debt at Newgate and Ludgate. His brother, Christopher, got 'two great flat bowls with a cover, a gown, a jacket, a doublet, a horse saddle and bugle with harness complete'. The rest of the furniture was bequeathed to Christopher's daughters. John Byass and Sir William Mountforth, both from the neighbourhood of Pocklington, also benefited.

CHAPTER 4

THE RE-FOUNDATION 1551 : THOMAS DOWMAN

The Guild and the School presumably flourished during the next twenty years. (There is a record of eight admissions to St. John's pro Dr. Dowman before this date, all but one Yorkshire boys.) There is a tradition that the aisle in the parish church, now known as the Dolman Chapel, which opens into the Lady Chapel, or north aisle of the chancel, through an arch in its own south-east end, was the one allotted to the St. Nicholas Guild. It was repaired during Hutton's headmastership, and five feet beneath the floor was discovered an obviously old stone slab with the initials J.D. carved on it. A schoolhouse building had been acquired, of which we know nothing except that it was often allowed to fall into disrepair throughout the succeeding centuries. The master would live in a separate house and possibly board one or two of the boys. There would be one, or perhaps two, large classrooms, capable between them of holding upwards of a hundred boys, if the numbers alleged to have been at the School during the next half-century are correct. It is not known how soon before 1551 an usher was employed; but a common practice was for a senior scholar to be deputed to hear the smaller boys recite their tasks, while the master devoted most of his attention to the better scholars. The College register of scholars' admissions begins in 1545, and the Dowman scholars are present in full force, for the entries at this period average one a year.

In 1547 Henry VIII died, leaving his throne to the nine-year-old Edward VI. The Reformation, sponsored by Protector Somerset, at once broke loose, and one of its first acts of destruction was to abolish the religious guilds. By a Chantries Act of 1547 all guilds were abolished and their property confiscated as from Easter 1548. Criticism is beside the mark. Doubtless these guilds were strongholds of the ritualistic, Romish form of worship, which the reformers purposed to uproot. The name of our own Guild suggests strongly that its members were not of Protestant inclination.

Provision was made for the temporary continuance of the Guild schools; and later a small part, usually a tenth, of the Guild property was set aside by the Commissioners for their maintenance. The result was that some schools disappeared while others, such as Sedbergh, managed to subsist on their meagre allowance, eked out by gifts from benefactors. The schools which Edward's advisers all but ruined are now called Edward VI foundations. Pocklington School escaped in an odd way. The Guild was dissolved. Its property was confiscated by the Receiver, and the schoolmaster continued at a salary of £13 6s. 8d., namely the whole of the income enjoyed by the Guild. Such generous provision was probably no more than a temporary arrangement pending settlement of a dispute about the rightful ownership of the property. For Thomas Dowman of Pocklington quickly came forward with a petition for permission to erect and endow a free school at Pocklington with the money and property with which John Dowman had intended to endow it. He claimed that John had never completed the transaction, and that as his heir, he, Thomas, owned the property in his own right. The fact that his plea was successful is enough to suggest that his claim to ownership was true. Yet it is strange that John, who was a lawyer, had not secured the property to the Guild. Thomas's claim to be John's heir is based on his being the son of John's first cousin, William,[1] who, according to Thomas's account, was co-feoffee with John and others of the property concerned, lands in Thryburgh, but surviving them all became sole possessor. At his death Thomas inherited the property. It is surprising, to say the least of it, that John Dowman only shared the endowment property with others. Whatever the answer, Thomas retrieved the Guild's property and gave it to the School.

He was a lawyer of Gray's Inn, presumably a barrister. He petitioned Parliament and obtained a private Act of Parliament establishing the Free School of Pocklington according to the terms of John Dowman's intended endowment together with certain necessary modifications and additions. A copy of this Act, passed in the fourth session of Edward's first Parliament, i.e. in January, 1551, exists in a document of Letters Patent dated July, 1552. The Act embodies Thomas's petition and is very long. A brief summary is all that can be given.

The petition states that John Dowman, 'for the zeal and love which he had to his country and to the education and bringing up of youth in virtue and learning', gave to St. John's College lands worth £15 a year, to support five scholars from the Grammar School freely erected in Pocklington by John Dowman; and among the deeds of composition between him and the College was contained a clause that vacancies among the scholars should be supplied by the nominations of the master, wardens and brethren of a certain fraternity or guild in Pocklington founded by Royal Licence. The Chantries Act did not intend to destroy 'good and godly foundations made

[1]Foster's *Yorkshire Pedigrees*

only for the increase of learning'; yet the said fraternity or guild, 'colourably, under pretence of a Fraternity superstitiously used', is now dissolved. So the benefit and preferment which the scholars of the School have always had is 'like to be clearly gone and taken away, most contrary to the meaning and good intent of the godly ordinance and foundation'; and yet St. John's College still possessed the properties given for the purpose mentioned; 'which thing is like to ensue to the great displeasure and loss of the inhabitants of the Town of Pocklington and of all the country there, unless it shall please your Majesty that the said godly ordinance may be ... recontinued and established'.

The petitioner held in his own possession the schoolhouse and all the lands and property purchased by John Dowman to maintain the School, 'without any use declared and no other device yet made for the more perfect continuance of the said Free Grammar School'. If the petitioner should die ('whereof he is most assured'), they would be lost to the School.

Be it therefore enacted:—

1. That the Master and Fellows of St. John's College, Cambridge, and their successors for ever, appoint one discrete and well-learned man to be Master of the School; and that the Schoolmaster and the Churchwardens of the Parish appoint one sufficiently learned young man to be Usher.

2. That the Master and Usher be a perpetual corporation with license to hold lands up to the value of £20 a year.

3. That the five scholars at St. John's be appointed by the Master and the Vicar and Churchwardens of the Parish, in the same way as they were appointed by the Guild.

4. That the scholars shall have all the rights and privileges previously enjoyed by the scholars sent up by the Guild, according to the College's composition with Dr. Dowman.

5. That in respect of the scholarships, the Master and Usher may do all that the Guild was allowed to do, and that the College shall treat them as they were bound to treat the Guild.

6. That the Master and the two Churchwardens, or any two of them, may enforce performance of the covenants in the deed.

7. That if the College fail to appoint a Master, or the Vicar and the Churchwardens fail to appoint an Usher, within two months of the vacancy occurring, the Archbishop of York may do so.

8. That the Archbishop of York and the Master of St. John's may make statutes and ordinances for the governance of the Master and Usher, so long as they are made within two years after Easter, 1548.

9. That the College be in no case made to shoulder any new burden or obligation, beyond those undertaken in the deed of 1525.

10. That Adam Lockwood, now Master of the said Free Grammar School in Pocklington, shall be the first Master to be appointed by this ordinance, and where he is so appointed, to continue in the same during his life natural.

The Colleges of Oxford and Cambridge had been exempted from the provisions of the Chantries Act. Thomas therefore bases his argument on the fact that St. John's have legal possession of valuable lands given for a definite educational purpose, which will be frustrated if the School is not allowed to continue. The Chantries Act, he pleads, aimed at strengthening, not weakening educational foundations. The lands used to support the Guild School are legally his, and he wishes to secure them for ever to the School in Pocklington.

Now that the Guild was abolished, the School had no governors. The Guild's place was to be divided between the master and usher themselves, the master and fellows of St. John's College, the vicar and churchwardens of the parish and (by default) the Archbishop of York. As it turned out, the College was too far away to maintain sufficiently close supervision of the master and usher. The arrangement was naturally very unsatisfactory.

The Archbishop and the master of St. John's never made the suggested statutes, probably because the Act was not passed till two years after the time-limit imposed. This seems to clear them from the charge of negligence.

Finally, the deed gives us the name of the first schoolmaster of the reconstituted Free Grammar School. We have a complete list from this time onwards. Another document, which we shall mention shortly, tells us that Alexander Smith was then usher.

Thomas Dowman is therefore in every way to be regarded as a second founder of our School. His act was very generous, and he wasted no time making over the property to the School. In an enquiry under direction of the Court of Chancery, in 1698, occasioned by a dispute over the lease of some of the lands at Thrybergh, the jury found that Thomas by an indenture dated 9 January, I Mary (1553-4) 'gave to the Master and the Usher, Alexander Smith, and to their successors for ever, all the said messuages lands tenements etc., to hold the same for ever'. This is the document which explains how Thomas came to be heir of the property : 'John Dowman, LL.D and William Dowman were jointly with other co-feoffees seized in their demesne as of fee of ... lands tenements ... in ... Thrybergh ... and William Dowman did survive the other co-feoffees'. Thomas was William's son and heir.

Thomas's tomb is in the parish church in the Lady Chapel. The arch opening from this chapel into the chancel was blocked by the organ until the removal of the organ at Christmas, 1949, and the arch opening into the Dolman or St. Nicholas Chapel was, until then, filled by a screen erected to conceal the back of the organ. Thomas is now rescued from undeserved obscurity and dust. The inscription on the monument tells us that he was a Justice of the Peace, that he married Elizabeth Vavasour of Spalding, and had twelve children, of whom five sons and three daughters survived his death in 1589. Most of his sons went up to St. John's College and doubtless all of them were at the School. Thomas was head of the family. Both he and his eldest son, Robert, played an active part in helping to run the School during their lifetimes. In the latter part of Elizabeth's reign he was suspected of being a 'subtle papist' though for that matter much of Yorkshire remained hostile to the Reformation.

CHAPTER 5

THE EARLIER (ELIZABETHAN) SCHOOLMASTERS

ADAM LOCKWOOD	Before 1551 to 1558 (?)
ANTHONY ELLISON	1558 (?) to 1581
ROBERT FAWCETT	1581 to 1598
JAMES NELSON	1598 to 1600

Adam Lockwood, gentleman, was perhaps a graduate of Cambridge University. In the Act in which he was appointed first Master of the Free School reconstituted by Thomas Dowman, he was said to be 'now master'. He may, therefore, have been Master of the Guild-School. He was buried at Pocklington on 2 August, 1558. We may assume that he remained at his post to the end of his life natural. During the conjectured period of his mastership, twelve boys went up to St. John's as Dowman scholars, which indicates a full school. One of them, Edward Hansby, afterwards became senior dean of the College. By 1553-4 Alexander Smith was usher. He was Dowman Scholar 1550, took his B.A. 1553-4, and was elected Fisher Fellow 1555. Yet according to Leadman's list of Vicars, he was collated Vicar in 1549; it seems unlikely that he received a benefice while still at school.

Anthony Ellison, B.A., of Christ's College, was elected Sympson Fellow by St. John's in 1555. There is thus some reason for assigning this date to his appointment as master, because to give the selected candidate a fellowship was the College's regular procedure on future occasions. He was buried at Pocklington on 27 September, 1581. During most of his long mastership the School flourished. Judging by letters (see pp. 22, 23) of a somewhat later date there were about 140 boys in the School at one period. Twenty-five Dowman Scholars went up, among them a Sothebye, three Dowmans (one from Leicester and perhaps not at the School) and Thomas Fallowfield. Others no doubt went up to the University as pensioners or commoners.

The Gonville and Caius Biographical Register and their College Admissions also contain a few entries of boys who must have been at the School under Ellison (though, where the name of the Ludimagister is given, it is written 'Ellis'. However, spelling in those days was less conventional and the entries were often copied down at the dictation of the undergraduate.) But these entries are of more interest than all the twenty-five scholars of St. John's. Two entries in the Register are worth quoting in full:

> *Anselm St. Quintin,* son of Gabriel St. Quintin, Esq.
>
> School, Pocklington. 3 years under Mr. Ellis. Age 18. Admitted to the Scholars' table, 1578/9... Complained of by the fellows as a papist; 'he did openly call Mr. Nowell of St. Paul's a heretic', and as favoured by the Master; 'the words being confessed, the Master promised due punishment for them ... yet this deponent ... could never yet hear so much as any private correction being taken for the same.' (Vol. 1, p. 101)
>
> *Christopher Langlaye,* son of Richard Langlaye, Esq.
>
> Born in Howthorpe, Yorks. School, Pocklington under Mr. Ellis. Age 20. Admitted fellow-commoner Oct. 17th, 1584. (Litterarum gratia adms.) ... His father was hanged at York, Dec. 1586, for sheltering Romish priests in his house. (ibid., p. 122)

The Admissions, among the seven other contemporary entrants — two of them, Robert Smythe and Marmaduke Constable, migrants from St. John's — contain the name of Edward Fairfax, who spent one year at Pocklington.

These notices show not only that the School at this time, as later, was attracting boys from the leading families in the county, but that it was strongly Roman Catholic in its sympathies. Caius College seems to have sheltered many papists. In his very interesting introduction to the Biographical Register (page xiv) Dr. Venn wrote:

> In the same period (1560-1680) no less that 200 natives of this county (Yorks.) entered our College. Many of them would have come in any case, but there was not a single scholarship connected with any Yorkshire school to account for their selection of our College. The explanation is to be sought in another direction, and is connected with that very interesting religious episode of which I shall have occasion to speak more particularly presently. In the reign of Elizabeth, as is well known, the North of England was still largely Roman Catholic; and our College in comparison with others at Cambridge had a decided reputation in this direction. Dr. Caius, it is supposed, never became a protestant; and his successor, Dr. Legge,... seems to have had strong sympathies with the old form of faith, and introduced as one of his principal tutors a man of like views with himself, Dr. Swale. These two, both Yorkshiremen, gave the College a distinctly marked ecclesiastical character. Of Dr. Legge it was complained that 'All the popish gentlemen send their sons to him. He setteth sundry of them over to one Swayl, also of the same house, by whom the youth of this country is corrupted.'

It must be remembered that Queen Elizabeth prosecuted the Roman Catholics with increasing severity after she was excommunicated in 1570. The invasion of Jesuit missionaries bent on securing the downfall of the champion of the Protestant cause compelled her to take precautions. In those days to be a Roman Catholic was to be a traitor; for obedience to the Pope meant readiness to take up arms against Elizabeth, whose position at times verged on the precarious. Her spies were busy and hundreds of families came under suspicion, among them the Dolmans. The following extract from a letter of information, supplied by one of Queen Elizabeth's pursuivants to the Council, is now preserved in the State Paper Office:

> Yoinge Dolman of Graies Ine and his brother. Hee (that is a seminary priest named Smith) is most lyke to haunt the company of yoinge Mr. Dolman of Grayes Ine, son to old Mr. Thom's Dolman of pocklington neare Yorke who laytly reported that his sayd sone was gone into Yorkshyere to be marryed. And it is sayd that Dolman's youngr sone is laytly gone over the seas.
>
> The father did belong to my lady Leaneuxe and greatly in her favore, and a subtill papist thought to be. Both his sons noated papists.
>
> For being of Graisine They lodged Thom's Anfild a not seamenarye now prisoner in the Tower who haunted the Northe. And hearde him saye a number of masses in there chamber, and in another man's chamber.
>
> And one of these Dolmans did accompany Anfild to Campyan's execuc'on took noats of his words and manr of execucyon, And delyvered the same to Rowlande the prynter in Smithfield, and
>
> Anfild did deliver iij of the books printed unto one of theis too Dolmans.
>
> And dyvers other seamanaryes did haunt to theis too Dolmans.

It is endorsed as follows:

> On the 29th May, 1582, the council ordered the Earl of Huntingdon to apprehend Wm. Nelson, James Clayton and Dolman of Gray's Inn, and to cause their houses to be searched.

Campion was one of the leading Jesuits who invaded England after 1574. The Lennox family were Mary Queen of Scots' chief support. The 'Young Dolman' is probably Thomas's eldest son, Robert, who had some of his estates confiscated in 1610 by James I as a punishment for nonconformity.

Numbers at the School were undoubtedly high during Ellison's reign, but towards the end all was not well within the house. For a letter dated a few days after his death is still preserved at the College, in which the Archbishop of York writes to the master of St. John's:

> Sal. in xto. I remember that you muche myslyked of the Scholemaster of Pocklington, for that he sent you rude and vnlerned Schollers oute of his Schole. And you prayed me to reform hym or remove hym. At your request I rode thither reproved his negligencie and gaue hym a monicion. I learne that yesterdaye he departed oute of his lyfe, so that you haue to nomynate another Scholemaster, And forsomuche as your College must Receyve Schollers owte of that Schole, Yt standeth you in hande to appoynte such a Scholemaster as will gyve youe Schollers accordinge to your expectacon, a man lerned, godly and discrete fyt for that Office. And I shall require youe to haue good consideracon hereof as well in respect of yourselves as of the Commonwelthe I am given to vnderstande that the Governors of that Schole deale not accordinge to the trust reposed in them. But if youe shall nominate vnto me a worthy Scholemaster, I will call the Governors before me. Loke owte the ffoundacion and ordinances of that Schole, and see that the Scholemaster haue full righte. ffare youe hartelye well. Bushopthorpe this xxixth of September 1581. your loving friend E. Ebor.
>
> Addressed : To Mr. Howlande, Master of the College.

The 'Governors' can only mean the vicar and churchwardens, whose duties were confined to helping the Master elect the five Dowman scholars. Perhaps the negligence had been shown in failing to perform this duty, or, more likely, the scholars were not up to a good enough standard of scholarship. Owing to the unlikelihood of a master being in a position to resign his post voluntarily, the School had to suffer under more than one nonage.

Ellison's ushers were Alexander Smith till 1558, then Peter Stainton, and from 1577 onwards Thomas Fallowfield.

The next master was almost certainly Robert Fawcett. For not only is he mentioned in the Dean of York's Visitations as Ludimagister in 1591, but he was signator of the following letter to the College:

> A Dowman scholarship vacant, 'whearof we receaued no knowledg from you according to the composition betwixt you and Dr. Dowman, which as we ar informed by Mr.Alvey one of the felowes ... was by reason of the oversight and negligence of Sir Hammon late scholler in the said place.' As the College desires Pet. Gyll late of Pocklington school to be admitted, 'we ar contented that for this tyme you do vse your owne pleasures therin, trusting that from henceforth the schollers of our schoole will better remember their dewties and othe in geving you knowledg, so that ther shall be no such omission.' 15 March, 1586/7.
> Signed : Thomas Dowman. Roger Sotheby. Robt. Fawcett. Alex Smith. Thomas Fallowfield.

The persons who should have signed this letter were the master, the vicar and the two churchwardens. All other names are known to us and it is certain that none of them was the master. By elimination, Fawcett must have been master. To confirm the view that he succeeeded Ellison is the fact that a Robert Faucet is given as having been a sizar of St. John's in 1576 and having taken his degree in 1581. He took his M.A. in 1584, but was never made a Fellow. The identification is at least probable.

In the winter of 1599, at the end of Fawcett's successor's brief reign, Robert Dowman, Thomas's eldest son, wrote a very long letter to the College, complaining about the conduct of the former masters and suggesting new statutes. The Archbishop's failure to make the statutes according to the terms of the Act of 1551 had left the School in an unfortunate position.

> yt may please you to be advertised That whereas my self Mr Sohebey and other the chefe of the Town of Pocklington have by our generall letters related vnto you the rewenouse estate of the Schoole of Pocklington by reason that the Mrs sent from you have more respected ther owne particuler personne than the commen good or carefull instruccon of ther schollers, and that wee have to all indifferent eares delivered vs from the surmised accusacons suggested against vs; I have presumed yet for my owne particuler earnestlly to intreat your speciall care and mature consideracon not only in curing our present sores but by your providence to prevent any lik future inconvenience; wherein I hold yt a matter of

some moment, To have such Lawes and statutes by your gravytyes considered of, and sett downe, as you shall think convenient to be observed by the next master you mind to send, Some elements or groundes whereof we have sent vnto you, reformable at your pleasures, which agreed vpon, and by your generall assent sett downe, indented, and one parte thereof revised to vs, to remain as directoryes, as well to the Master and Vsher as to vs of the parish, vnder your seal. Then yf yt would please you (after you are agreed vpon a master) to taik him sworne and bound vnto you, to observe and kepe the same Lawes and statutes, so by you made, and that when he is not content so to do, then that he shall surrender up his place to you againe, yt semeth probable to me, that this Course will do good. Otherwise I knowe you may not be Ignorant, that yf you do not taik this Course (Vpon letters of conditons) to admitt your master, and not otherwise afore he be invested Master; he being once by you absolutely and without condiCON nominated and presented will then do as thes later masters have done, stand vpon the Statut and foundacon; That (being once masters and vshers) they hold the Schoole, and the possessions thereof, as free (yf not freer) then the Persons doo ther personages, that is as Lordes of the fee simple thereof to geve, grant, demise for what time they list and the lik. Which as I have said, to prevent, is always to Admitt your masters to the Schoole but condicionally that they shall possesse ther places so longe as they do not obstinately violat your lawes and statutes ordeaned for the regine and the good disport of the facultyes of the Schoole. That much I have out of my care as being more interessed in the foundacon as well by affinytty to the founder as otherwise being the only surviving feffe thereof, presumed to advise vnto you requiring That as my father, who in troth was a second founder of the Schoole, being the only man that gott the same Reestablished by K.E.6. after it was dissolved and confiscate by the Statutes of dissolving Gildes &c, did taik from his posteryty and name the preeminencyes which by the founder was first attributed vnto him above others, both in the eleccons and direccons of that bodye corporat, and transferred the same wholy to you as most meet for your Larninges and Judgment to dispose thereof freely, you would (the rather yer att my sewt) be carefull or rather more than carefull in sending to our Schoole men of more gravity and Larning. And yf here you will say to me That our wages will not maintaaine such as we desier, I will yeld vnto you, that the ould stipendes will not. But therfor you shall see in my draught of statutes that we are very willing to inlarge the same so the rest might orderly be accompted for and laid vp in the Treasury chest which the founder ordeyned for that purpose to be yssued out in pious vses &c. And yf yt shall seem good to you I think the masters wages may be made xxvj li or xxx li and the vshers x li. So the landes might be a little rased and some ouerplus yerly remaine also for common treasor with which I would have the master and vsher not to medle, other then to geve accompt thereof at the Accompt day. And yf yt could be drawne to this, then I think yt would be more answerable to a man of more Respect for gravyty and Larning both which your wisdomes know are inseparably necessary to a Schoolmaster that should both teach and moderate. The Contry that do depend vpon this fundacon is great, and therefor your care had not nede but be also. And thes thinges thus digested, the Master being once of any fame, would renewe the decayes thereof, and gather of Strangers good Rewardes extraaordinary, for I (in my tyme) was one of the (xx vij) schollers that larned ther, and now ther ar not much more then one Schore, and these not much better then Catonistes which is pitesfull. But I must crave pardon that haue thus longe vsurped vpon your patiences in Reding thes tedious lines, and now will taik my leave of you referring all thes premisses to your good consideracons expecting your carefull reformacons of what is past. ffrom my house att Gouerby this 12 of No. 1599.

Your wor : in all offices
of kindnesse at your dispose
Rob : Dolman.

I am going to London whether yf it plese any of your society to writ to me by way of consultacon what may be the best course in these causes, I dwelle at the signe of the blew Bell in holborne and ther I doubt shalbe occacioned to stay till Candlemass tyme whereof I thought good to advertise you.

To the Worshipfull the master and Seniors with the fellowes of St John's Colledge in Cambridge be thes.

Robert was a man unsparing of words, but his argument was sound. There really was a deplorable lack of control over the masters and ushers. His suggestion that the College should make statutes for the School and bind the master to them before his appointment was good sense if not good law. No doubt the master and the usher had made pretty free with the property under their control; not, one imagines, by selling the School lands, but by granting too long and too favourable leases in return for a lump sum of money. From the reference to Thomas's act of beneficence, it looks as though the founder gave the Pocklington Dowmans, and particularly Thomas, some sort of control over the Guild-school's conduct. The suggested raising of the master's income to £26 or £30 and the usher's to £10, to be paid as a salary, is the first mention of the usher's share in the income. The value of the land has gone up by nearly double. The writer is just in claiming that the School served a large district. It never was, never has been, a village school erected by Pocklingtonians for Pocklingtonians.

The masters whom Robert criticises must be Fawcett and James Nelson, who had been master just over a year at the time the letter was written. Ellison cannot very well have been meant, because Robert was at School under him in about 1570-75, at which time, he says, there were 140 boys attending. Numbers would always drop when a good master left. But it seems to be Fawcett who is indirectly said by the writers of the next letter never to have had less than 80 boys at the School. Nelson in his single year of office must have reduced the numbers to a few more than 20, and the scholarship from unmentioned heights to sorry grappling with the elementary Latin translation book *Cato*. But complaint about 'rude and unlerned schollers' was made in Ellison's time, so the responsibility for the poor standard of learning is not wholly Nelson's. In a well-conducted school the older pupils would have known their accidence and syntax thoroughly and been able to write good Latin prose and translate the more advanced authors — Virgil, Cicero and Seneca — without undue difficulty. Greek was again studied in England in the Reformation period, but chiefly as a means to a Scriptural end; while Latin remained the chief subject.

It remains to add that James Nelson was admitted Lupton Fellow of the College on 21 March, 1593-4. He was appointed to the mastership on 2 August, 1598, and he resigned the post on 18 February, 1600, in order to become Rector of Croft, Yorkshire. He was of St. John's College; B.A. 1593-4, M.A. 1597. His usher was Thomas Fallowfield.

CHAPTER 6

THE REGRETTABLE AFFAIR OF
MR. MARTIN BRIGGS (1600 to 1613)

The College was unable to put Robert Dolman's suggestions into effect. During the next sixty years the correspondence between the School and St. John's is taken up with complaints against the various schoolmasters. The worst of them all was Martin Briggs, whose story is neatly told in Latin in David Morton's manuscript history of the College. Translated it reads:

> Mr. Martin Briggs, elected Feb. 18, 1599. In consequence of the complaints of the townspeople that he neglected the instruction of the boys and was wasting the revenues of the School, after being admonished in vain by the Master and Fellows in 1612 to return to good ways, he was in the following year removed.

For twelve years Mr. Briggs, elected Fisher Fellow on 30 March, 1599, stood upon the statutes and the foundation, without paying overmuch attention to his duties; while the sullen townsmen of Pocklington waited for an opportunity to eject him. Really they deserve every sympathy; for the School, after a long initial period of prosperity, had now for the first time fallen upon bad days, solely through the incapacity of one man. The Dowman Scholarships were being given to boys from other schools (the lists at this period are for that reason not trustworthy as evidence of numbers at the School). Mr. Briggs was proving, it seems, as bad a steward of the School lands as he was an indifferent instructor of the boys committed to his charge. The building was in ruins. At last, in October, 1612, when the School was all but closed down, Mr. Briggs intimated to the townsmen that he was thinking of leaving. Next month he accepted the living of Barmston, Yorkshire. Let the correspondence speak for itself:

In August John Bourchier wrote to the College recommending Mr. Nesfields for the mastership. Briggs had apparently already made plans for departure. Then followed these letters:

The townsmen to the College:
> Reverend Master and right worshipfull fellowshipp, We haue vnderstood (thoughe not soone ynoughe) of the purpose of our Schoolmaster to leave our Schoole. And knowinge the well orderinge of that business, to make choyse of another, dothe especially belonge to you, we haue thought good to intreate you in your graue consideracons to respecte the necessitie

of the place as a painefull man may haue the preferement thereof, els, in your favoures you wilbe pleased to take the whole state of our Schoole into your handes, and to make triall for the restoringe and reducement of the same to its former and pristinate worthe. Longe haue we Indured the miserable wantes of so necessarie a benefitt, and hopefull promisses haue made vs forbeare to suggest these wronges and Indempnities we receive by the neglect and non-performance of ther duties in this callinge. Whereof yf you will not take notice by pregnant luculent testimonies of the best of our Country : Then do we craue you will looke into these fewe yeares bypast and measure who haue bene sent from vs to succede in these Schollerships belonginge our Schoole, alwaise till of late supplied sufficientlye by our owne, nowe transferred or transverted to straungers. Our nombers vnder our Cheife master was in our tymes never vnder fourscore persones, now with small a do brought to two children, the eldest not exceeding twelve yeares. We are loth to trouble you with seuerall harmes which hereby growe to the common welthe of our towne, and in a worde because we will not be tedious and troublesome to yow, desire that in your discreete thoughtes yow will thinke of vs and regarde vs as welwillinge members of your howse, to which we wish all good in him which is the Author of all goodnes And so rest

Pocklington, 4 October   your loveinge friendes.
1612   (Peter Dolman and others)

A postscript contains a recommendation for the mastership of Mr. Fowberie, of Hull, and also of Mr. Pettie, of Beverlie, a Christ's man 'who haue hadd the bredinge of divers of our youthes for want of a diligent master at home ...' Mr. Fowberie is wrongly stated by the writers of the letter to have been a Johnian.

Letter from the College to the townsmen:

After our verry hearty Commendations remembered etc, whereas yow haue been pleased to advertise vs by letters of certeyne graue disorders in our Schoole of Pocklington, and sollicited the redresse thereof, eyther by speedy reforming of the present Master if he continues, or by a careful nominacon to the place if he relinquish it. These arre most kindly to acknowledge your discreet and moderate dealing, withall to intreat a little patience, till we may gyve full content. We haue by this bearer addressed letters to Mr. Briggs expecting his speedy answer, when we shall provyde for these wrongs respectively to your desyres, and the Statutes of the Schoole. In the meantyme hoping of your good affection to the Schole and vs, we commit you to the grace of God and rest

Cambr.   Your loving frendes,
Oct. 20. 1612   the Master and Seniors.

Letter from the College to Mr. Briggs:

After our hearty commendations remembered etc. Yow shall hereby vnderstand how the Townsmen of Pocklington, offended at your misvsage of the Schoole there, haue ioyned in complaynt vnto vs. They charge yow with deepe neglect of your duty, breach of many promises of amendment; that by your extreme negligence, the number of Schollers is not decayed but perished, of fourscore persons only two small children left. Which imputations as they immediately touche your credite, so they needs cast some reflexion vppon the Colledge, who sent yow thither vppon better hopes. These are therefore to request, and as

far as we have power to requyre yow, forthwith to repayre hither for the clearing of these obiections. Otherwise be assured of such proceedings as the statutes of the Schoole shall autorize vs vnto. We expect yow in the beginning of the next moneth. Marvell not that we confyne yow to so short a tyme, longe negligence calling for speedy reformation. Then we shall looke for yow, and till then committ yow to the All-mighty and reste
Cambr.   Your loving ffrendes
Oct. 20. 1612   The Master and Seniors.

Meanwhile and later, the College received several applications and recommendations for the post, together with the news that Mr. Briggs had departed for Barmston without giving them notice. The first of these letters came from the Earl of Cumberland, recommending Mr. Fowberie and Mr. Pettie at the request of the townsmen. It was written from Londesborough on 5 October, 1612. The second, dated 16 October, was from Mr. Fowberie recommending himself. 'I am verie desirous as to continue in this latomious course of life in framing and fashioning young wits to some good use hereafter.' 'Latomious' seems to be a metaphor from stone-quarrying. The third of this group was from Sir Roger Wilbraham, Master of Requests to King James I. He recommends William Nesfield; the King having received testimonies from the hands of the Lord Bishop of Bristol and the Dean of York, and of Dr. Hodson, Chancellor, and divers other Prebends. Written 27 April, 1613. To this last the College made the surprising reply:

May it ... plese yow to vnderstand that vpon the vacancy of the place, now first known to vs by your worshipps letters, we have ... respited our election for certeyne dayes ... Sir the great wrong the Country hath susteyned, and no lesse the reproach fallen vppon the Colledg, by the neglect of the former teacher, doe force vppon vs a more then ordinary care of a successor, one experte, not only to manage a schoole setled vnto him, but to plant and erect it decayed and overthrown.
Camb.
May 3rd. 1613.

The complacent attitude taken up by the College is aggravated by the improbability of Mr. Briggs having obeyed their instructions to come up to Cambridge; since in November he definitely accepted the living at Barmston and went off to live there. A second letter from Mr. Fowberie, of Hull, was written on 1 May. It was backed up by two of his pupils in person as samples of his schooling. 'The place,' he writes, 'is something ruinous both School and house, and by reason of some neglect in these later years altogether at this time disfurnished of scholars...' Both had left in Mr. Briggs' absence. While the College was wasting valuable time making up its mind to comply with what amounted to a royal command, the townsmen lost all patience and wrote to threaten legal proceedings, sharply reminding the College of its allegedly illegal transference of the Dowman scholarships:

Reurend Maister and Right worshipfull fellowshipp. Thoughe we doe agnise the dependencie of our Schoole of Pocklington from your colledge of St. John's in some speciall perticulers, as in the Acte of Parliament, to nominate ye Maister els by graunt from Doctor Dolman, as in the gifte of our Schollerships. yett when wee see and consider what wayes are given to appayrant wronges partely out of the vnsufferable neglect of our Maister, beneficed twentie miles from our schoole where he hat not been present since Michaelmas last. And partely by the transferrence of our schollershipps to straungers never so intended by that worthie donor. We cannot but complayne and exclame bothe in Courte and Countrie howe vnconscionablie we are vsed by such a maister and howe carelessly we are respected by such a venerable fellowshipp. And for these causes before we proceed to litigacon in places where we will make overture of all theise Iniuryes we thought good to lett you know, that vnlesse we may haue spedy reformacon and releefe in this so weightie a busines, wee intend godwillinge to addresse our complaintes to the Lord Chancellor, and then demonstrat the Iniuryes, Indignities and Indempnities wee suffer and by him feare not but to haue equall hearinge, and so purchase the infranchisement of this our thraldome, yf to take the fleece and then appropriate the carkasse be ether paternall or pastorall care over pupylls, lett the decree of his Lordshipp or who els shalbe appoynted to censure our cause, be accordinge to the truth and proofe of the same. But lett this be a taste of the infelicitie of our schoole which we desire yow will please to redresse, so as we be not inforced to proclame our greves before the highest magistrates. And even thus commending the orderinge of this business to your wise thoughtes, we take leave, and rest

Roger Sothebe,.. Thomas Dolman (and
seventeen other signatories.)

Postscript. Mr. Briggs hath promised before the Lord Bishopp of Bristoll and some of his highnes Councell, here at Yorke, to resigne and giue vpp his place of Maistershipp in Pocklington nowe at Whitsontyde, wherefore we shall intreate yow will please to make choyce of one who may trewlie and rightlie Judge what is fitt for him to do in the breedinge of youth in manners and learninge, which we found of late to be farre from younge men transported by the pleasures and idle delights.
Pocklington xvijth of May 1613.

The College duly elected William Nesfield on 27 April, 1613, to the vacant mastership. He apparently refused; for on the 19 May of the same year Richard Elcock was nominated. The College wrote to Sir Roger Wilbraham informing him of the appointment and adding that Elcock was 'a man so approved vnto vs for sufficiency of learning and integrity of lyfe, and of himself so desyrous to follow that course, as we conceive assured hope, that by his paynes and discretion the Schoole may be re-established and well ordered...' A day after the appointment and the writing of this letter, was sent a pathetic letter from Robert Fowberie, 'a long and troublesome suitor for Pocklington'; it was a last request for the mastership. Too late.

The upshot of this regrettable affair was that the College wrote to the Archbishop of York asking him to secure from the Crown a second term in which the Archbishop might legally make statutes for the School:

(To Toby Mathew, Lo. Archbishopp of Yorke.)
Right honourable and most reverend ffather in God, may it please your Grace hereby to

vnderstand how his Majestye of famous memory King Edward the Sixt, vppon petition to his Highness made, vouchsafed by a speciall Act of Parliament to graunt power and libertye to the Right Reverend ffather in God the Lo. Archbishop of Yorke and his successors with the Master of St. John's College in Cambridge and his successors to enact and establish certeyne lawes and Statutes for the better government of the ffree grammar schoole in Pocklington, vnder this proviso. That the said L. Archbishopp and Master of St. John's should effectually execute the tenor thereof within the space of two years next following. And for as much as the Lo: Archbishopp and Master of St. John's then being forbearing to proceed accordingly have lost the benefit of that Royall graunt and so left the schoole destitute of those good orders and statutes wherby it shold be ruled. If it may therefore please your Grace to afford vs your honourable favour and assistance in procuring from his majestye a second term to the vses aforesayd both the Schoole now labouring of an Anarchy shall have cause to honor your Grace as a cheef benefactor and we ever bownd to pray for your Graces long lyfe and prosperity. Thus fearing to be troblesome we humbly take our leave and rest

St.John's in Camb.   your Graces to be commanded
Nov 8th 1613.   The Masters and Seniors.

From the fact that no mention of these statutes is made in subsequent letters of complaint from Pocklington we may safely assume that the Archbishop failed to give the School the help which it needed.

Briggs' ushers were probably Thomas Fallowfield and John Dobson (Vicar of Pocklington).

CHAPTER 7

THREE SCHOOLMASTERS
FROM 1613 TO THE END OF
THE CIVIL WARS

RICHARD ELCOCK . . . . 1613 to 1624
JAMES SOTHEBY . . . . 1624 to 1630
ROBERT SEDGWICK . . . . 1630 to 1650

Richard Elcock, M.A. and Fellow of St. John's (1611), a Cheshireman, arrived at Pocklington to find the buildings in ruin and the School empty. He at once set about repairing them. In 1616 he wrote as follows to the College:

...I have dared (beinge hindred from comminge vp to the commencement by weakness of bodie) to interrupt your serious imploymente with these few lines, wherein I ... humbly crave the continuance of your favor in granting my request for a vale ... How ruinous I found the buildings here at my first cominge, and what cost hathe been bestowed since in repaire I spare to write...

The bearer hereof Mr. Thomas Dolman is a gentleman livinge in our towne of Pocklington, of the name and kindred of the founder of our Schoole. He hath brought up his eldest son with him to the Colledge, for your lawful favor and countenance towards whom both he and my selfe are humble suitors...

Pocklington
June 18, 1616.

The 'vale' was a distribution of money often at this time made to Fellows on the vacation of their fellowships. Who paid for the repairs is not mentioned. Perhaps the Dolmans helped. The letter implies that some of it came out of his own pocket. A Marmaduke Dolman was given a Dowman scholarship in November of that year. Another letter, written to the College in June of the following year, asked for expenses in an impending lawsuit against the parish of Millington, who were alleged to be liable to contribute to the repairing of Pocklington parish church. It is not clear why he expected the College to be interested in the matter.

Collated vicar of Pocklington in January, 1619, Elcock held the living until March, 1622. He was succeeded by James Sotheby, who also took over the mastership from him in July, 1624.

How far he repaired the fortunes as well as the buildings of the School it is difficult to say. Between 1613 and 1624, thirteen Dowman scholars are given (including a Francis and a Robert Elcock, both 'Cestriensis' and so probably his sons). Most of the entrants are Yorkshire boys; among them is a Dowman, a Sotheby, and other boys with familiar names. The College may, however, have continued to give some of the scholarships away to boys from other schools. The Gonville and Caius 'Admissions' give us three entries, mentioning Elcock by name: Robert Sherlocke, son of a husbandman, one year at Pocklington under Mr. Elcock, admitted sizar 1622, ordained at York, 1625; Robert Kidson, son of a wool-draper, four years at Pocklington under Mr. Elcock, Sizar, 1624 (he succeeded the errant Mr. Briggs in the living of Barmston); Michael Richardson, son of a husbandman of Barmby Moor, at Pocklington seven years under Mr. Elcock and Mr. Sotheby, sizar, 1625. If boys of humble parentage could win Open Sizarships to Caius from Pocklington, Mr. Elcock must have been a good enough teacher. Nor were there any complaints made about him. His usher was Obadiah Chossip (or, by a ruder spelling, Gossip).

James Sotheby, a member of one of the two most notable families in Pocklington (the Sotheby monument may be seen on the north wall of the north transept of the parish church), was admitted Dowman Scholar in November, 1618, and he took his M.A. in 1624. (The identification is not certain.) He was buried at Pocklington in August, 1630, very young it seems. Eight boys took Dowman scholarships in these six years. No complaints were made against him; and, indeed, as a member of the Sotheby family he would be secure from attack. We shall guess that he was a satisfactory master. His usher was Chossip.

The next master was Robert Sedgwick, of St. John's College, B.A. 1624-5, M.A. 1628, ordained priest 1634. From the date of his appointment the St. John's College Admission Registers begin, providing valuable evidence of the condition of the School at any given time; as not only the scholars but all the boys who went up to the College are from now on entered, together with the name of the School and its master or masters during the boy's term there. The entries also include the name and the profession of the boy's father and the boy's age is noted. The Registers are exceedingly well edited and indexed under several useful headings and valuable notes have been added to them. A specimen entry is:

1632 (31) Hammond Baldwyn, co. York, son of Henry Baldwyn, vicar of Barneby, Yorkshire; school, Pocklington (Mr. Sedgwick) for six years; admitted sizar for Dr. Ambrose, surety Mr. Robinson, 17 April, aet. past 16.   (Vol. I, p. 10, l.30)

There are eighteen entries, with only six sizars, for the nineteen years of Sedgwick's reign, all of them Yorkshire boys and most of them gentlemen's sons. It is, however, significant that the average time spent at the School by a boy at this period was one year and, in one case only, eight weeks. Two names call for further notice. Sam. Drake, of Halifax, was by Charles I's orders given on 14 March, 1643, to be elected Fellow, 'any statute to the contrary notwithstanding'. He was made Fisher Fellow six days later. A Dowman scholar, he was made D.D. by mandate in 1662, early in the Restoration. Joseph Hill, one year at Pocklington, was admitted in 1646, and later became a Fellow of Magdalene College. He was ejected for non-conformity and became minister of the English Church at Middleburgh in Holland. He was the author of several printed sermons.

Sedgwick was perhaps a Royalist, for no complaint was made until the Commonwealth had begun. But as soon as that happened a vigorous effort was made to get rid of him. Among the signatories of the letters written to the College against him were 'preachers of the Word', who were put in to replace the parish priests at that time, known Parliamentary men and men whose names have been hitherto unfamiliar to us. On the other hand, some of them seemed just as glad to evict a Puritan ten years later. No member of the Dolman family wrote against Sedgwick, for they, at any rate, were all Royalists. Most of them were deeply involved in the struggle to uphold the Crown. One of old Thomas's sons, Marmaduke, of Messingham, Lincolnshire, fell fighting for the King at Marston Moor. Of his son, the younger Marmaduke, Peacock has the following account: 'In June, 1648, when all hope for the Royal cause on the field of battle was over, he and his following formed a portion of the four hundred horse and two hundred foot who attacked Lincoln Castle and released therefrom all the prisoners who were confined for murder, felony and debt ...' He went on to recount how the Royalists were routed at Willoughby, Mr.Dolman and many others of the Cavalier gentry of Lincolnshire and Yorkshire being made prisoners. For joining in this wild escapade Marmaduke had his property confiscated and sold by the state. He was a Roman Catholic.

The correspondence began in 1649 with a letter dated 14 November from Sedgwick himself; in it he resigns his post:

Right worshipfull,

Vpon such dislike of some gentlemen in the country haue thought me vnworthie to continue in that poore preferment in the free schoole in Pocklington, I thought it my duty (having received it from the College) to resigne it back into your power, that soe you might present (as of just power you ought) to the place. And therefore I humbly desier you to take care for a man able for that purpose with what convenient speede you thinke fitte, which is the desier of

Your worships Servant
Robt. Siggeswicke.
Witnesses hereof : Ri. Marby, Tho. Waite, Mar. Prickett.
Cha. Campteshorm.

The following February a disclaimer arrived. The resignation was not legal, he pleaded and, almost in the same breath, offered to sell the College his legal resignation in exchange for other preferment:

> Reverend Sir obleiged duty presented etc.
> I am informed of a report should come to Mr Burnbies eares of my resigning vp my place in this schoole to your selfe and senior fellowes of your house. Sir there is a paper to that purpose may chance to salute your hands : but as it was vpon threats as also large promises (without any performance) of a tender care over my wife and tenne children by the Committee for Sequestrations wrested from mee : So it is altogether illegall no Publicke Notarie being a wittnes therto, and therefore I disclaime from it : and yet vpon other preferment I wilbee readie to make a legall resignation but to noe other but to the Master and Senior fellowes of your College whatever befalles mee...

A paterfamilias with such a family to maintain could not afford to give up his only means of sustenance without a struggle. At the same time the correspondence which follows makes it clear that, however great the political prejudice against him may have been, he had shown himself a far from ideal schoolmaster. The explanation of the appearance of the same signatures against a Royalist and later a Puritan is probably that they were both bad schoolmasters. As the man, who was next appointed on the very warm recommendation of the complainants, turned Roman Catholic less than seven years later — a thing no man would do in response to a sudden whim — it looks as though Sedgwick's enemies used the Puritanical element in Pocklington to get rid of a man they disliked for non-political reasons. How the townsmen suffered from a bad master at the School is made clear in the correspondence. On 24 July, 1650, Seth Elcock, preacher of the Word in Pocklington, and thirty-two fellow citizens — among them Jasper Belt, of whom more anon, but none of it to his good — wrote in complaint to the College:

> Whereas the inhabitants of Pocklington, and parts Adjacent haue long groaned vnder the burthen of a Negligent Schoolemaster whose carelessenes hath not only much ruinated the fabrique of the Schoole, but exceeding ecclipsed its former Honour, by diminution of the number of Schollers. Thereby much Impoverishing the Towne. Which some worthy Gentlemen taking notice of preuailed with him for a Resignation ... We ... doe earnestly desire ... That Mr. Edward Llewellin, a man of an honest, and pious conversation, very well approved of for his sufficiency of Learning and Diligence in his calling, May be elected... Soe as you shall reape much Honour and the now much displeased Town and County much content.

Four days later nine of the neighbouring ministers wrote a lengthy letter at the instance of the townsmen. The burden of their complaint was much the same, with a few additional points of interest:

> Its former Schoolemasters ... through their care and diligence did much advantage to the towne, not only in their trading, but also in the education of their youth ... Not only the cuntrie and parts adiacent, but alsoe the inhabitants of the towne have been necessitated to bestowe their children in Schooles abroad. Vpon which there has risen, in the hearts of many, very great indignation against your college...

They recommend Lluellin.

On 1 August Thomas Fairfax and seven other Yorkshiremen repeated the charges against the unhappy Sedgwick in a fulsome condemnation of him, written from York, bringing in a new hint of peculation or financial mismanagement, and pricking the College's conscience with the only weapon available, mention of the continued abuse of the Dowman scholarships:

> ... By whom (Sedgwick) also we feare, some detriment hath accrewed to the revenuewes and profitts belonging to its maintenance ... But we are very unwilling to look backwards in any other way of procedure because hee hath resigned (which resignation is herewithall sent unto you)... As also to specify those more particular damages wee are informed have bin sustained by this Country in the disposing of those Scholarships and Sizars places ... bestowed upon the aforesaid Schoole by worthy Patriotts of this Country... But we will not remember anything of this nature, because wee conceive it hath principally proceeded from the School's deficiency.

They recommend Mr. Lluellin.

The most interesting point in these letters is the information, subsequently confirmed, that the boys were boarded out in the town. So that the townsmen (especially Jasper Belt, the publican) had the strongest interest in the number of boarders attending the School. The purse as well as politics urged Sedgwick's departure. Edward Lluellin was appointed on 23 August. The School had now endured nearly fifty years of ill success, with an interlude of fair achievement under Elcock and Sotheby. It is unfortunate that our most illuminating evidence is all of this prejudiced complaining kind; the picture is apt to be painted too dark.

To name the usher during this headmastership is difficult. The lists give three names: Obadiah Chossip; James Hudson, vicar from 1641 to 1673; and (queried) Foley. From Lluellin's time the list of ushers is complete and accurate.

CHAPTER 8

THE SCHOOL UNDER THE COMMONWEALTH

SEPTENNIUM OF EDWARD LLUELLIN, 1650 to 1657

Edward Lluellin had been recommended to the College by the townsmen in the warmest terms of praise. A graduate of Pembroke Hall, he was admitted to St. John's as pensioner on 23 August, 1650. There is a record in the Admissions Book that he took this step in order to be a candidate for the mastership of Pocklington School. He does not seem to have been given a fellowship, or to have taken his M.A. degree. Indeed, 23 September is the date of a letter written by him to the College from Pocklington, thanking the master and fellows for his appointment in choice Latin. His admission must have been purely formal.

Of all the early masters Lluellin is the one of whom it would most profit us to have been bequeathed a little information. The Latin letter and the vellum-bound manuscript register of admissions to the School contain the only clues to his character. A translation of the letter is given for the benefit of Catonists[1] and worse:

Worshipful Sir,
    I cannot say why it is, but very often most men forget their patrons as soon as through their kind help they are able to swim without a life-belt; and either neglect, or wholly disdain, to display the slightest sign of gratitude. Of course men of this kind (or rather shadows of men, since they have so stripped themselves of every vestige of humanity) are like the Stoics in this particular; for the Stoics, according to Seneca, teach that willing acceptance is in itself abundant repayment. But fie on this ungracious Stoic paradox, so abhorrent to good manners! There is no doubt at all that we ought to make some repayment to our benefactors, if we are not to be branded with the monstrous stigma of ingratitude. Let the poorest man pay back something. Poverty, nay destitution, and gratitude can make bed-fellows. If a man cannot pay back a kindness, at least he can try. No one who has paid back as much as he can is an ingrate. Nay, he were deservedly thought to have made great restitution; since all actions are to be judged by their intention and measured by the good will which inspired them.
    As for myself, Honourable Sir, I can give you for the present nothing except words, but those, believe me, are sincere. In the future I am hopeful of offering you some solid harvest of my labours. For I most solemnly promise that, as far as in me lies, I will make it my

[1]See pp. 22, 23

ceaseless endeavour that from this Seminary — alack, at this moment in absolute ruin — of which by your own special kindness and by that of certain members of your learned Society I am become the gardener, there shall be transplanted saplings to grow up into trees under your wise and more illustrious guardianship, so as finally to bear the choicest fruit to both Church and State.

I meditate often on the number and importance of the considerations which spur me to the resolute execution of this task. But there is within me that which drives me on ever more fiercely. How ineffable a consolation a mind conscious of right and fidelity will be, when I am called to give account of my stewardship in the presence of that awful and supreme tribunal.

Nonetheless this does not depend upon me. Alas, that I am all infirmity! Wherefore I call to mind that saying of Augustine, 'If thou standest upon thyself, thou standest not' and Bernard's 'He that leaneth not on Him strives in vain'; and I burden God, the Giver of all good things, with untiring prayers and repeated supplications that He may deem worthy so to strengthen my weak efforts with His own blessings, and there may redound glory to Himself, service to the Church and benefit to the State. That he is earnestly toiling to carry out all these tasks, is the constant avowal of him whom you will ever find

Yours etc,

Pocklington   Edward Lluellin.

Mr. Richard Darley gives you most hearty greeting and is delighted to have received your letter.

Baker Street itself would hardly dare to deduce the writer's character from such slender evidence, all the less revealing because the letter is written in the formal Ciceronian of the Schools. The opening words are taken, as by any schoolboy, straight from one of Cicero's Philippics. The exaggeration of sentiment and expression is the rhetoric of the Roman Forum. The only two deductions that we can make from it are that Lluellin was a capable scholar and a religious man.

He was also business-like. If he was not the first master who kept an Admission Register of the boys, he was certainly the only one to bequeath it successfully to posterity. Nor do we hear of an earlier one being kept. The reason why we have so few documents and records of the School is partly that the masters of a school regarded them as their own property and treated them accordingly. This register, after two centuries at the School, was carried off by one of Hutton's immediate predecessors and only recovered for the School a few years before the close of the nineteenth century by the energy of Mr. Leach, who did so much to preserve our history for us.

The Register was kept in a white vellum-bound book, and on the first page is written in a somewhat elegant hand, *Liber Admissionum Scholasticarum in Grammaticalem Scholam Pocklingtoniensem*. Beneath is added in the same hand *Haec laudabilis (absit invidia verbo) invaluit consuetudo:* 'This laudable custom, if I may call it so, now prevails.' Lluellin's first pupil, thirteen-year-old Christopher Little, spoiled the first two pages by adding in scrawled characters his own unimportant name and the unnecessary grammatical definition *mos fuit consuetudo*. Discipline has been reasserted by page 3. The first entry is dated 23 September, 1650. Lluellin had had a few weeks before this in which to repair the 'utterly ruined' buildings and to canvass the County for pupils. We are entitled to assume that he did both; for on the first day of entry he admitted twelve boys, and on the next, eight. The total of admissions was forty-three by the end of November and seventy-three before next September. At the end of two years it was one hundred and eighteen. The entries are evenly distributed over the year : it almost looks as though there were no holidays in these strenuous years. The father's name and rank or occupation are generally given together with the boy's age. An analysis of the occupations of the fathers who had boys at the School during Lluellin's six and a half years' mastership will give us some idea of the School.

Gentlemen (generosus)	52
Husbandmen (agricola, i.e. labourer)	28
Esquires (armigerus)	10
Clergy (presbyter — a Commonwealth term)	8
Merchants (mercenarius)	7
Knights (miles or eques auratus)	5
Yeomen (i.e. one who farms own land)	4
Blacksmith (fabrius ferreus)	2
Butcher (lanius or lanio)	2
Lawyers (iuris peritus)	2
Tailors (sutor or s. vestarius)	2
Baker	1
Scrivener (scriba)	1
Soldier (militaris)	1
TOTAL	125

There were some parents merely described as 'deceased'. While there is thus revealed part of a perhaps unconsciously democratic tradition, it is likely that the social differences would make more difference to the seventeenth-century boy than they would to those born since the Great War. What is rather unusual during the early part of our history, hardly any of the poorer boys went up to St. John's. Though the boy's home is rarely mentioned, we may take it that they came from all parts of the County. Several came from well-known Yorkshire families such as Hesketh, Fairfax, Saville, Beaumont, Darley (five brothers of this name on one day),

Vavasour, Wilberforce (the grandfather of the slave liberator), Gower and Askwith. Many of the other names are already familiar to us, among them a Dolman and a Sotheby. The town must have benefited considerably by such an influx of good customers. There is no means of estimating the precise number of boys in the School at any one given time after the first year, but there are not likely to be many omissions from Lluellin's Register which gives one hundred and sixty-four names (there is one other to be added from the College Register). Although boys often stayed less than a year at Pocklington, Lluellin must have had about a hundred boys in the School for at least some of the period. The ages at entry range from six to eighteen, the great bulk of them being between eight and fifteen; the average age was twelve and a half. A scholar and an ill-paid usher to cope with a hundred boys of all ages from infancy to adolescence in perhaps two rooms! But this was indisputably one of the School's greatest periods. Eleven of these boys went to St. John's and a few to other colleges, only six as sizars. Statistics grow wearisome; it will suffice to say that in after-life a number of these boys seem to have become fairly prominent, some as 'eminent divines', including the master of Sidney Sussex College; nine became fellows of Oxford and Cambridge Colleges, three were styled baronets and others became soldiers. Though one was tried as a Jacobite at Manchester during William and Mary's reign, none of them, so far as we know, was hanged.

The Vellum Book was used for other purposes than that of an Admission Register. The appointment of new ushers is noted in it; and it was sometimes used as a rent-book. In 1652 John Sturdy was elected usher by Lluellin and the churchwardens; in 1654 John Winne, a Johnian. Meagre as our record of this great mastership is, and still more meagre our knowledge of the master himself, the manner of his departure is grandly told by David Morton[1] in a single sentence, '*In campos Pontificios transfuga post septennium recessit :* After seven years he deserted to the Roman Faith and departed.'

[1] Manuscript History of St. John's College

CHAPTER 9

ROWLAND GREENWOOD, PURITAN, EXPELLED FROM HIS DIONYSIAN KINGDOM OF POCKLINGTON
(1657 to 1660)

The College elected a Richard Thistlethwaite, B.A., on 5 August, 1657, to fill Lluellin's place. But he died 'priusquam in actualem possessionem admitteretur'. In a letter to the College, dated 16 September, several ministers and schoolmasters from neighbouring villages wrote to recommend Rowland Greenwood. He was a Johnian, B.A. 1619-20, M.A. 1623, B.D. 1638, and ordained priest 1622-3, and he had been master of the Brewers' School at Aldenham in Kent from 1623 to 1634, a post which apparently only carried a meagre emolument. Since then he had been vicar of Wimbish, Essex. The College elected him on 28 September. In October he wrote to Mr. Ffothergill, president of the College:

> Good Mr. President, I am comed so far as the Crowne in Cambridge onward to my Dionysian Kingdome at Pockl :

He continued Lluellin's practice of keeping the register in the Vellum Book; it is uncertain with how much accuracy. Lluellin's last entry was on 1 March. Greenwood's first was on 16 October. In the remaining three months of the year he re-admitted two of Lluellin's pupils and admitted an orphan, Ralph Witty, aged nineteen. This boy became a fellow of Peterhouse in 1666 and later held two livings in Yorkshire. In the next year there are sixteen entries, two re-admissions. In 1659 there is only one entry, but two pages have been torn from the book. The figures are interesting enough, because, if we may assume from the mention of a few boys being re-admitted that all the boys left on Lluellin's departure, it would seem that Leach was wrong in stating that the School continued to prosper. On the other hand the chief reason for Greenwood's unpopularity in the town was the fact that he was a Puritan. For this very reason he would be unlikely to attract many of the Yorkshire gentry to send their sons to Pocklington and only a few did. Already the Commonwealth was dragging to its end and late in 1659 General Monk's army dislodged the Rump Parliament and set the stage for the Stuart restoration. In October of that year the College received 'The Humble petition of Rowland Greenwood Master of your Schoole in Poclington':

> Sheweth, Whereas some of our disaffected and popish persons together with our Alehouse Birdes (fluttering after the glimmering Light of their dark Lanterne guided by a tipling Maltster) have stirred up two justices to move you for my removall : Theese signify that by reason of a Quartane feaver my intention was and is to leave the place about the end of May next when I have finished the repairs to your house; And in the meane Time the Schoole shalbe carefully attended by myself and Vsher : Further be pleased to take speciall notice, that the said Maltster, as this enclosed paper makes it plain, because hee could not corrupt mee basely to take aduantage of one who forfeited his Lease, for non payment of rent at the very day, And because I would not be bribed to sell another Lease at an vnder valewe (vnto which if I had yielded, great wrong had been done in leauing the house vnrepaired) hath ever since being stimulated by his Alehouse Customers who cry out because parte of their gain is gone by reason Boarders, because of my sicknes, come not to them as formerly, sought occasion of revenge
>
> Wherefore your petitioner having no means at all save only 12 li per ann. to maintaine himselfe and a servant and having, not long since, suffered great Losse by a private fire and the publique Sword, humbly beggs for his Continuance heere till about the end of the said May next; and then rowling himself vpon Evidence, will cast himself and the College Seale at your feete, And daily pray etc.

This abruptly is added:

> As 12 handes were privately sent against mee, so cold I send above 60 handes neare to the Towne for my continuance.

Within the letter is folded a slip with these words:

> Mr Greenwood you desired to speeke with my counsell about that busines that is betwixt you and me, he is now in towne & goes away shortly if you please to meet me there let me know by the bearer
>> Your friend J.B.
> This note came in synnce and this J.B. is Jasper Belt, the Maltster and Incendiary to our Tinder Tappe houses.

It seems almost sacrilege to offer comment on so delightful a masterpiece of spirited English prose. And surely that sinister note must have convinced the master of St. John's of Jasper Belt's wickedness. A few words of explanation are all that is needed. The corrupt demand for the sale of a lease below its proper value is curious, because the next schoolmaster accepted a bribe to perform a similar service to Sir John Reresby. If serious repairs were needed to the building, Lluellin must have been unable to afford more than the patching up of these perpetually ruined buildings. We have already mentioned that the boarders were a source of wealth to the townsmen; and now that, as Greenwood admits, there was a serious drop in numbers, they would have a just pretext for complaint. Robert Dolman (1599) had suggested £26 or £30 as a suitable salary for the master and £10 for the usher, and had added that with careful management some margin would be left. Greenwood is either exaggerating the smallness of the income or referring to his private means. His losses by a private fire and the public sword it is beyond the writer's knowledge to conjecture what they were. Twelve hands means the signatures of twelve witnesses. This and the next letter make it plain that the townsmen had already complained about him to the College, for on the 8 October they wrote as follows to the master and fellows:

> In answeere to yours We doe signifie that the intimacon alreadie giuen yow of Mr Greenwoodes negligence and evill behaviour is true and also that he exactes and requires monies at everie Schollers entrance and yearlie compositions to be paid him quarterlie beinge a thinge altogether contrarie to custom, the freedome of the Schoole and the founders donacion : by all which meanes the Schoole is brought to soe lowe and lost condiCON that it is never like to be raised again by him, and herebie our Towne is much impoverished and learninge discountenanced. For now here is not aboue eight or nyne little boyes in the Schoole, where as formerlie by the paines and industrie of some former masters there hath bene six or seven score Schollers in our Schoole, of which three or four score of them hath bene tablers, gentlemen sonnes, which was a great benefit to our Towne, and thereby Learning was much advanced and the Vniversitie enlarged by the number of Schollers that were yearly sent from hence. Moreover we heere that Mr. Greenwood hoped to obtain your fauours to resign his place to the present Vsher, who either married or is to marrie his daughter which we do not approve of nor commende as fit for the place, but we desire rather that yow would procede to an election in the Colledge that by that meanes we might have one able, discreet and well learned man according to the mind and will of the ffounder ...
>
> (Signed by James Hudson, Vicar, Jesper Belt,
> ffrancis Field, one of the feoffees, and eleven others.)

It is clear that these writers would not agree with Leach's contention that a 'free' school was simply one where there were no tuition fees. Only a few boys went up to Cambridge in these years; but then Greenwood was only at the School a very short time. We may note with relief that it was the presentation of the usher to the mastership, not his marriage to Greenwood's daughter, which was disapproved. He was James Dayson, and had only been appointed the previous June. This alleged effort to bring off a diplomatic marriage was Greenwood's last unavailing effort to preserve his attachment to the School revenues. His successor was appointed on 27 September, 1660. But according to Northcliffe his resignation was dated 26 January, 1661-2. It is easy to believe that it was difficult to get him to sign such a document.

CHAPTER 10

FROM THE RESTORATION TO THE END OF THE CENTURY

FOUR MASTERS

JOHN CLARKE .... 1660 to 1664
THOMAS ELLISON .... 1664 to 1693
THOMAS DWYER .... 1693 to 1698
MILES FARRAR .... 1698 to 1702

Having rejected the unfortunate Roundhead, the town apparently settled down to a period of contentment with the School's prosperity. The evidence is scanty; but there are a good number of admissions to St. John's College and to Peterhouse to suggest that the School was still doing well. During Clarke's short mastership, six boys were admitted to St. John's, and during Ellison's long one, forty-four boys to St. John's and nine to Peterhouse. There may, of course, have been others admitted at other Cambridge colleges or at Oxford. In any case two a year is a good average. All but one of these boys came from a Yorkshire home, but only seven from Pocklington itself. Under the heading of 'father's occupation' we find a wide range, though gentlemen and clerks together total slightly over half the recorded occupations. Only three are noted as the sons of husbandmen. As it would normally be the wealthier families which sent their sons to the university, these entries probably reflect a fairly full School, drawing its boys from all walks of life and offering a real opportunity of advancement to boys from humble homes. The figures for the masterships of Dwyer and Farrar show rather less than one admission a year to St. John's. Dwyer's great work was to rebuild the School (1698), for which the reader should refer to the chapter on the buildings (p. 150).

Farrar was preoccupied with the one incident in this era of the School's history which is well documented. For a bribe of £20 and perhaps the promise of preferment, John Clarke (with his usher, John Dayson) gave Sir John Reresby, of York, an eighty-one years' lease on some of the School's land at an annual rent of £24 against its proper value of £133 6s. 8d. per annum as subsequently valued. Thomas Ellison began legal proceedings in 1680, and after twenty-three years of litigation, during which Ellison and Farrar had acted with commendable honesty and energy, the lease was annulled and a small portion of the arrears was recovered. The proceedings are interesting in themselves and show the weakness of a system which allowed the master and usher, acting as a corporation, to mismanage the School's property in this way. Part of Sir John Reresby's defence was that the strips of land belonging to the School were inextricably mixed up with his own property (at Thrybergh, near Ripon), a common enough state of affairs under the prevailing agricultural system. The College gave considerable help in the legal actions, Ellison was firm with Sir John, and Miles Farrar resisted several offers to settle for a smaller sum than the Commissioners first fixed as owing to the School. Farrar was at this time only receiving £24 a year from the endowment, and this he had to share with the usher.

A little silver bell, inscribed with Clarke's and Ellison's names, is now in the possession of the Governors; it has been handed down from headmaster to headmaster with the tradition that it was the School cock-fighting bell.

These four masters were all clergy and all Johnians, though Dwyer took his degrees at Trinity College, Dublin. Dwyer went from Pocklington to Leeds Grammar School, and thence, in 1706, to Sedbergh. Farrar came to Pocklington from Leeds, thus changing schools with Dwyer.

The Cockfighting Bell

CHAPTER 11

THE FIRST HALF OF THE EIGHTEENTH CENTURY

There follows a long period when little or nothing is known about the School's history apart from the names of the masters and a few names of boys in the Admission Registers of the School and of university colleges. It was a time when grammar school education had fallen into a decline throughout England, partly as a consequence of the Act of Uniformity (1662) requiring schoolmasters, among others, to conform to the liturgy of the Church of England. This applied to private as well as public schools, but it resulted none the less in nonconformist masters leaving the grammar schools to set up schools of their own. It was a period when the gentry employed private tutors and in many cases sent their sons abroad. The universities were largely neglectful of their responsibility to educate their undergraduates, and the gulf between the rich students and the poor distressingly wide. As if in compensation, this was an age in English history which fostered individual brilliance and, significantly, by far the most famous of our Old Boys, William Wilberforce, was at the School during the latter half of this century.

For the first fifty years the bare list of headmasters must suffice:

John Foulkes . . . . 1704 to 1709
John Drake . . . . 1709 to 1714
Joseph Trebell . . . . 1714 to 1716
Christopher Lantrew . . . . 1716 to 1717
John Baker . . . . 1717 to 1740
Robert Robinson . . . . 1740 to 1749
Edward Birckbeck . . . . 1749 to 1754

All these masters were Johnians and clergy. Only nineteen boys are known to have gone up from the School to Cambridge during this long period. And there is one entry of fourteen boys in the Vellum Book, admitted by John Baker in February, 1717-18.

CHAPTER 12

REV. KINGSMAN BASKETT, M.A.
(1754 to 1807)

The eighteenth century, as has been said, saw a great decline in the effectiveness of grammar schools. For over two centuries they had supplied education to the middle and labouring classes, in the best interests of democracy. Trevelyan mentions the 'young gentleman sitting on the bench (in the schoolroom) with the cleverest sons of the farmers and the townspeople'. The Admission Register of Pocklington confirms this practice from the beginning. Grammar schools were also numerous. In 1547 there was one grammar or secondary school for every 8,300 people, with which one compares very disadvantageously the proportion in 1865, when there was one for every 23,750 people. Various causes led to the decline in the eighteenth century : insufficient revenues of the foundations, owing to the lowering of money values, political interference after the Restoration, when nonconformists were disqualified for office, with a resulting shortage of good schoolmasters and, thirdly, the rigidity of the curriculum fixed by the founders in face of a growing demand for other subjects than Latin and Greek. Moreover, the bad conditions of boarding-school life deterred parents from sending their sons. Locke mentions the 'ill-bred and vicious boys', and even at the big public schools of Eton, Winchester, Rugby and Harrow, revolts marked this period of their existence.

Pocklington, however, except for a short period, did not suffer from lack of revenue, and the income was sufficient to attract a good master. Nor was the curriculum confined to Latin and Greek. From the viciousness of schools admitting only boarders the attendance of day-boys and the watchful eye of the townspeople no doubt helped to keep the School immune. It seems that education at Pocklington went on quietly and more usefully during the eighteenth century than in many other old foundations. The parents of William Wilberforce would not have placed him at Pocklington unless the School had been reasonably conducted. But all depended upon the conscience of the headmaster. The old age of Baskett and the absenteeism of Shield brought Pocklington eventually as low as the rest. The position came almost to resemble that of Whitgift, Croydon, whose headmaster, according to the report of the Schools Inquiry

Commissioners in 1868, had held office for thirty years, but was teaching no pupils.[1] Yet as soon as a master like Gruggen succeeded at Pocklington all went well again.

In the next ninety-five years of the School's history after 1754 we have a remarkable phenomenon, two headmasters only covering this period, Baskett and Shield. The headmastership of the Rev. Kingsman Baskett, appointed in 1754, is wrapped in obscurity, lighted only by that 'bright particular star', William Wilberforce. The records available, admissions to St. John's College, Cambridge, continue to show Pocklington sizars entering the college in 1754, 1755, 1759 and 1766, the age of the sizar on entry being eighteen or nineteen, which indicates at least some higher work in the School.

It was a curious reason that brought William Wilberforce to the School. He had been living in Wimbledon with an aunt, and when this lady became sympathetic to the Wesleyan sect, whose popularity at that time was frowned upon by society, the family, in alarm at her tendencies, brought the boy back to Hull, fearing the danger of his conversion to Wesleyanism, and shortly afterwards placed him in 'the costly seclusion of Pocklington School' (Coupland, *Life of Wilberforce*), costly, because his parents apparently paid the headmaster £300 a year! It is obvious that his position at School was to be similar to that of the gentleman-commoner at the universities in those days. He would no doubt have a room of his own, dine with the headmaster and be specially tutored by him. In any case the atmosphere seems to have been congenial, for he stayed five years, 1771-1776, and proceeded in due course to St. John's College, Cambridge. Baskett must have found him a serious student. It is not often that a boy at school is so moved by a public evil as to write to the papers about it. His letter to the press, which is extant, denounces slavery as 'that odious traffic in human flesh'.[2] The sequel shows that there has been no greater moment in the School's history than when the Emancipator began his lifelong work by penning his first public protest from some study or living-room in the Schoolhouse. The conclusion of his great work and the centenary of his death in 1833 were duly honoured by the unveiling of a panel in the new School hall at the Commemoration of 1933. Another illustrious pupil belongs to this period, William Etty, the painter. He left, however, at the age of eleven.

Baskett certainly stayed in office too long, if we accept the evidence of his successor, Shield, who reports upon the lack of pupils in the first years of

[1] An interesting summary of this period is given in *The English Grammar School* (published by Hosking).

[2] A recent account of this letter, given by a junior boy of the School in an essay, was that Wilberforce wrote his first letter to the Press 'about the abolition of slavery in schools'.

William Wilberforce

the nineteenth century (see p. 52). We may suspect that he became too old for this job and kept the post as a sinecure after he had ceased to earn the income. Even this he frittered away by leasing the properties at small rentals, thus storing up trouble for his successor. A tablet in his memory hangs in the parish church near the Dolman Chapel, of which the inscription reads:

In memorial of
Kingsman Baskett, Clerk,
Formerly Fellow of St John's College, Cambridge
Fifty-three years Master of
The Free Grammar School in this place
Who died April 17th, 1807

He retired to Hull after his resignation and is mentioned in correspondence, preserved in the library of St. John's College, as late as the year of his death.

CHAPTER 13

REV. THOMAS SHIELD, B.D.

(1807 to 1848)

After the obscurity of the eighteenth century it is good to possess some contemporary evidence of the mastership of Thomas Shield. It is an extract from a *History, Gazetteer and Directory of the East and North Ridings of Yorkshire* by William White and dated 1840. As most of the information is personal to Thomas Shield, it was almost certainly supplied directly by himself:

> The School property produced in 1828 £1,020, and now about £800 per annum, and consists of land and buildings at Pocklington, Duggleby, Barmby, Wetwang, Lutton, Acklam and York, partly received in 1824 from Colonel Fullerton in exchange for two farms of 188 acres at Thrybergh. The School has also £1 16s. 8d. yearly from land at Wetwang, left by a Rev. Thomas Mountforth.
>
> The old School and Master's house were taken down in 1818, and rebuilt on a more commodious plan by the Rev. Thomas Shield, B.D., the present Master, who was inducted in 1807, when the school income was only about £100 per annum, and when he commenced a series of suits in Chancery, which terminated in 1820, and by which he succeeded in setting aside the long leases and small rents, under which all the school estates had previously been held. It is not distinctly provided in the school-deeds, in what proportion it was originally intended the master and usher should share in the school revenues; but before 1807 it was usual for the former to receive two-thirds and the latter one-third of the income.
>
> In consequence of the present master having alone incurred a considerable expense in recovering the possessions of the School, from the lessees, and thus increasing its yearly income from £100 to £800, it has been agreed that he shall allow the usher £200 per annum, and retain the rest for himself. By the spirited and praiseworthy exertions of Mr. Shield, during an expensive litigation of thirteen years, the school has been raised to the rank of one of the most liberally endowed scholastic institutions in the kingdom. It is free for classical learning to all the boys of Pocklington and the neighbourhood, on the payment of an entrance fee of five shillings.

This extract reminds one of the satisfaction of Little Jack Horner who 'pulled out a plum and said, "What a good boy am I!".' When he claims to have 'raised the School to the rank of one of the most liberally endowed scholastic institutions in the kingdom', and that it was 'free for classical learning', he draws a veil over one of the worst periods of neglect of that learning, classical or otherwise.

On 24 April, 1807, a Mr. J. Singleton, of Givendale, wrote a letter to the Bursar of St. John's College, Cambridge, saying, 'Mr. Baskett, on whom I called, said "All the leases are for 21 years"...'

This word 'leases' has great significance for the fortunes of the School during the next forty years. No doubt the carelessness of Baskett in his old age in letting the properties at such low rentals had to be met by exertions on the part of his successor, if he was to have a decent income. He was able to claim at a still later date, 1846, that for ten years previous to his own appointment that School income had been about £110 a year, whereas his labours had restored it to £950, exclusive of two fields allotted to the master and let for £13 10s. A stroke of luck helped him in 1842, when the railway bought School land at Dringhouses, York, for £4,500, which sum was invested in 3 per cent. Consols. All the same, his efforts to get the leases set aside, involving frequent visits to London, caused him to be a very unfaithful shepherd to the School. In any case there is little excuse for him after 1820. His heart was certainly not in schoolmastering.

His absenteeism provoked chronic complaints, which numerous visits by representatives of the master of St. John's College seemed powerless to cure for long. About this time Parliament itself was much exercised by popular dissatisfaction with the management of endowed grammar schools. During the sittings of Lord Brougham's commission hard things were said to the master of St. John's College, among others, for lack of oversight of Pocklington School. But to do him justice, in spite of the slow journey, as it was in those days, from Cambridge to Yorkshire, the master did send frequent 'visitors' to instruct Mr. Shield in 1817, 1819, 1825, 1827, 1842 and 1847, besides writing many letters. In 1827 Mr. Shield actually denied the authority of the College to 'visit' the School. He was 'decidedly of the opinion,' reported the bursar, Mr. Blick, to the master, 'that neither yourself as master of St. John's College as a corporate body has any right or authority whatsoever to visit the School, that the authority ceased at the deposition of the Guild, when the College received the power to appoint the master in lieu of the power of visiting to ascertain his qualifications.' Without actually flouting the College, he continued to 'kick against the goads' until, in May, 1847, Mr. Bateson of St. John's, after seeing counsel in London, wrote to Shield saying that ' "a visit" authorised by the Master and followed by an act of College will suffice to amove either master or usher or both.'

The first scandal was concerning the usher, who evidently did most of the teaching; Shield, when in residence, taking the more advanced boys, rarely as many as half a dozen. A good usher was the more necessary to give the boys a grounding. By October, 1817, the complaints to St. John's were so serious as to warrant an immediate visitation. Nearly fifty inhabitants of the town signed the remonstrance. From deafness and infirmity the usher, the Rev. T. Brown, was incapable of teaching, and the master seldom or never attended — he had not been for nearly twelve months and 'none of us has seen him during that time'.

Evidently Shield had procured a 'cheap' usher to save his own pocket and, moreover, 'Mr.Brown had offered to act as usher for £200 a year and *give up the office to Mr. Robert Shield* (Shield's son) on his attaining the age of 21 years.' The scholars, when this usher was in charge, hearing their prepared work, 'omitted passages they did not know or mumbled anything over, as the usher was too deaf to hear!' Yet Shield told the visitor that he conceived the usher to be 'perfectly competent with the exception of an infirmity, that of deafness, under which he has lately laboured'. Shield could be very vindictive if the complaint of the local surgeon, a Mr. Hornby, was true, that because he, Mr. Hornby, had subscribed to a petition to the Archbishop of York against the employment of the Rev. T. Brown, Shield had the next day most barbarously punished his son, who was a pupil, without giving any reason, so that the boy was unable to sit on his seat for a considerable time afterwards. To add insult to injury he also refused to admit the boy to school.

Other serious complaints were that Shield had let the schoolroom to a carpenter for some years, who used it as a sawpit and filled it with lumber, that the School was in a most ruinous and dirty state, that he had received a sum of money for dilapidations and never applied it, and that he had absented himself so much that 'he had been publicly proclaimed in the churchyard of Pocklington on 1 June to appear in one of the courts of Westminster in order that he might be proceeded against to outlawry!'

In 1817 therefore, on 27 October, the first visitation of inquiry by St. John's College resulted. Mr. Shield in answer to questions had to admit that at present only one boy attended the School. Since 1809 there had been a bare sixteen in all, with a maximum of ten at any one time, 'previous to which time there had been none for eleven years, and only three or four for twenty years under his predecessor'. It was high time the College intervened if a School with a potential revenue of £1,000 a year had taught only twenty boys in thirty years. No wonder such an abuse of trust excited the wrath of the Lord Chancellor.

The visit was effective, but, to make sure of it, another inspection was held on 25 August, 1819. Meanwhile the master of St. John's, Mr. J. Wood, sent a copy of some simple regulations about prayers and demanded the keeping of a register of admissions. Above all, an efficient usher was to be appointed without delay.

The visitor's report of 1819 reads:

> The schoolroom is new and extremely well suited ... the schoolhouse of which it forms
> part is wholly new in front, and of white brick, handsomely finished and covered with
> slates. The interior of the house is not yet completed.' .... There are ten scholars in the
> school, six having lately left to go out as apprentices ... There are two classes. No Greek is
> taught at present. The school hours are 7-8 and 10-12 a.m., and 3-5 p.m. The usher seems
> well qualified and the business of the school is extremely well conducted.

Whether this usher is the deaf Mr. Brown or an assistant paid by him (a
Mr. Jones, who taught about this time for some years) is uncertain. In
carrying out his inspection the visitor interviewed the churchwardens of
Pocklington, who reported that there was no complaint from the town in
any quarter. The parish was satisfied with the regularity and good conduct
of the usher, and *the master was attending regularly*. A register was kept.

A request for a writing-master Shield resisted on the ground that 'the
boys had abundant means of improving themselves at their intervals of
leisure in the town'.

Mr. Shield seems to have avoided scandal for some years, since a visit by
the president of St. John's and Mr. Tatham in 1825 not only approved the
schoolroom and master's house 'newly built and under the same roof', as
effected in 1819, but found twenty-two scholars on the roll, the eldest being
thirteen years, and these were divided into five classes, of which the first two
learnt Greek. There were eight boarders among them, under Mr. Jones,
assistant usher. Admission was at eight years if a boy was able to read.
Besides the entrance fee of five shillings, seven shillings a year was charged
for 'firing'. Mr. Shield had given way about the writing-master, who
attended daily. Mr. Robert Shield and Mr. Jones are mentioned as
assistants, making a staff of five, if we include the writing-master and the
usher. But Mr. Brown was probably a sleeping partner for, according to
Shield, he was paid £200 a year still, but paid out of it his own assistant
(Jones). The proportion of income shared by the usher was later to cause
much trouble.

The practice was for master and usher to come into School before
breakfast, and again in the afternoon, and 'since last holidays, also during
the whole of school hours'. (Remarkable devotion to duty, but not for long!)
The churchwardens, however, while stating that the inhabitants of
Pocklington were 'satisfied with the School as conducted by *Mr. Jones*',
remarked that Shield was frequently from home. This was ominous. The
report is signed by T.W. Hornbuckle and R. Tatham on behalf of the
College.

The peace was again broken in 1827 when a William Cook wrote to St.
John's to complain that the School in February was left entirely to Shields'

son, Robert, Shield being himself away and having sacked Mr. Jones. Shield defends this action in a letter of 16 March to Mr. Blick, the Bursar, on the ground of Jones' 'disgusting behaviour', and apologised at the same time for his own absences. But in October, 1827, in spite of his protest against 'visits', as mentioned above, the Bursar, the Rev. Charles Blick, came and made a further report, which mentions the keeping of the register and the attendance of sixteen scholars aged eight to fifteen years. 'There were fourteen in school when I went in, and one, aged 15, in class I, was reading classics.' Two new assistants are named, the Rev. Richard Higgs, B.A., of Wadham College, Oxford, and Mr. Daniel Carter. The watchdogs, the churchwardens, reported 'no complaints', but the buildings were still incomplete, as in 1819.

A welcome note under October, 1830, appears when a William Cross was nominated by Mr. Shield as 'Dowman Scholar'. A curious threat follows in March, 1831, from seven Pocklington inhabitants to take legal proceedings against the College if their scholar is not given more adequate help to live at St. John's!

A shocking decline ensued. In 1836 Shield at last appointed his son, Robert, as usher, with the consent of course of the vicar and the churchwardens, and promptly quarrelled with him. First it was about salary, about which they went to law, in chancery, the Chancellor ordering the master to take two-thirds and the usher one-third. Shield again writes complaining to St. John's that Robert had not behaved well and disobeyed his orders and, moreover, entered the master's house and broke windows. For this the usher had been fined by a magistrate. That bad relations continued may be inferred from the refusal of Robert to sign the conveyance of land by Shield to the railway company in 1842, but the Court of Exchequer ruled that under the Railway Act Robert's signature was unnecessary. Meanwhile, in 1842, in consequence of a protest from Archdeacon Wilberforce of Burton Agnes, dated 1 January, 1842, about the School's neglected state, a further visitation took place. 'We found Mr. Shield,' runs the report, 'instructing two pupils (the only ones in attendance) ... the usher has not been there for many months. We visited him (the usher) at his house and he admitted non-attendance. He had been teaching one pupil turned over to him by the master owing to some disagreement ... We then went to the Inn and interviewed the vicar and the Churchwardens, two neighbouring clergymen, and twenty respectable inhabitants.'

But Shield seems to have been beyond remedy. Money affairs intrigued him more than teaching, and with less success than formerly, for on 29 April, 1847, Mr. Blick, the Bursar, mentions to Dr. Tatham that Shield had creditors (perhaps owing to his lawsuits in chancery) in spite of an income of over £600, very ample for those days, and on 30 November Shield writes that he is 'hurt by the hostile tenor of the Bursar's last letter' about Shield's debt to the College. Again on 3 December he begs for 'no hostile proceedings' about his mortgage, while admitting all the claims of the College except the interest on the bond, to which letter Dr. Tatham replied in kindly reassuring terms. Between 1843 and 1846 only one boy attended the School, leaving in 1846. He may have been the Hudson referred to by J.A. Spender in his *Memoir of Robert Hudson* (Cassell, 1930), a prominent Liberal party organiser, whom he describes as the grandson of Charles Hudson, of Pocklington, who 'is still remembered as the man who revived the now famous Grammar School in that town. For, finding it closed, though well endowed, he is said to have insisted on its being opened, in order that his son might be educated there. Opened it had to be, though for a time young Hudson was the only boy in the School.'

It seems that, after the bursar had reported upon Shield's debts and his law suit against his son, and Tatham, as mentioned above, had found it necessary to assure Shield that St. John's *had* the power to remove him from office, the old man made a pathetic last attempt to set his house in order. Though he still reported in June that the usher was an absentee, on 16 July he is able to announce that the Rev. Samuel Wilson of Warter 'is coming as assistant, giving up his own school of twelve boys, who will probably accompany him'. Though Robert had written promising to resume his duties, Shield 'cannot depend upon his regular attendance'. On 30 November Shield reports that 'the School was re-opened in August with ten scholars, since increased to thirteen, and attendance has been satisfactory by these, by the usher, and by my assistant, Mr. Wilson'. He makes a last defence of his tenure of the mastership: 'I have improved the revenue of the School by more than £800 a year.' He still harps on this without much sense of the neglect of the first object of this income, the training of scholars, in all those forty years. 'It is my anxious wish,' he adds, 'that whenever it please God to call me home, I may be able to leave the world with credit.' But 'I find that at 80 my mind is not so easily made up on doubtful questions.' In December he promises Dr. Tatham to come to London to discuss School business. His reign came to an end in 1848, when this melancholy period was followed by the brighter era under the able and conscientious F.J. Gruggen, whom the College appointed from its body of fellows, that the School might resume its proper function in the sphere of higher as well as primary education.

The School as rebuilt by F. J. Gruggen, 1851

CHAPTER 14

REV. FREDERIC JAMES GRUGGEN, M.A.

(1848 to 1872)

The year 1849 opened a new era for the School and, however important the advances that followed the intervention of the Charity Commissioners in 1875, and the coming of Hutton in 1889, the mastership of F. J. Gruggen was perhaps the greatest turning point in the School's history. The fifty or more years of torpor were ended. A strong personality, blessed with scholarship as a Cambridge wrangler and fellow of St. John's College, and also with business acumen, justified the discernment of the College Council in making what was to be its last appointment. An extant portrait, the first likeness of a Pocklington headmaster that is preserved, shows the resolution of the man who revived the School, rebuilding the premises in much the form which they show today (for above all he was a builder) and devising a curriculum which for the first time may be said to indicate the broader lines of modern education.

Games fanatics would be interested to see the extract from the scorebook of the Londesborough Cricket Club, which records a game played in 1857(!) between the School and Market Weighton-and-Londesborough United, in which the headmaster himself scored eleven and took three wickets, while in the return match he helped the School to an innings victory by scoring twenty! (Evidently the ball beat the bat in those days.)

A story shows his determination and acuteness in overcoming obstacles. When the common land called West Green was enclosed by the local council with railings, Gruggen also put railings round the School front to preserve his lawns. Unfortunately for his privacy there was a seat just outside the dining-room window on which yokels came to sit and which was now within the ring-fence. This they still persisted in doing till Gruggen conceived the idea of keeping the seat freshly painted and made it impossible.

A 'prospectus' of the School survives in the form of a leaflet in small print setting out the date of foundation and the founder's name at the top. It gives prominence to the Dolman exhibitions just below and the advantages offered by them to pupils of Pocklington. Next we have in larger type:

Patrons and Visitors
The Master and Fellows of St John's College, Cambridge
Headmaster
Rev. F.J. Gruggen, M.A., Late Fellow of St John's College, Cambridge, and late Vice-Principal and Tutor of St Bees' College, Cumberland
Second Master
Rev. E.B. Slater, M.A., late Fellow of St John's College, Cambridge, and late Assistant Master of the Grammar School, Sedbergh, Yorkshire
Assistant Master
Rev. S. Wilson, Vicar of Warter

Notice first that both headmaster and usher have had experience in good public schools and, secondly, that the staff is growing, like the cast in ancient Greek drama. An assistant aids the usher and the headmaster and we see a reinforcement of 'visiting teachers'. Then follow details of fees, boarders paying sixty guineas per annum and four guineas for washing (laundry). 'Masters for French, German, Drawing, Music and Dancing, attend on the usual terms, viz. four guineas for each of the three former, and six for each of the two latter accomplishments.' Boys under twelve were charged ten guineas less.

School hours are then noted: 8-9 a.m., 10-12, 3-5, and evening preparation 7-9. Wednesday and Saturday are half holidays. 'The Sunday services in the parish church commence at 10.30 a.m. and 6 p.m. The boys also assemble at 8.15 a.m. to repeat the Collect, Epistle, and Gospel for the day, in whole or in part, and again at 4 p.m. to write a short essay on some religious subject, or a short comment on some portion of the church service for the day.'

After noting the times of meals as 9-0, 1-30, 6-0 and 9-0 respectively, the leaflet adds : 'The Master and his family invariably dine with the boys, and each boy has a separate bed, chest of drawers, washstand, etc.'

A photograph of September, 1866, described in *The Pocklingtonian* of Michaelmas, 1907, and now hung in the School lobby, shows Gruggen and his small family with a group of boys around. The School register, which Gruggen kept carefully, was unfortunately lost, but an honours list handed down to Hutton and included in his School year-book of 1896-7, has preserved the chief scholastic successes from 1857 to 1879. The numerous 'wranglers' and lower honours in mathematics are evidence of the teaching power of Slater and Gruggen, their former pupils securing third, fifth and eleventh places in that Tripos. A memoir by a pupil, Morris, complains of Gruggen's late arrival for lessons, compensated by hustling tactics which sought to make up for lost time. A double first in classics and moral science was won by H.M. Hewlett. College prizemen abound in the list, which records over twenty open scholarships and exhibitions, mostly at St. John's College, Cambridge, but including two choral scholarships at Oxford and foundation scholarships at Christ's and Pembroke and at Durham. The prominence of Pocklingtonians in university and college sports and boating clubs is equally marked. Two Old Boys are credited with 'winning university races' at Cambridge, the hundred, the quarter-mile and the half-mile in or about 1858, but whether this refers to Freshers', Seniors' or Inter-Varsity Sports is uncertain. Successes in Army and Navy examinations give variety to the record.

One well-known old pupil of Gruggen's had an obituary notice in *The Times* in 1923 — Rawdon Levett. This stated that after graduating as eleventh wrangler in 1865 Levett became mathematical master at King Edward's School, Birmingham, where he 're-organised the teaching of mathematics, and soon became known for the fertility of ideas by which he initiated the reform of mathematical education in English Public Schools. His success was extraordinary. For many years he sent a succession of boys to Cambridge, who won high places in the mathematical tripos. Many of them became college lecturers and public schoolmasters, and so spread his ideas and methods through the country.' To him more than to anybody else, it seems, was due the abolition of Euclid as a text-book in this country. In 1880 Shorthouse dedicated to him his famous novel, *John Inglesant,* 'that he might have the opportunity of calling himself his friend'.

In October the number of boys in the School is given as forty-three, of whom twenty-five were boarders, thirteen Pocklington day-boys, and five rural day-boarders.

Only too often in the history of schools a headmaster has not resigned in time before waning powers or interest undo previous success. According to the account of his successor (given orally to the present writer), the position in his last years, 1870-2, deteriorated. Mrs. Gruggen turned Roman Catholic, which frightened away boarders, and the sudden death of Gruggen in 1872 'left the School in a muddle' and nearly empty. We leave the sequel to the next chapter.

A very pleasing engraving shows us the Schoolhouse as rebuilt by Gruggen in 1851, practically as it is to-day, but without the large dormitory and classrooms underneath erected in 1898 at the east end, and also without attics in the house portion. Stately trees rise as background, but the fine lime tree in the middle of the front lawn and the row of trees that now line the front are yet to be planted. Virginia creeper and pyracanthus on the walls have begun to give them that softness and colour which graced them till 1948.

Rev. F. J. Gruggen, his Children and Boarders about 1860

An inscription in gilt and colours over the front School door, crowned with the Dolman arms, runs as follows:

> Schola Pocklingtonensis
> A Joanne Dolman
> Utriusque iuris doctore
> Suffolciae Archidiacono
> Fundata A.D.MDXIV
> Impensis Frederici Jacobi Gruggen A.M.
> Instaurata est A.D. MDCCCL
> Hoç qualecunque
> Avitae in municipes suos
> Monimentum munificentiae
> PC
> Joannes Thomas Dolman M.D.

'The School of Pocklington, founded in A.D. 1514 by John Dolman, Doctor of both kinds of law, Archdeacon of Suffolk, was erected anew in A.D. 1850 at the expense of Frederick James Gruggen, Master of Arts. This humble memorial to his ancestor's munificence towards his fellow-townsmen was placed and established by John Thomas Dolman, M.D.'

The memorial refers to the Dolman arms above the doorway.

In 1858 Gruggen erected Wilberforce Lodge for the use of the second master or usher, as the inscription over the front door testifies:

> Scholae Pocklingtonensi
> Haec domus
> Hypodidascali in usum
> Condita et attributa est
> A.D. MDCCCLVIII

'This house was built and assigned to Pocklington School in A.D. 1858 for the use of the Second Master.'

Nor was that the limit of Gruggen's building activities. It is said that he frequented sales and bought up old oak and other valuable things and then built houses to put them in. Anyway, Dolman House and St. John's Lodge beyond were his work which, alas, were sold later so that Dolman had to be re-purchased in 1924. A beautiful staircase in the Schoolhouse, a set of four doors in the diningroom, three of them adapted as panelling, another pair in the bedroom above, and in Dolman House an Adam mantelpiece testify to Gruggen's taste and initiative. But whence the funds? Gruggen's own estimate of his expenditure upon the restoration of the School is £4,000. Of this sum £1,200 was lent to him by St. John's College at 4 per cent. interest and repaid by him. A further £300 was borrowed at 5 per cent. for the enclosure of the School premises, of which two-thirds 'was discharged by order of the High Court of Chancery out of a fund belonging to the School then in Court'. (Perhaps this was a residue resulting from the efforts of the former headmaster, Thomas Shield, to increase the value of the leases through the Court of Chancery.) The rest of the cost was borne by Gruggen himself. The report of the inspector of the National Society, published in 1870, explains how he was able to provide such a sum: 'Though the investment has probably not yielded so speedy a return as he expected, as the number of boarders is still small in proportion to the accommodation provided, it will be seen that the income he enjoys as landlord of the estates and from the fees of the pupils, is exceptionally high for so small a School.'

There were then forty-four boys in the School, of whom fifteen were boarders with the headmaster and eleven with the second master, paying fees 'usually charged in expensive private schools'. (Yet they were only sixty guineas a year plus extras!)

The inspector referred to above was sent out by the National Society in 1865 to report on all Yorkshire endowed schools. His visit to Pocklington stirred the ancient grumblings of the townsfolk, whose two main grievances had always been, firstly, that if the headmaster neglected the boarding side they lost considerable profit from supplying the boarders' needs; secondly, that if his tuition, along with the Dolman exhibitions to Cambridge, attracted scholars able to proceed to the university, the less able pupils from the town were correspondingly neglected. What the tradesmen wanted seemed to be elementary instruction, the general demand for secondary instruction being hardly awakened. The real purpose of a grammar school was still vague. No doubt, before the School Board Act of 1870, it had the duty of supplying the primary instruction needed by all and sundry, but the provision of closed entrance scholarships to the University and the connections of school foundations with particular colleges, as of Eton with King's, of Winchester with New, and of Pocklington with St. John's, make plain the founder's intention to produce scholars as well as boys who could merely read and write.

The second error of the townsfolk was to ignore the intention of the founder to cater not merely for Pocklington but for a much wider area, to attract pupils from Yorkshire and beyond. The share of Pocklington in the foundation was provided for by free tuition supplied to day-boys. When a meeting was summoned to discuss the School with the inspector, Mr. Fitch, Mr. Gruggen complained with reason that it had been called 'no doubt purposely' in his absence and that he was never officially informed of it. As to 'the leading inhabitants of the town', as the newspaper called them, who had suggested the meeting, Gruggen writes with irony: 'I think I am right in stating that no one of them ever had a son in the School, or indeed possessed a son at all to send to it.' Mr. Fitch, however, dismissed most of their complaints as trivial or untrue, and also their demand to appoint the usher. His report, published in 1867, had little but commendation of the position and management of the School: 'Under the skilful management of the present head the estates have greatly increased in value. The premises have been enlarged and almost entirely rebuilt. Advantageous changes have been made with neighbouring landowners, fields drained, wall and outbuildings erected, and rents advanced. With the sanction of the Charity Commissioners nearly four thousand pounds have been borrowed on mortgage and judiciously expended. This debt is being gradually cleared off, and in seven years the Grammar School of this little town will possess an unincumbered income of £1,500, with large house, fields and farm buildings besides. *In the hands of any but a headmaster of extraordinary energy, to manage so important an estate will doubtless diminish attention to the proper business of the School.'*

Here the inspector lays his finger upon the difference between Gruggen and his predecessor, Shield. For the proper business of the School, he goes on to say, has received close attention. He praises the wider curriculum, even while he looks askance at the extra fees charged for such a subject as French. 'So long,' he says, 'as the School maintains its character as a high-class grammar school exclusively, it cannot well render greater local service than at present .... The one great want of such a town as Pocklington is one good school which is on a sufficiently large basis to admit the boy who is going to University side by side with the boy who will leave earlier, and which knows how to do full justice to the requirements of both. As education improves, the proportion of lessons applicable to both classes will probably increase ... and we shall avoid the vulgar expedient of separating boys early in life as "a commercial class" and giving them an ignoble education on that pretext.'

What prophetic discernment!

The least favourable comment of the inspector was that the whole establishment 'partook too much of the character of a private school'. This, of course, was soon to be remedied by the Charity Commissioners' Act of 1875. The local press, by the way, when publishing the inspector's report, congratulated the town on the success of Gruggen in rescuing the School from 'the scandalous neglect prior to his appointment'.

F. J. Gruggen then, if anyone, deserves from all Pocklingtonians to be remembered at the reading of the passage which honours benefactors — 'Let us now praise famous men' — in the service of Commemoration. Suitably his name is preserved with those of Dolman, Wilberforce and Hutton as one of the names of the 'Houses' that compete in games.

There are some interesting letters from Gruggen to St. John's College which show that even so able an administrator was not free from calumny. A long letter of 17 November, 1862, defends his stewardship of the School properties. After reporting to the master the following items:

(i)   sale of property by order of the Charity Commissioners;
(ii)   re-investment of £3,850 of the railway money and income from Barmby Field farms;
(iii)   exchange of Duggleby for Greenland farm and other exchanges;

he mentions among the costs: 'my own labour in planning buildings, writing innumerable letters, managing with Mrs. Rives' solicitors all arrangements connected with the business, journeys and like — 0 £.'

> I may very likely have omitted some items, but, as I have done ever since I have been here, I am quite willing to let these go into the estate for the good of the school. I can assure you this is the first time I have been supposed not to have been working for the good of the school property. Almost every one who has seen or heard what I have done, has attacked me for neglecting the interests of my family to increase the value of the property, and doing too much in that way. If I can show that in each exchange, as I put them before the commissioners, the school gets a substantial advantage, and that I reap none privately, I have done all that can be required of me, and instead of incurring censure, I ought to receive praise ... The result of my work here is that the school estate, which, when I came, was worth about £1,000 a year, will with the proposed changes be worth about £1,500, which I think is no trifling matter to have been brought about in the space of 14 years. That it has not been effected without great personal cost to myself, you are well aware. F.J.G.

Another letter reflects seriously on the corruptness of the churchwardens of his opening years when he had to nominate his first usher. Three neighbouring clerics were all regarded as promising candidates for this ushership. They were 'informed by the churchwardens that they could hire a young man for £50 a year to do the work for them. The churchwardens offered, you will remember, to take £50 each for their votes on that occasion. The vicar told me of the arrangement proposed to him by these authorities.'

The ushership of Slater, fellow of St. John's College, whom Gruggen insisted on appointing, covers almost the whole of Gruggen's mastership. His ability and desire to take boarders, while helping the School, led to friction with Gruggen in 1867. We find him complaining of paying the poll-tax of £5 on his own boarders, and wanting to enlarge his house so as to take more. Gruggen wrote to St. John's opposing this.

In that same year, 1867, Gruggen sent in the following return to the Charity Commissioners, from which it would appear that the income did not increase as he had hoped:

	£	s.	d.		£	s.	d.
Land rents	994	14	9	Subtract expenses[1]	583	3	1
Dividends	64	4	9	(including usher's			
[No details available	5	5	0]	share — £195)			
				Leaving master's			
				income at	481	1	5
	£1064	4	6		£1064	4	6

The average income is given as:
Master £381 7s. 0d. — with house and piece of land.
Usher £175 18s. 0d.

Lighter reading is Gruggen's exposure of a man named T——, who with another local cleric opposed the exchange of properties mentioned above, probably as piqued by Gruggen's appointment of Slater as usher over their heads. This T—— also wrote to the master of St. John's complaining about the inconvenience of school hours, and wanting to know why there were only ten pupils, with a threat of legal proceedings if the number were not increased! Gruggen deemed it time to let the master know the type of man the complainant was:

> T——, our Vicar, G——, and others came into the neighbourhood years ago... on a speculation matrimonial, clerical and otherwise, as curates. T—— married a woman much older than himself, as he then allowed, for her money, and in hope that he might have no family. He recommended our Vicar to follow his example. He purchased of the Dean the livings of Barmby and Fangfoss. When the Dean's nephew disgraced himself here and left, our Vicar, as *he* told me, bought Pocklington and Meltonby. G—— got hold of one of old Singleton's daughters as a wife, and so got an easy purchase, from the Dean, of Fridaythorpe and Millington... T—— himself has been in a lunatic asylum; his wife killed herself by drinking....

If all Gruggen wrote is true, it is good to know how much the last century has done to raise the standards of both the patrons of livings and of candidates for them.

---

[1]Under expenses are given: Drainage £127, Agent £30, Manure £77 6s 0d.

CHAPTER 15
REV. CHARLES GILMOUR WILKINSON, M.A.
(1872 to 1884)

On the death of Gruggen in 1872 the usher, C.G. Wilkinson, M.A., of
Pembroke College, Cambridge, was left with few boys to teach and without
real authority to act, except that he was the sole survivor of a 'corporation'
of two, and in that capacity he claimed jestingly to have appointed himself
headmaster. It was still the business of St. John's College in Cambridge to
appoint, but evidently, pending action by the Charity Commissioners, who
were inquiring into the government of schools whose trusts they
administered, the College Council thought well not to disturb the acting
headmaster.

Mr. Wilkinson has stated that during his two years as usher the School
was 'in a muddle' and that Gruggen left him only two boarders and a few
day-boys. This number he gradually raised to forty and with the aid of three
masters, one of whom was a visiting teacher of French, he managed to
maintain the usefulness of the School. A photograph shows him in the
middle of five dignified Cambridge Old Boys, and his pupils included the
Foxley brothers — Charles, who won a double First in Classics at
Cambridge, and Allen, Dolman Exhibitioner of St. John's, who later was
architect of the School hall; also A. Summerson and H.S. Powell,
afterwards to become Governors of the School, and A.E. Brett, who first
portrayed Sherlock Holmes on the stage, and whose photographic memory
enabled him to mystify the examiners for the Cambridge Previous
Examination. Finding his answers on *Paley's Evidences* word-perfect, they
suspected cribbing and challenged him. His reply was that they should ask
him to recite from any point of the book they liked, as he knew it by heart,
a book of over two hundred pages.

When the new Board of Governors was established in 1875 under the
chairmanship of Admiral Duncombe, the headmastership was thrown open
to competition, but Wilkinson was invited to stand and was appointed at a
salary of £400 a year. During the next few years, as extant printed
examination lists show, the total number of boarders and day-boys varied
from forty-two in 1879 to thirty-eight in 1883, arranged in three divisions.
The Honours Lists included Dawson Williams' fellowship (in Medicine) at

University College, London, a Lightfoot University scholarship, a classical scholarship at Durham, and the usual Dolman exhibitions at Cambridge. Charles Foxley's classical success at Cambridge has already been mentioned. Though the School was small and could not boast great doings in scholarship or games, yet the closed exhibitions to St. John's kept the staff on their mettle to preserve the succession of pupils proceeding to the University, and ensured the presence of one or two boys with brains at the head of the School able to take learning seriously and at the same time to mould the junior boys. A rugby fixture list of 1881 includes games with Ripon Grammar School, High Harrogate School, and York Commercial School, besides Hull Town and York Town, all of which clubs were defeated. Athletics sports programmes of 1877 and 1885 (under London) surprise one by their similarity to those of the present day, though notable differences are pole jump events, open and under thirteen (!), and an event curiously styled 'French and English', open, also a 'consolation scramble' quarter-mile at the end. It was also under this régime that the first Pocklington School magazine of any note appeared, so far as we know from extant copies, and in its review of the cricket season of 1881 it mentions games at Catton and Cherry Burton and refers to fixtures with Doncaster Grammar School in 1879 and 1880. A fixture list of 1883 has the name of Archbishop Holgate's School, York.

Speech Day, as developed or initiated by Wilkinson, was a 'Speech' Day. Programmes of the years 1878-1883 give a list of speeches from such authors as Terence, Shakespeare, Schiller, and others, while another extant leaflet announces the 'Opening of New Buildings' on Friday, 4 April, 1879, and prints psalm, prayer and hymn in Latin, for the last of which A. E. Brett, mentioned above, composed a very creditable English translation. These new buildings were a substantial addition to the premises, comprising two classrooms and a dormitory above, erected on the site of an enclosed courtyard at the back of Gruggen's buildings, and with a corridor between the new and the old. Unfortunately, the narrowness of this corridor was not a convenient legacy to the bigger School of the future.

In 1883 Wilkinson resigned on the ground that 'the School worried him and his wife was not strong' (so he told the writer of this memoir) and he retired to the vicarage of Waresley. He lived on till 1938, visiting the School to open the Assembly Hall in 1928. Before his death, sitting in a bathchair, he received the writer with a kindly welcome, answered questions about his headmastership, and gave a guinea to the Wilberforce scholarship fund. This gift appears to have been a mere token donation, for in his will in 1938 he left a sum of £2,000 to provide leaving exhibitions tenable at Cambridge, a great and grateful benefaction.

The Charity Commissioners. The year 1875 saw not only the official opening of Wilkinson's headmastership, but the epoch-making reform of the Charity Commissioners, which we must now examine.

The schemes of this body for the better government of the educational trusts under their control were the outcome of public clamour during many years for the removal of abuses in this class of education. Their work was done with considerable foresight as well as concern for what had been considered past abuses. The new Boards of Governors, as will be seen later, not only maintained old traditions of representation but were wisely recruited by a measure of co-option. Local interest in the case of Pocklington was provided for by a rather clumsy election of two governors by the parents of day-boys, an election later transferred to the District Councils. While preventing waste of school revenues by forbidding the sale or re-investment of School properties without their own consent, the Commissioners earmarked £2,000 of the Trust's stock for improvement of School buildings, with the proviso that this capital sum must always be replaced in a term of years out of revenue if more than the interest on it were so used. This allowed for expansion if boarders became more numerous.

With some broad-mindedness they allowed boarders to be admitted on two systems, either that of lodging with masters who received the profits, or on the hostel system, profits accruing to the Trust. The two might be combined. The first of these two systems, the running of the boarding-house for private profit, was later discountenanced by the Board of Education[1], but the wisdom of the regulations as a whole is justified by the Board of Education's subsequent adoption of them, with modifications, in its own schemes for schools.

Curriculum. The prescribed curriculum has, of course, been modified again and again since 1875, but Greek was now to be paid for as an extra at a fee of not less than £3 a year, and an extra fee might be charged for special laboratory instruction in natural science, though this subject was one of the prescribed ones. Few things in the history of education are more interesting than this evolution of the curriculum. Subject after subject, at first treated as a special item to be taught at an extra charge, is afterwards included in the general fees. In the sixties it was modern languages, in 1875 it was Greek, in 1900 it was laboratory instruction, in 1920 there was still a subscription for games, and in 1960 there may still be a charge for instruction in swimming and lessons in instrumental music. But it is easy to see that some day the ambitious programme of teaching any and every subject, including Italian and Russian and golf, for one inclusive fee, or for no fees at all, may

[1] Now the 'Ministry' of Education

be realised unless the public goes bankrupt in this praiseworthy pursuit of culture.

Finance. Other aspirations of the Commissioners were to see £150 a year set apart from the revenue of the Trust to provide leaving exhibitions to the University and £200 a year to promote the education of girls in the East Riding, for which 'a supplementary scheme may be made'. The second of these provisions it is difficult to bring within the original terms of the foundation and may have arisen from pressure on the part of the Commissioners' wives or from a natural indignation that such small provision was at that time existing for the education of girls. For neither of these projects, however laudable, was any money ever found available. In fact, a letter of protest from Pocklington parents and ratepayers against the draft scheme issued in 1873 is extant, asking that all the income should be devoted to paying the headmaster an adequate salary and providing an efficient staff. The income of the Trust was, indeed, so inadequate to meet the growing cost of education that in an extant document of 1876, which horrifies the modern reader, the Governors apply to the Charity Commissioners for permission to *sell* Wilberforce Lodge, as 'such house is not required for the purposes of the School and is *deemed too far distant* from the School premises to be made available for school purposes'. The Commissioners' reply asks for more particulars and, fortunately, the application seems not to have been pursued, for the house was re-let, not sold.

In a schedule of 1889 the School properties appear as so many farms (see Appendix), a few pieces of land and an 'oxgang' held by Sir Tatton Sykes at Wetwang, from which the income was £1 16s. 8d. and which was redeemed by the Sykes family about 1920. These properties, which had once sufficed to maintain the School in what were considered essentials, nowadays merely relieve the funds to the extent of a few pounds per place. The amount of £60 a year ordered by the Commissioners to be set aside for repairs and improvements would now fail to meet the annual bill for painting. It was the income from boarding-fees that eventually proved the main source of income and the Commissioners were only re-stating the original object of the foundation when they laid down that the School 'shall be a Day and Boarding School'.

So the long licence of headmasters and ushers to abuse their trust was ended, though many of them had no doubt been conscientious during the preceding three centuries. Further failures were due rather to excess of zeal than to lack of it, and the wilful neglect of duty which could lead to the closure of the School, as in the early nineteenth century, was no longer possible.

CHAPTER 16

REV. HERBERT LONDON, M.A.
(1884 to 1889)

Mr. Herbert London, M.A., of St. John's College, Cambridge, started his short, vigorous, but ultimately unhappy reign in January, 1884. Its character may be gauged from the first *Annual Register* of 1886, which replaced the *Chronicle*. This *Register* shows London to have been modern in ideas and progressive and to have anticipated in several things the twentieth-century trend in public schools.

A modern note is at once sounded by mention of an extension to the heating apparatus just effected and for the first time we find a Speech Day described at length and an examiner's full report on the work of the School. Still more modern things were to come, for the second *Annual Register* records the instalment of electric light in dormitories and workshops. 'The old-fashioned paraffin has been exchanged for the latest form of energy, electricity, which has already proved so useful a servant to man's needs... It has been found that the same amount of light from oil lamps would vitiate in each dormitory no less than 1,400 cubic feet of air per hour.' Sententious writing, but it is claimed with just pride that 'the installation has been put up without the aid of an expert'. Mr. London, a keen scientist, managed it with the aid of his pupils. The experiment did not last and electric lighting did not arrive till 1934, after successive trials of coal gas, petrol gas (1913), a miserable failure, and again coal gas (1916).

Another intelligent anticipation of the future was the suggestion for a reconstruction of the swimming pool! A plan was drawn up for converting the existing pool in the corner of the cricket field, contemptuously designated in after-years the 'frog-pond', into 'a handsome and well-equipped place for this valuable recreation'. The plan was commended by the chairman on Speech Day. This plan, too, fell through, and the pond continued to be used — mud, minnows and all — till 1919, with occasional sallies to the canal beyond Riverhead. Certificates for swimming were awarded notwithstanding, one of which came to a boy named Fairweather, afterwards the Governor who opened the new swimming bath and gave the trophy for swimming.

There are other items of interest in the *Register*. The passing of 'the

Twelve Apostles' is heralded, and an intention is registered to plant a new row of trees as a memento of the Royal Jubilee of 1887. These trees (the big chestnut excepted) which now enclose the School's lawns, were a happy thought for which posterity is grateful. Even in those days an epidemic of measles interfered with cricket, but not with Past *v* Present, which match may have been first arranged in 1886. Speech Day, being continued on the same lines as before, opened with a Greek speech from Euripides, and included an English speech from Shakespeare, a French speech from Florian's *Fables*, and a speech from the chairman of the Governors, with a vote of thanks to him in conclusion. Most splendid of all is the first page of the *Register*, its list of titled patrons and, above them, inscribed as Visitor, Her Majesty the Queen! This is explained by the passing of this duty from the master of St. John's College, Cambridge, to the Crown, under the new Act, 1875.

It is easy to see that London was anxious to do his best for this small School, reinforced by eleven new boys in 1886, and nine in 1887, whose names are recorded in the *Register*. To encourage boarders he instituted two House scholarships. The curriculum comprised most subjects taught to-day, including Greek and chemistry, the absence of which latter subject from the curriculum of public schools was censured by the Commission of 1862. The results in chemistry were specially commended by the examiners. London was a keen chemist and might have done much with this subject had he stayed on, new as it was in the curriculum of schools at the time. Physics was the subject of the future. 'Owing to the wide range of studies,' says the examiner, 'it is difficult no doubt to secure great proficiency.'

The *Register* was to be a 'hardy annual', but only two numbers have survived for us and no further magazine is extant to our knowledge, until it started again under Hutton as *The Pocklingtonian* and so remains to-day. The explanation is a sad one. In the next two years, 1888-9, the School, largely owing to bad catering, sank as low in numbers as it had been for years, so that only ten remained to fuse with the forty brought by Hutton in 1889. After so promising an opening Mr. London's zeal for discipline led him to fall foul of a parent, who took him to court for a severe beating administered to his boy. The boy himself afterwards affirmed that he deserved the beating, but before the magistrates London, flustered by questions, put up a weak case, and he was fined £20. This seems not to have been the cause of decline but merely the climax. Tales have come down from a contemporary of a present of a sheep, kept overlong for his limited number of boarders to consume and still served to them when 'high', of a jam roll which they refused to eat, but which appeared at eight successive dinners until they capitulated and gulped it down. By all accounts London's discipline did not err in mildness.

Of life in the School from 1880-6 *The Pocklingtonian* in 1919 published a lively impression from the pen of Allen Foxley, which should be allowed to speak for itself. After paying tribute to the teaching powers of both Wilkinson and London, he goes on:

It is strange to remember that scarcely forty years ago the School was, like many others, largely in the Middle Ages. When I joined, there were no workshops, no laboratories, no gymnasium save a small room having a few bits of antique apparatus and known as 'the gymmy'; no school music, no pictures, nor any of what may be called the amenities of life; the sanitary arrangements, then but recently improved, were those of the tenth century, and for washing by day we were content with a pump at the head of a long stone sink, up and down which slithered a few zinc basins. There was neither cloak room nor changing room, and though the boarders had hot baths at intervals, the bathing arrangements were primitive. In my last year, when near the top of the school, I was permitted a morning tub, but this was a personal privilege, and I underwent it more or less *coram publico* in a flat tin vessel disposed at one corner of the general dormitory.

School fittings were equally venerable. The seats were long forms without backs; there were long plain deal desks, some even attached to and facing the wall, while others had a double slope like a roof, with a narrow flat strip along the ridge. At these we sat facing each other and shins were an easy target.

The school buildings ended square beyond the third window to the east of the columned main entrance; just inside this entrance were doors right and left, leading respectively into the third master's room and the second class-room. Facing the main door was the second master's room, while the passage to the left led to the first and third class-rooms, and to the right into the washhouse where the pump lived; near the pump a doorless opening led into the 'gymmy' aforesaid, which was lighted by the last window of the school front.... What is now the dining-hall was divided midway by a panelled wooden screen ceiling high, never removed save for Speech Days .... The front half was the dining-room, the back part the first class-room. There were only three classes of which the first was the highest.

'The Apostles' were then a row of lofty and magnificent elms, falling however into sad decay. Here a secluded plot of grass was dedicated to courts of summary jurisdiction, ordeals by combat, and such gear generally as was more comfortably managed away from masters' eyes; and here against the blank end of the school was built a fives-court, now gone, where we played without gloves, and with little solid rubber balls, such as then cost a penny.

Some of the masters took their duties lightly. I have mentioned the desks with double slopes; these were set at an end touching the wall. One good easy man, after giving out some work to keep us busy, was wont to lay his limbs along the flat top, and slumbered so long as there was peace in the room. He was naturally in a strong strategic position for marking what was done amiss, were we rash enough to disturb him; as may be imagined, this was not often; but, oh, the deadly dullness of it all.

Mr. Foxley has a lively sketch of the visiting French master, apparently in those days a very common type, lacking any gift of discipline over English boys: He kept no notes of work done and we presented the same grammar and translations time after time. This saved trouble all round, and, though

Monsieur looked doubtful occasionally, he seldom interfered. In expansive mood, with a little judicious encouragement he would favour us with long yarns about the successes achieved in business by the "young marchants" who had been privileged to study with him …. If he tried to embark us on French conversation, we had an unfailing cure for that worry. The boy appealed to would gaze blankly towards the window and ask wearily, *"Que pongsay voo est le tom (temps)?"* Whereat Monsieur shrugged his shoulders and ceased from troubling.

The same writer laments the hour's early school before breakfast and 'the added pang, as with food beneath our noses, we had to last out prayers', but remembers with pleasure being allowed 'to mess about to his mighty content' in a little private laboratory which Mr. London made out of the boot-cleaning shed. The same hands converted the 'gymmy' into an engineer's workshop and fitted a gas-engine and dynamo, from which he lighted the dormitories and parts of his own house.

The Cadet Corps was another of London's daring inventions, replacing the drill taught by a Sergeant Smith from the town. Instead of swords the officers carried single-sticks, with which on parade they saluted punctiliously the master commanding: 'There was no uniform except a black glengarry with flying tails and a red knob on top …. I well remember as captain, and thus accoutred, heading one Speech Day a grand assault on the school railings, and blushingly receiving the encomiums of the gentle colonel of volunteers who was there, unofficially, to inspect us.'

Rugby was the official game until Mr. London changed it to Association and substituted for the red and black 'hoop' colours, dark blue and white 'quarters', a change 'deeply resented at the time'. Blazers, colours and caps for games were, with other niceties of costume, despised at Pocklington as elsewhere. Tennis, Mr. Foxley claims to have helped to introduce, making for it the court beside the large chestnut.

The more one reads of these brief years of London's the more one is impressed by the introduction of so many items that go to make public school life to-day, expanding the curriculum and filling in the boys' leisure. The beer is perhaps small but it is not flat.

Rev. C. F. Huton, M.A.

Rev. F. J. Gruggen, M.A.

CHAPTER 17

REV. CHARLES F. HUTTON, M.A.

(1889 to 1910)

New life was given to the School in 1889, when the Rev. C. F. Hutton, known always as the Chief, descended upon the almost empty Schoolhouse from Daventry, 'bringing his sheaves with him', for some forty boarders accompanied him to Pocklington.

With very indifferent school buildings, in the byways of the East Riding, this shrewd Irishman set out to make the small grammar school notable once more in Yorkshire and beyond and familiar to both the older universities. He found no science laboratory but a primitive makeshift in some outbuildings, but he looked round for some commodity that could be distinctive of Pocklington and he found it in the study of Hebrew. A fair Hebrew scholar himself, he was fortunate in attracting a valuable colleague in P. M. Stewart, a first-class scholar in Semitic languages and theology.[1] Hence began a succession of scholars who passed to Oxford and Cambridge and shared with Merchant Taylors' School most of the special scholarships and prizes which the study of Hebrew offered at those universities. It was a shrewd policy and even to-day, when the study of Hebrew has long been abandoned at Pocklington, and lost most of its vogue elsewhere, to many people Pocklington is still known as the School which taught Hebrew.

But the policy did not end with the dead language of Hebrew, which was at the university often a preliminary to Sanskrit and Oriental tongues, which in turn were a step to important posts under Government in Egypt and the East. It was a Pocklington Old Boy, O. L. Prowde, C.M.G., whom Kitchener selected in Egypt as engineer for the construction of the Sennar Dam, and another, G.E. Iles, by his administrative work earned the Order of the Blue Nile. Nor were scholarships won in Hebrew only. Hutton chose a staff that secured awards also in science, history and classics, so that in 1897-8 Pocklington headed the Yorkshire schools with five open scholarships and won twenty-three in a period of twelve years. Names on the staff that may still be remembered are those of W. J. Sharples, E. C. Marsh, F. B. Welch, R. Johnson and L. V. Wright. The last two of these

---

[1] *See* Appendix C

had taken Firsts in classics and science respectively, while mathematics were in the care of a Wrangler, T. H. Kirby. Few schools of the size of Pocklington could have boasted such a strong staff at this time.

Hutton's second emphasis was on games. He was no player himself, but his enthusiasm was obvious. In fact, as one contributor says, 'games were a very serious business, because C.F.H. was the worst possible loser. He loathed the first XI being beaten and made a private grievance of it.' Two or three of the masters he appointed excelled in cricket and football and were keen coaches — Picton Davies, E. C. Marsh and R. Johnson. In those days cricket and football with a little hockey were the only activities besides the annual athletic sports, whereas now the corps, gymnastics, swimming, shooting, fives and tennis all compete for a share of the time available out of school. The result was that the School side reached a high standard. In 1892 the cricket XI under C. H. Cooper won all its matches, and in 1904 in the time of C. E. Anson, who later played occasionally for Yorkshire, the first XI was only defeated once, the second XI won all its matches but one, that was drawn, and the third won all its matches easily.

Whatever the initial discomforts of the School, common to many schools in those days, C. F. Hutton and his staff evidently communicated to the pupils a wonderful vigour which lasted beyond school life. Blues in soccer, athletics and cycling(!), the positions of eminence attained in the Church (which included the primacy of Scotland, and several deaneries and archdeaconries) and a considerable number of honours and sacrifices in the first Great War were all evidence of the vigorous spirit bred of spartan living and fostered by an enthusiastic staff under a lively Chief. The School kept abreast of the times. Hutton wished to offer all that in those days could be offered. His prospectus even claimed to provide a good commercial education, specially mentioning that the typewriting was taught on a Remington! From the first he was bent on having better instruction in science, and in 1891 applied to the East Riding County Council, who made him a grant out of the so-called 'whisky-money', part of which went to the science master's salary and part for new equipment. His laboratory, gymnasium, manual room, and fives-court are mentioned in the chapter on buildings and his appointment of an instructor in gymnastics, Mason Clark, gave gymnastics a rare and lasting popularity. In 1897-8 a new wing was added to the Schoolhouse (see p.152), and, while it was being finished in the Christmas term, Hutton took the surprising step of removing the senior boys to accommodation at St. Mary's, Harlow, where they played against Chigwell, Forest and Bishop Stortford Schools. In the meantime thirty boarders had already been placed at Wilberforce Lodge, the house originally built by Gruggen in 1852, and for some time at the close of the century ten more were housed with Mr. and Mrs. P. M. Stewart at Ivy (now Burnby) Hall.

The social life of the School was, as early as 1891, reflected in the new magazine, *The Pocklingtonian*, which showed a great advance over the old *Chronicle* and the *Register*. Prosperity continued in a marked degree till 1905, when a decline began. Numbers had risen to one hundred and fifty, of whom about one hundred and ten were boarders.[1] The tone also had been good, scholarship and games and a steady procession of boys to the universities all made the School well known and its head was invited to be a member of the Headmasters' Conference.

Under the Chief life was never dull. 'He was,' says an old pupil in a character sketch, 'almost the typical Irishman, with the quick impulsiveness, the generous affection, and the vivid inconstancy that combine to make the Celt so fascinating a study to the rest of us and so inevitably misunderstood, except by those who learn to know and love him. With all his oddness and wilfulness, which increased as he grew older, he had a large heart. He was recklessly generous and would have given the coat off his back to one in need. Many a lad going up to the university or into business-life had reason to thank him for the timely "fiver" or "tenner" and some of us for more substantial help still.'

It was this generosity rather than the desire to get boys that no doubt caused him to admit pupils, especially sons of clergy, for extremely low fees. It was this, too, as well as the lack of a good bursar to help him with his accounts, that led him into financial embarrassment. The same trait endeared him to the boys, to whom he gave on occasion bun-feeds, sweets, and teas of ham and eggs as rewards, or excursions with teas to crown them, as easily as he dispensed beatings. 'How long have you been in the School, B——?' 'Just over a year, Sir.' 'Have you had the cane yet?' 'No, Sir.' 'Then it's time you had. Stand out.' And B—— was caned. He would take a boy by the scruff of the neck and give him what he called a 'circus.' One boy escaped during the performance and the Chief chased him round the School, out at the front and in at the back shouting, 'Come here, you little devil,' to the joy of the onlookers. In a wild moment he would put his cane under his arm, take a candlestick in his hand, and go the round of the dormitories, suddenly select a victim, and chase him between or over the beds with cries of, 'I see you, I see you.' This was mere mad humour out of control. He was equally irresponsible when he walked along the corridors in

[1] A prospectus of 1897-98 prints the list of scholars, including seventy-eight boarders in the Schoolhouse, twenty-four in Wilberforce Lodge, and twenty-eight day boys. This was before Mr. Stewart's house was opened to about ten boarders.

school hours and pulled faces at the boys through the door-panes, to the confusion of the master-in-charge, who asked the cause of the laughter. 'Only the Chief, Sir.' At the railway station he indulged himself so far as to mimic the porters and call out, 'All change,' and disappeared as the surprised passengers disembarked, and he would tell with glee how another time he imitated the guard's whistle and sent off the train without a guard. But sometimes his temper was dangerous. Even in 1890 his long bout of insomnia in the summer term caused boys and masters to be greatly relieved when the last day of term arrived, while in later years it was not unknown for a master to have to intervene. His nicknames for people stuck: 'Codfish G——' designated a boy with prominent eyes; harmless enough, but more offence was given in his retirement, when his curate had to hear his own wife called 'a one-eyed slab of toffee'. When desperately badgered by dunning tradesmen threatening the law, the message he sent to convey the uselessness of it was, 'Don't try to bolt a door with a mashed carrot.' Some flaw in the cooking made him once throw a whole leg of mutton through the dining-hall window.

Petitions for 'leave-off' were a perilous business in certain moods and a queue of boys outside his door would arrange for a boy in his good books to break the ice for the rest. 'He could be wild, he could be charming, and his tremendous sense of humour was a great attraction, a soft brogue enhancing the effect of his stories.' Asked to preach at neighbouring churches or patronise sales of work, he was a well-known figure sallying out on his bicycle with his frock coat tucked up on either side. Standing by a stall and talking rapidly all the time, he was asked to buy a resplendent table-centre. 'Oh, yes, how beautiful, how beautiful, I will buy it,' and as he talked of other things he unconsciously rumpled up the work of art into a ball and stowed it away in his pocket, ruined for ever. He loved to wear red socks, which showed to more advantage under trousers worn by him well above the ankle. His cigarettes he would smoke so short as to singe his upper lip and suggest a moustache. 'One of the untidiest men ever known,' says one who knew him well, 'and one of the most undisciplined, in the ordinary meaning of the word. His clothes were the despair and his hats the constant scandal of the good lady who looked after us all at the Schoolhouse (Miss Woodman), and his unpunctuality made life very difficult for his staff. As a teacher he was uneven. He was a sound Hebrew scholar and his Greek Testament classes were a real joy and illumination to us, but his history was shaky, and his classics inexact and sketchy. His Confirmation classes could hardly be taken seriously, and his anecdotes and illustrations were wont to startle the good citizens of Pocklington and the country round.'

As the annual summer excursion to Bridlington, to which he treated the

School, was one of the best-remembered items in his reign, a quotation from the account of it in the mid-summer number of the magazine of 1898 will convey some idea of the affection he aroused. 'Cheer after cheer for the Chief, who had given us such a delightful time, closed a memorable outing …Even the return to the School could not check the enthusiasm that had been growing in the train as we recognised what we owed to the Chief; the renewed cheering on the platform was the heartiest that has ever been given, but it could not fully express our appreciation of his kindness.' Making allowances for the exuberance of a schoolboy writer after a day's holiday in term time, one cannot doubt that at this particular time Hutton reached the high-water mark of his headmastership.

For, as his buoyancy and wisdom had advanced the School to a position of some note, so certain defects of his, accentuated by worry and nervous strain, led to a sad falling-away. For some time the buildings had needed repairs and rats had runs in the dining-hall and dormitories. It is true that this appealed to the sporting instincts of the residents and one master used to shoot the marauders from the high table at breakfast. But in 1909-10 the number of boarders had sunk to fifty, graver disorders passed unchecked, and the Chief had let his own affairs and those of the School get into financial chaos. His own debts were settled soon after 1908, when he married an Irish lady of means, but the School's overdraft rose to over £4,000, then considered a high figure. For some years he seems to have neglected or resisted the attempts of the East Riding County Council to get him to put his house in order. This body, constituted in 1889 and encouraged by the new Act of 1902, empowering local authorities to foster secondary education, was extending along with its grants its interest in the schools of the Riding. Aware of the School's decline it pressed the headmaster to seek for the recognition of the Board of Education, which would follow upon a satisfactory inspection and result in a Government grant. Hutton still hoped to preserve his independence, but faced with bankruptcy he did, in 1906, when there were forty-nine boarders and sixteen day-boys, accept an inspection by the Board. The report was unfavourable, criticising especially the dinginess of the interiors and the lack of organisation of the teaching of certain subjects. Evidently no Government grant was forthcoming, for in 1908 the East Riding Education Committee again reminded the Governors that its own grant would be conditional upon their securing a grant from the Government. Hutton had himself innocently invoked the County's aid in 1891. 'The man who pays the piper calls the tune,' is the motto of public authorities, and in fact the cost of education is too heavy to be borne unaided by a small school without a very large endowment or high fees, if the education is to be of good quality.

So in 1910, after a reign of twenty-one years, Hutton was presented by St. John's College, Cambridge, to the living of Frating, near Colchester, only to lose his wife soon after and suffer from a complete breakdown. From this he happily recovered and paid several visits to the School, taking the liveliest pleasure in its renewed prosperity. On one occasion, when at his own request he preached the sermon at Commemoration, his clouded mind gave the congregation the strangest mixture of personal reminiscence, heraldry and history that was ever heard. On another occasion he unveiled the memorial to the Old Boys fallen in the war. Then heart trouble supervened and, after a final very cheerful visit to Commemoration in 1931, he passed away the following November and was buried at Frating.

A last memory of him waiting for the train which was to take him away from Pocklington for the last time, recalls him walking up and down the platform, talking in his old quick way, with his umbrella up to keep off quite imaginary rain.

O times, O manners, O the lost romance
  Of Chas. F. Hutton's reign!
What changeful weather did that lightning glance
Portend? Sunshine or — pain?

The waiting queue without the study door
  Questioned what doom would meet
Their peccadilloes or defective lore;
  Would it be cane or sweet?

  The generous boy forgives quixotic ways,
  Sensing the old Chief's flair,
And subtle strokes of genius, that blaze
  The trail to laurels rare

Of sport or learning. What if snuff-stained coat
  And visage marred by wart
Proclaimed him no Adonis? Yet he wrote
  Upon the schoolboy heart

His tune of signature, his haunting tune
  Of mingled grave and gay,
And left affection glowing, as in June
  A rose upon the spray.

CHAPTER 18

GEORGE HAYDN KEETON, M.A.

(1910 to 1914)

The departure of the Chief was at once followed by a new scheme for the government of the School drafted by the Board of Education. This draft, issued in August, 1910, was adopted and published with some alterations in May, 1911, under the Charitable Trusts Acts of 1853-1894.

Clause 3 dropped the word 'Grammar' from the title of the foundation, though it had been preserved in the draft and the School was henceforth to be known as Pocklington School. The abbreviation was aimed to align the School with other public schools, but the venerable term 'Grammar' was more easily dropped in official correspondence than in 'town' talk locally, and it still persists, although the old name 'Grammar ducks' for the pupils is rarely heard.

Clause 4 broadened the composition of the Governing Body by a useful admixture of national, county, and local representatives with others who maintained the connexion with the universities. The Member of Parliament for the division may rank as national, standing for the country in general. The Chairman of Quarter Sessions and six members of the East Riding County Council watched the County's interests and secured its grants in aid. The Archbishop of York's nominee maintained the interest of the Church in accordance with the original statutes. St. John's College kept its connexion through the appointment of two of its dons, and Leeds University also nominated one. Local interests were watched by one representative of the Rural District Council and two of the Urban District Council, the latter afterwards being elected by the Parish Council when Pocklington was de-urbanised.

In general the scheme confirmed the wise provisions of the Charity Commissioners in 1875, but added details concerning free places, exhibitions, general management, and school properties and income, of which it appended a complete schedule. An important feature of the scheme was the rule imposed by the Board as a condition of its grant that 12½ per cent. of the pupils should hold free places. This did not seriously affect the character of the School. The Board of Education exercised its supervision by an inspector and by a periodic full inspection by several inspectors. The headmaster who began the new régime was George Haydn Keeton, M.A., of Emmanuel College, Cambridge, of which he had been a scholar. He held a first-class degree in classics (1900), was a rugby football Blue and had gained his cap for England. He came from Fettes College where he had been sixth form master.

His first task was literally to set his house in order and with the aid of the County Architect carry out a thorough restoration of the interior, expelling the rats, and by the use of concrete floors preventing further inroads. The place was thus made more comfortable, if less exciting, for the inmates.

The number of boys in 1910 was forty-eight only, of whom thirty-seven were boarders; in October, 1911 it was fifty-one, of whom thirty-six were boarders. These latter were now concentrated in the Schoolhouse, Mr. Keeton bringing down the small number from Wilberforce Lodge, where they had been under W. J. Thomas. This master's services were retained, but the rest of the staff was new, composed of three young men, who helped the headmaster to infuse the old-time spirit and vigour into work and games. Among these were W. J. Perry, who coached four winners of open mathematical scholarships at Oxford and Cambridge. The football code was now changed back to rugby (discontinued by London in the eighties) and Hymers College, Hull, and Ampleforth College were persuaded to make the same change. Bridlington refused, but made the change under a later headmaster. Within two years the School, though so small, had produced a useful rugby side and in 1914 was strong enough to beat Leeds, St. Peter's, Ripon and Hymers by good margins, losing only to Wakefield and Ampleforth. This was a considerable feat.

The second task of the new headmaster was to prepare for the second inspection by the Board of Education in October, 1911, which this time was very favourable, mentioning the tone and discipline of the School as admirable. It testified to the successful re-organisation by Mr. Keeton and the internal improvement of the buildings, while suggesting further useful improvements. It assessed the income from the Trust as just over £800 a year, supplemented by a grant of £750 from the County Council, to be continued at £500 in succeeding years or such other sum as should meet deficiencies. The Board itself promised a grant. But attention was called to the small number of pupils as uneconomical at the present fees, resulting in an overdraft of £1,000. The cost per pupil was roughly £70 a year, towards which the tuition fee brought £15 and the boarding fee £47, without allowing for loss on free places and scholarships.

An interesting paragraph classified the boys as follows:

Professional men's sons . . . . 49 per cent.
Farmers' sons . . . . 8 per cent.
Traders' sons . . . . 23 per cent.
Labourers' sons . . . . 2 per cent.
Unclassified . . . . 18 per cent.
40 per cent. of the pupils came from Pocklington and the East Riding and
60 per cent. from the rest of England.

Another change made at this time, though unwelcome to the
townspeople, was much in the interests of the boarders. On Sunday evening
the boys now had their own service in the School hall instead of attending
the parish church as in the morning. This form of service was shortened
and more suitable, the address could be less formal and more direct and the
singing was more confident.

The chief event, however, of Mr. Keeton's four years was the celebration
of the fourth centenary of the foundation in July, 1914, when the Duke of
Norfolk gave away the prizes at Commemoration and a large number of Old
Boys and their Chief, Mr. Hutton, came down to celebrate the occasion.
Representatives of the Dolman and Wilberforce families also attended. To
mark the anniversary a scheme to build a swimming bath was mooted, and
a subscription list opened. But within a week the first Great War had
commenced and the scheme was postponed.

In spite of the sounder régime and improved discipline and conditions it
had proved difficult to get boys. Several factors contributed to this. First,
there was no large body of Old Boys to recommend the School, for the
numbers during some years before 1890 had been negligible and since 1906
rapidly dwindled after some years of prosperity. The reputation of the
School had sadly suffered too during this period, when the nerves of Mr.
Hutton were suffering from strain and control was relaxed. There was also
the new rivalry of Bridlington School, with its new buildings and its
situation near a seaside health resort.

But a further cause was undoubtedly the friction between the headmaster
and the Governors. The Governing Body, being committed already to the
re-purchase of Consols sold to finance the additional building in 1896, were
loth to reduce the endowment much further. They had, however, to do this
to re-condition the premises. Trouble arose when the young headmaster
ordered further work without the previous consent of the Governors. More
friction arose later over the control of the catering and house-management.
Bickerings at Governors' meetings were frequent. It was a happy relief to
both sides when Mr. Keeton's desire to seek fresh fields was realised by his
appointment to Reading School in October, 1914. But in the meanwhile his
growing dislike of his surroundings and task, resulting in absences during

complete vacations, did not conduce to the getting of fresh pupils and in December, 1914, the number of boarders had sunk to twenty-seven, while day-boys numbered about a score. This was the lowest number of boarders since 1889 and they looked very sparse in the dining-hall and dormitories.

But there was a good spirit among them and they were led by excellent prefects of ability and character. A newcomer could not help but be struck by their all-round activities in work and games. One pair of brothers in particular, the Alldreds, who later became scholars, one in mathematics, the other in classics of St. John's College, Cambridge, besides their literary ability (the younger one at fifteen edited the magazine with the skill and touch of a mature journalist), shone as gymnasts, and in games and athletics, and yet found time to rule the small school as prefects and get through a prodigious amount of study as well.

84

CHAPTER 19

PERCY COOPER SANDS, M.A.
(1914 to 1944)

Note (By C. M. Haworth). — Desiring to bring their history of the School up to the latest possible date, the authors decided to include the whole of the headmastership of P. C. Sands, despite the obvious difficulties involved. I therefore suggested to my co-author that he should write a factual account of this period, without any special effort to be impersonal or detached, a slight flavour of autobiography being likely to afford a pleasant contrast to the earlier part of the book. I helped him only in the general planning of this chapter. To round off the story and bring it into line with the accounts of other headmasterships, J. M. Cobban was invited to contribute a verbal portrait of P. C. Sands.

The reader hardly needs to be told that the responsibility for including this outspoken tribute is entirely mine; indeed it represents the one occasion in my life when I have succeeded in browbeating my old headmaster. — C.M.H.

1. DIFFICULTIES

A small but well-disciplined School awaited the new headmaster in January, 1915. Its good discipline reflected the soundness of Keeton's régime, and at this particular time owed much to his selection of excellent prefects and resident housemasters, three in number. His successor came to the School in some trepidation, having gained his experience in day-schools. No change could have been more complete than that from a day-school of over seven hundred boys in the centre of London to a boarding-school of fifty boys in a rural area.

It was, of course, war-time, and a crisis soon arose in 1916 when War Office emissaries demanded to take over the premises. To this demand, which caused great anxiety to everyone else, the great Bickersteth, Clerk of the East Riding, replied, 'What nonsense! Of course they can't have it,' and pointed them to the empty Waplington Hall two miles away, an obvious and successful substitute.

But no sooner has this cloud blown over than danger arose from an unexpected quarter, the Local Education Authority, which threatened to withdraw its grant on the ground that the School's small numbers were too expensive! The first intimation to the headmaster was from a man in the street who said. 'So they are going to close your school!' The L.E.A. had allowed their minute to be published without any previous communication to the Governors or hint to the headmaster of their resolution. Though they had no power to close the School, their withdrawal of grant, in view of the history of Hutton's period, was likely to be followed by that of the Board of Education.

It was the reverse of helpful, in a single-handed struggle to attract more boarders, to be faced with a published minute of the Authority which could deter parents from entrusting their sons to a sinking ship! Nor was it helpful that the Governors' attendance at meetings, owing to the emergencies of the war, was now so thin as three times to fail of a quorum! The chairman had gone to live in London to avoid Zeppelin raids and never appeared. Nor did it avail to appeal to the Authority for delay. Its uncompromising reply was, 'They (the Authority) will not be content with the answer that they must go on giving large grants in the hope that things will mend after the war. We do not know how long the war may last.' Again: 'It may be the best thing for Pocklington to suspend it for a time. Unless *by some miracle* you can increase the number of pupils, I much fear the School cannot be continued on the present basis.' Yet the grant then being made was only £700 a year. It seems a small subsidy to an ancient classical foundation, which might well have been a source of pride, but at that period it seemed much more vital to keep rates low than to keep education at a high level. Even Bickersteth gave way to the economical chairman of the Higher Education Committee.

The best thing to do in this desperate situation seemed to be to approach first of all the only wealthy Old Boy known to the headmaster and ask for help. He, Mr. T. F. Brewster, at once promised £500 to tide the School over the crisis, if public grants were withdrawn. In the sequel this generous gift was not needed, but it was given notwithstanding towards the cost of the swimming bath later on. The second step was to send a letter of protest to all the Governors, appealing for more support and more confidence in the School's prospects: 'Such an old foundation as Pocklington should be given a chance to survive. It was still doing good work and had just won three open scholarships at Oxford and Cambridge. One could not be expected during two years of national crisis to remedy a state of things which one had had no hand in creating.' The third measure was to seek an interview with the fearsome chairman of the Higher Education Committee and offer to cut down the staff to the bone. This soothed him somewhat, but it meant a thirty-two period week of teaching for the headmaster, tackling classics, history, divinity and English, besides supervising the boarding-house and coaching in games, with no resident house-tutor except one lady.

The headmaster liked to recall the visit at this juncture of H.M. Inspector: Mr. Wager, a dour man, who like the L.E.A. despaired of Pocklington's prospects: 'We tried to cheer him up with a good lunch and a cigar, but he remained in the doldrums. After lunch we walked out upon the lawn. While we paced up and down discussing all the drawbacks, I saw his eye suddenly light up as he stooped to peer at the grass and took out a pocket lens. He had discovered a very rare fungus. Already he had two hundred and fifty-six varieties and this was the two hundred and fifty-seventh. His outlook changed at once. He brightened and began to discuss the School with a new interest. No school was a matter of despair that could produce so rare a fungus! It had a future. He proceeded to write a more hopeful report to the Ministry.'

The Governors meanwhile met in full force and elected a new chairman. They prevailed upon the County to increase its grant for a further year. But as boys came in more rapidly no further crisis arose. In 1919 the still growing numbers warranted the opening of a Junior House. The only other period when the number of boarders caused anxiety was in the financial slump of 1929-31, when the depression caused parents to cut down expenses and favour day-schools. Wilberforce Lodge had temporarily to be closed as a boarding-house and Dolman's numbers fell to fifteen. But three years of recovery more than made up for the four lean years. In 1939 the outbreak of the Second World War repeated the process of filling boarding-schools to overflowing. The buildings that arose in succession and the purchase of Dolman House and of Lyndhurst to accommodate the overflow are described elsewhere (Chapter 25). For the first time since 1896 came the satisfaction of providing for too many rather than too few.

One happy feature about the new influx of boarders was the number of counties from which they were drawn. In the twenties one batch of thirty-two boys derived from sixteen different counties. A boy in a kilt arrived from Glasgow and at ten years old announced himself solemnly as an Anglo-Scot. Aberdeen and Ayrshire sent others and Poole in Dorset and Wales also contributed. Yorkshire boys as ever preponderated, but the Newcastle area, Durham, Lincolnshire and Worcestershire sent their quotas. This variety had better effects than the usual closed policy of the county authorities, which encourages a local type and a narrower outlook. In fact this had to be pointed out to the chairman mentioned above, who objected to what he deemed 'foreigners' enjoying education in the East Riding. But as by that time the Riding's grant was nominal and did not at all cover the cost of educating their day-boys at the School his objection could not be pressed. It is worth mentioning, however, as evidence of the outlook of some controllers of educational policy.

In the main, boarders represented the homes of professional men, industrial managers, business men and farmers. The flourishing farmer will usually invest in boarding-school education because of the lack of society in country districts. Nothing was a clearer index of agricultural depression

P. C. Sands

Headmaster and Prefects, 1936

than the sudden fall in recruits from the farming fraternity in 1921 and 1930. The vigorous spirit of the northern boy, his initiative and robustness, are often remarked upon by masters who have taught also in the more 'polished' south.

II. POLICY AND PROGRESS

'I take my stand on detail.' — *Thring of Uppingham.*

There are several ways to make a boarding-school attractive. One is to make it distinctive in some special line and so draw the attention of press and public. One well-known school, for instance, is said to have won repute in the first place by its powerful rugby teams, since to excel in games is a sure way to the heart of the British public. Hutton had brought Pocklington to notice by the winning of scholarships and prizes in that rare commodity, Hebrew. But the study of Hebrew was dying and, if it could have been restored, its narrow field of usefulness made it hardly worthwhile, when even the vogue of classics was declining.

A second way is, putting it bluntly, to give value for money, to attract the bargaining British parent by offering good buildings, well situated, and good food. When schools are competing for boarders, parents are very critical of accommodation and only the largest public schools by their size and prestige can weather persistent criticism, not schools as small as Pocklington had become. Of course, when parents are competing for places in schools, they put up perforce with many drawbacks such as overcrowding, carelessly prepared meals, and untidy premises, and write to the papers in protest from time to time. But a fine building by the sea or in pleasant scenery that will provide an object for an outing by motor when coming over 'to see the boy' is a great inducement. Neither the situation nor the buildings of Pocklington were remarkable in 1914, though not without charm in summer. Moreover, the East Riding is rather a backwater and Pocklington was not on any main route.

Some discriminating parents will scan first of all the staff list in the prospectus and inquire of recent parents about the masters, but these are few. Centuries have passed since pious founders endowed the master and not the building of the school, in the belief that the master was the school.

In the long run any school will succeed which produces a good type of boy. A school is known by its fruits. But production has to begin. Keeton had said how difficult it was to get boys at all and the last years of Hutton's decline had advertised the School unfavourably.

The only solution seemed to be to build on the sound beginning Keeton had made, but to overlook no detail in any department (and a boarding-school has many) which could improve upon former standards, whether in teaching, games, catering, buildings and social amenities — to look for excellence in embryo and develop it — all to ensure that a report should go out from within that the School was a good one and that a younger brother might be happy there. Obviously this meant that the master should be always there and it also meant husbanding the small financial resources available. Fees were absurdly low, at that time £65 a year inclusive, and even that had often been reduced in favour of boys of promise. Endowments were no more than £1,000 a year and the L.E.A. was in no liberal mood.

Academics. Plenty of old foundations have sunk into the grade of ill-equipped private schools, barely subsisting because they could not qualify for grants. This was the danger here in 1915. Mainly it is the difficulty of staffing, so as to be able to offer the advanced education demanded of a secondary or public school, for which, of course, specialists are required. In 1916 the staff of four included a good mathematical coach who produced scholars in that subject, while the headmaster could coach the odd classical scholar, but the teaching in science was not strong. To remedy this quickly engaged the headmaster's attention. In 1919, when it was at last possible to increase the staff, he 'angled for' a first-class science man, the bait being the resident house-tutorship, which induced a nephew of the great chemist, Perkin, to leave Bradfield and come to lay the foundations of a good science course at Pocklington. He was a scholar of Trinity College, Cambridge, C. S. Kipping. A first-class mathematical man was also secured to maintain the high standard reached by the departing Perry. The policy deliberately pursued was to get good specialists who would teach their subject through all forms. To each was assigned a form for his particular shepherding, but in a small school one must choose between specialists and those valuable all-round form-masters, who teach most subjects at a lower standard and assume a paternal attitude to their forms. These were due later when increased numbers allowed. At present it was essential to teach as many subjects as possible to university standard, win scholarships, earn grants, and keep the School above the level of a small private school. The inspectors conducting a general inspection in 1920 were struck by the high qualifications of the small staff. After their visit a modern language specialist was added, and history and English also received more expert attention from Mr. T. W. Pay, who has taught these subjects with skill and enthusiasm for thirty years.

The policy bore fruit. Open scholarships and exhibitions were won at Cambridge and Oxford in classics, science and mathematics and also in history. About this time there was a loud demand for the teaching of biology in schools. Teachers were rare, but one was at last found, and within three years two pupils in this subject qualified for a scholarship award. An eminent biologist was invited to Commemoration to distribute the prizes in order to mark this development. Between 1920 and 1944, in spite of the larger numbers of schools now competing, many boys became Scholars or Exhibitioners of universities, not to mention the regular succession of Dolman Exhibitioners.

But another obstacle had to be surmounted to enable boys to take up the awards gained. The cost of a university course after the first war rose from £150 to £250 a year, and the open scholarship award did not go far enough. Grants were needed to supplement. The East Riding at that time offered only six major scholarships a year, eked out amongst all their schools, both of boys and girls. State scholarships, just inaugurated, were also severely limited in number. Hence the effort in 1933 to raise funds for a Wilberforce Memorial Scholarship, completed in 1938, while overtures to the old headmaster, C. G. Wilkinson, prompted a bequest of £2,000 in 1938 to provide two more exhibitions.

Then came more trouble. A battle had to be fought with St. John's College Council over the awards of the Dolman Exhibitions. It was a one-sided battle, for the Council had all the guns by virtue of an Order in Council (House of Commons) overriding the Dolman deed of bequest and empowering the College to set the standard required of candidates. As competition for College awards had become fiercer, the standard was raised and the College was tempted to award closed exhibitions also away from the School to which they rightly belonged. This would have been an almost fatal blow to smaller grammar schools, to which closed exhibitions induced many parents to send promising boys.

The headmaster's remonstrances were politely but firmly rebutted. He pleaded that the original bequest aimed at supplying boys to the College and linking School and College together. He insisted that any boy who was capable of taking an honours degree was 'a suitable and fit scholar' as Dolman defined in his deed of bequest. An outstanding case of a boy passed over as not qualifying, followed by an indignant protest from his father, prompted the headmaster to ask permission to put the case in person to the College authorities. This was graciously granted and in order to stress the seriousness of the occasion he asked the Governors to depute one of their number to go with him. The College Council was sympathetic, granted the pupil in question a special examination (a very great concession) and duly elected him. When this pupil, nobly playing his part, eventually gained a first-class degree and as usual was made a Scholar of the College, the

School's case seemed proved to the hilt. Later on the headmaster did not fail to send the College tutor a list of pupils whom the College had rejected for open exhibitions and yet afterwards had elected to scholarships because they had graduated in the first class, a list which included an anthropologist, a biologist, and a classic.

The policy of appointing specialists bore other fruit besides university honours. The specialists, as men with high degrees, were frequently appointed to headmasterships which not only brought the School to notice, but attracted other good men to take their place. Eventually, fourteen from the staff were so promoted, which counted a good deal when the School sought recognition by the Headmasters' Conference. The housemastership of Dolman, which was coupled with the post of second master, proved a great attraction when a key man on the staff needed replacing, and four of these housemasters succeeded in turn to the control of large schools.

Athletics. At the same time a constant watch was kept to improve the School's games and athletics. Most of the new men were also good performers in some branch of sport and their devotion and expert coaching produced cricketers and footballers who won a number of county caps or played for good clubs, besides athletic performers and swimmers of repute. Certain measures were needed to ensure this result. Hockey was abandoned in the Lent term and replaced with rugby House matches, to give newcomers time to learn the game and build up the next season's teams. The House matches, fought with extraordinary keenness, were a useful nursery for junior talent. Another measure was to divide the School into 'thirties', graded according to playing ability. Previously the captain of games had with much time and labour put up lists for games every day. Now the smallest junior knew his engagements beforehand, for each thirty took the field on certain days. Better still, a master took special charge of each thirty, coached and observed form and recommended players for promotion to a higher thirty. He had the satisfaction of training his own unit, while every boy was sure of his game and could aspire to promotion. Day-boys thus mixed with boarders were a great strength to the sides and their country physique an asset. And this provides an apt transition to a third important step in policy.

Boarders, Day-boys and Houses. The division between boarders and day-boys is an artificial one, a matter of where they sleep and feed, but it can develop into a real cleavage. Keeton had said to his successor, 'The boarders have a hearty contempt for the day-boys — a very proper feeling, I believe.' The obvious answer to this was to incorporate them in the same Houses for games and not to confine day-boys to a House of their own. Modern practice was anticipated by extending the wearing of the uniform grey suit to day-boys also. This went far to assimilating the son of the labourer, who might enter under the quota of 'free-placers', to the son of better-placed parents. The democratic tradition of earlier centuries was preserved and the way prepared for the 'equalitarianism' of the present day. Anyway the mixture was stimulating and healthy, and probably plays a large part in breaking down class distinctions and promoting good fellowship in the House of Commons!

Large public schools for the sake of convenient administration are bound to be divided into Houses, the inequalities of which, arising from inferior accommodation in some, or poor house-management in others, may cause odious comparisons. House feuds have also been known, which are more serious. There was one such in Hutton's time between the Schoolhouse and Wilberforce Lodge. Moreover, a boy may spend his whole school life in the small world of one house with a too limited outlook. To avoid this, the new Houses of Wilberforce and Dolman were graded according to age. Boys passed from these into the larger Schoolhouse as vacancies occurred but first had the advantage of living in a smaller family under the motherly care of the house-master's wife. This passing up provided a stimulating change of environment, as well as of companionship. All boys got the chance of sharing in the fuller school life and the headmaster of gaining a closer knowledge of all who became seniors. The School, as it grew, remained a unity.

Food. To the average boarder good food and comfortable and clean surroundings, affairs of every day, and of most of the day, are more constant concerns than scholarships and athletic results enumerated at Commemorations. Letters are always being written to the papers about school meals. Food grievances arise in all institutions that have an unimaginative cook, though, however good the food, there will always be grumblers, even at a college high table. Keeton's matron had a weekly menu, the same dishes on the same day of the week, an elementary but very common error. As Desmond Coke says in his school novel, 'On Wednesday it was pie. What was wrong with the pie? Nothing; but it was Wednesday's pie, and that spoilt it.' An element of surprise whets the appetite, monotony kills it. This was soon altered and the boys were kept guessing.

In the last war Parliament received complaints that the rationing at public schools was too severe and a team of experts was sent round to four typical schools, of which Pocklington was one, to inquire. Whole classes of boys were inspected in the gymnasium, stripped to the waist, weighed and measured. The report on Pocklington was 'pre-war standard' and 'very satisfactory'. At the outbreak of war in 1939 the headmaster's wife, guided by experience of the first war, built up reserves of provisions at once and

The Dining Hall in 1939

kept these reserves in three separate stores in order to meet the threats of bomb damage and compulsory evacuation through hostile invasion.

Interior decoration. When Thring remarked that he 'took his stand upon detail', he was defending the decoration of a classroom against a critic who objected that old desks and ink-stained walls made a boy just as happy. The influence of a clean, well-painted interior upon the residents is immense, especially on a wet day. At Pocklington the dingy pink distemper gave way quickly to paints in brighter and varied colours and a thorough spring-cleaning every vacation presented a spotless school for the boys' return. The old, dirty worn boards of common-rooms and class-rooms were replaced in time by polished red-jarrah wood blocks, and the old benches by shaped seating, not luxurious, but certainly less spartan. Pictures were hung in classrooms and common-rooms.

The School front. The exterior of a school can vary from the delightful warmth of some ancient public school pile to the repulsive hardness of unrelieved brick. Pocklington in 1914 through the mellowing of the white brick and the creepers already started had lost the more barrack-like look of earlier days. Care was taken to develop its attractiveness by fostering the evergreen pyracanthus with its flaming berries, which relieved the bareness in winter, and by pruning the virginia creeper which filled up the gaps in summer and blazed magnificently in autumn. Newly-planted hedges, well-kept lawns and flower-beds combined with the row of Jubilee trees planted in 1887 to present a front that arrested the attention of passing cyclists and motorists, rather resembling that of an old manor-house. The effects of such premises upon those whose home they remain for some years are subtle and lasting.

One last point : schools must be warm when seasons change. Too many boys suffer from the stupid rule that fixes the 1 October or the 1 November as the day when central heating must be started, whatever frosts intervene. Fuel may be saved, but colds will multiply.

Discipline and Punishments. The admirable Crichton's great conviction was that, 'What is natural is right.' According to others the keynote of good manners is B natural. There creep into the life of boarding schools as into other institutions practices that are unnatural, for what is natural for us is human, and boys, and sometimes masters, are apt to become inhuman.

When a crowd of boys live together, extremes of discipline must be avoided. A natural policy is to keep the prevailing temper human and humane. Abuses in the twentieth century were trivial compared with those of the olden days. There survived, however, excessive freedom of prefects to punish, of bigger boys to worry smaller boys, and of all boys to worry new boys. To a new boy the first entry into boarding school brings sufficient strain without the threats of what he will go through from the older hands, threats often empty but liable to depress. The new boys' concerts were harmless enough but, when they developed into pitching the singer suddenly off a table, resulted in such accidents as to justify forbidding them in future. The fact that one of the accidents incapacitated a first XI bowler was a good *casus belli* and helped to silence objections to the abolition of a 'tradition'. The decree was that 'all baiting of new boys as new boys' was to stop, and action would be taken retrospectively if breaches were discovered. Though attempts were made *sub rosa* in the dormitory, on the whole new boys were left in peace. Evidently, the aim was achieved, for an O.P., returning after some years of absence, wrote to the magazine in 1932 : 'It was not only in the buildings that we notice changes. A more subtle change has taken place in the School and its functioning. Gone is the old power of the senior changing-room, a factor which played such an important part in School life and politics a few years ago. That mixture of admiration and dread with which the "plebs" were wont to regard the seniors is noticeably absent ... In fact, a new régime is fast being established. The place seems more civilised in its views. It no longer requires a term of misery and a year of subjection to mark the entry and initiation of a new member of the community. A new boy steps right into his place of citizenship from the first day, and the privileges and the rest depend on him.'

The fagging system called for improvement. It was really stupid that a lot of small boys should be waiting for a prefect's whistle and have to leave whatever they were doing and run to its call in order that the last arrival might lace up the young lordling's boots. The remedy for this was afterwards nicknamed by the juniors as the Fags' Charter. Under the new arrangement, introduced about 1923, and so anticipating by some years the criticisms in the papers of fagging at public schools, fagging for prefects was restricted to two half-hours a day, when juniors tidied up the Club by rota. As a boot boy was provided by the management, there seemed no reason why a fag should clean a prefect's shoes, and as coals came by the same boot-boys, coal-carrying was also banned. The ringing of the bell and duties done hitherto at the order of the prefects were now arranged by the headmaster and posted up each term, and the tendency was for these to increase in number until, in war-time, every boy in the Schoolhouse had his special job. Nobody minded much so long as the distribution was fair. Thus a kind of general conscription replaced the haphazard drudging of the willing or submissive junior.

Caning by prefects could be excessive through a heated temper or adolescent sadism. The natural limits of a prefect's power of corporal punishment seemed to be those already prescribed for masters, corporal punishment being reserved for the headmaster's administering, except that if a prefect's authority were openly flouted, the headmaster could depute the head prefect to cane in the presence of the other prefects. Breaches of this rule, if discovered, were regarded seriously. The authority of the prefects was thus upheld.

Lines can be a real bugbear. Masters, aroused by some peccadillo, used to fire off an order to 'do five hundred lines' and any one of half a dozen prefects set one hundred or two hundred at his caprice. An Old Boy complained in 1916 that his handwriting had been ruined during his first fortnight at School, because he received in those few days nine hundred lines for various people. Boys went to school to learn to write and were promptly turned into scribblers. To impose such a load on a callow new boy was hardly humane. As he was unable to deliver his quota to all concerned, it was ridiculous that staff and prefects should be competing for the obedience of one small boy. To prevent this, 'copies' on special line paper, printed like the old copy-books, turned a scribbling effort into a writing lesson, one copy counting as twenty-five lines. Detention included a quarter of an hour's drill in the open air to keep the victim fresh. These items may seem trivial, but the aim was important, to secure the boarders' health.

For the rest it is a common practice now to follow the Mikado's famous plan and 'make the punishment fit the crime', as when the breaking of bounds is corrected by 'gating' (close or less restricted), instead of by caning. For misbehaviour off school premises, including smoking, gating seemed more adequate. A special circular to parents asked for their co-operation in checking smoking, as the old plea, 'He will smoke even if I try to stop him,' was no excuse for the encouragement to smoke often given by parents in the holidays. Most parents could, if they would, persuade their offspring to wait until they leave school or even later. Smoking is bad for discipline and leads to slackness. The boys themselves condemn it when they ban it in training and during the football season. Lastly, small fines for untidiness in changing-rooms were better than all other checks, and silence imposed in dormitories for talking after lights out saved much friction. Variety is the spice of punishment as of life and never was Aristotle's golden mean more salutary.

Religious Instruction. Though the English grammar school has played a great part in forming the religious tradition of this country, religious instruction called for more preciseness and definition than it had received before the First World War. Morning and evening prayers were an unconscious influence, but the divinity lesson was too often a failure. The policy pursued was to entrust religious instruction to masters who had convictions themselves and who viewed the subject as important. Emphasis was laid upon the New Testament rather than the Old, and one Gospel was studied carefully every year with the School Certificate form as a guide to Christian belief and practice at the present day and not merely as a subject for examination. Services on Sundays were deliberately kept short and, as boys like hymns, ten minutes now and again were given to practising a new hymn. To reduce the bad effects of the apathy of pagan parents in the holidays a letter was sent to the parents of all new boys asking them to support the efforts of the School by attending services themselves with their sons during vacations. What effect this had one cannot tell, but it is only too true that the absenteeism encouraged by their elders between terms dulls the good impression made upon the youth during term.

The verdict on this policy as a whole is pronounced by an old Boy who writes:

My impression of life as a boarder at the Schoolhouse in the late twenties is that life was fairly easy, unless perhaps a boy was unusually shy or nervous in disposition. The traditional bullying of juniors had all but died out; it remained as a topic of conversation rather than an actuality. Dormitories were warm and pleasant, but early prep in the summer term meant being roused by an always unwelcome bell at 7 o'clock. Work in the class-room was about normal, I suppose, with rather less than the average output of energy expected in a day-school. Masters were pleasant and fond of a joke, and some were real enthusiasts for their subjects, and there was every chance for the budding scholar to do well.

Prefects had a lot of responsibility for ordinary discipline, but (very wisely) restricted powers of punishment; they had a club of their own and some other privileges. They came under a good deal of criticism from the senior boys if they misinterpreted their duties, and some, if they did their job well; but this modernised version of the prefect system worked well on the whole and most of the lines one got were earned by pretty ostentatious misbehaviour.

I feel that if I speak too warmly about the meals, my past will rise against me. The food was good and there was plenty of it, but except on special occasions it was mostly that plain wholesome fare we recommend to our children, with memorably thick slices of bread and butter, and it was unfortunate if you disliked rhubarb.

We did a large amount of preparation, two and three-quarter hours on several nights in the week. However some of this was devoted to the surreptitious reading of English literature.

Sundays were pleasant, despite a compulsory church parade in the morning. We all went together to the parish church, with many of the masters and their wives and children. The vicar was Ian McNaughton Smith; his services were short, lustily sung, and well suited to boys. His sermons were exceptionally interesting; some of them I still remember, and his Confirmation lessons were a model of all that they should be. In the afternoons we went for a walk, sometimes a real one, sometimes for the stipulated hour only. The swimming-bath was of course open in the summer. In the evening we had a half-hour service, with a talk by the Head or his deputy on some topic of interest, not always directly concerned with religion. And then I think we must have had reading prep until supper time.

There was little or no privacy at school — not even a library — and the loss of this was felt.

The Cadet Corps we took lightheartedly, but we were glad enough of the training afterwards. Anyone who could form fours could manage the simple modern drill with patronising ease. Games we took — most of us — with deadly earnestness, and we heeded not the speeches at Commemoration warning us to put first things first. Perhaps post-war boys are more sensible; but I doubt it.

Discipline was a sensible balance between the rigorous and the easy-going. It was possible, though not easy, to get what seemed an unfair decision reversed, if it was something important. There was little chance to be lonely, for there was a friendly atmosphere and the Head, chary as he was of interfering with our personal relationships, quietly helped if a new boy found it difficult to fit in at first. Eccentrics we ragged and are now ashamed of it. It is easy to feel that one account of life in a boarding-school is exactly the same as another, and just as dull, but Pocklington School had a very distinct character of its own, a rugged school, but a good nurse of young men, if a misquotation is permitted.

Boarders have spoken of the delight of hearing thrushes on awakening in the dormitory or during evening preparation through the wide-open windows in summer. Some recall the few yards run across to the bath before breakfast for a plunge. Small cricket in the Dolman field, sunbathing in the bath after a swim, tobogganing down Chapel Hill in winter, and the keeping of wild pets — squirrel or hedgehog or young daws or owl — all helped to carry one through the serious business of term. Then there was the cinema, installed as soon as suitable models came on the market. The Saturday night show, several times a term, became a popular change from lectures, conjuring displays and gramophone recitals which were interspersed. Form plays, mostly uncoached, signalised the end of the Christmas term, a play by the staff that of the Lent term, and the boys' School play proper that of the summer term, all conducing to better elocution apart from the fun of rehearsals, and leading up to the declamation contest in July. The Sixth Form Club provided a pleasant mid-week break by its papers and debates.

All these affairs are now general in most schools and on an even more lavish scale. It is, however, notable how all these elements of school life were at Pocklington blended or caught up, so to speak, in the annual Commemoration, with its cricket match, swimming sports, School play, gymnastics display, garden party and church services. A film taken in 1938 gave a faithful picture of the 'cavalcade' of events, and Sir Arnold Wilson, M.P.,[1] then editor of *The Nineteenth Century and After*, gave a free description of them in his article called 'Walks and Talks' in that magazine after he had distributed the prizes here: 'The prizegiving was one of the best I have attended. The attendant ceremonies of Commemoration followed lines which would have rejoiced the heart of Milton, who in 1641 urged our magistrates to take into their care the "public sports and festival pastimes"

---

[1]This great man was killed in an air-raid upon Germany. To do penance for his deception by Hitler at an interview and for a favourable article on Hitler's aims, he volunteered for the dangerous post of rear-gunner on a 'bomber' at the age of fifty-eight.

that "inure and harden our bodies, and civilise, adorn, and make discreet our minds".' After mentioning the 'admirable' gymnastic display and other events, he winds up: 'Service in the parish church ... brought the day's proceedings to a fitting climax and a close. It was opened with the traditional Bidding prayer, which mentioned the name of the founder and benefactors, and closed with Luther's great hymn, "Now thank we all our God". We filed out uplifted and, after dinner, we enjoyed, again in the Hall, a detective play, admirably staged and faultlessly played.'

III. WAR RE-ACTIONS

The impact of the First World War was less felt than that of the Second, as bombing was rare and evacuation from bombed areas unnecessary. Blackout came later and was less rigorous. Curious outstanding memories are the use of maize in puddings instead of rice, and of rhubarb leaves as spinach, experiments hastily abandoned. Bread was scarcer, meat more liberal, than in the second war. Two grim experiences in the North were the Zeppelin raids and the influenza epidemic. In these days of lightning bomber raids it is strange to remember the threatening hum of the comparatively slow airship, faintly seen above like a colossal cigar, avoiding moonlit nights and cruising about to find a well-lighted town. Decoys were lit then as later and a fire purposely made on Barmby Common saved York Minster but caused the demolition of a pig-sty. The airship's engines so alarmed the Pocklington townsfolk that they sent a message to the headmaster, asking him to quieten the boys' voices for fear they should guide the Zeppelin crew in dropping their load!

The influenza germ was a virulent one and spread havoc on the Continent in 1918 before crossing to England, where it struck down whole families, even in remote farmhouses, and deaths were frequent. All the School boarders fell victims in two spasms, and most of the teaching and domestic staff, but came safely through.

The shortages of the submarine campaign of 1917 were eclipsed by others between the wars when the miners' strike of 1924 necessitated cooking porridge by hay-box and the General Strike of 1926 other expedients. Even water had long been in short supply, because some 'riparian owner' had refused the local water company his assent to the installation of a wider pipe-line. The chairman of the water company, a Governor of the School, when invited to open the swimming bath in 1921, must have felt embarrassed when the ceremony revealed an almost waterless bath.

The impact of the Second World War upon the School was more severe. Though inconspicuous towns like Pocklington were regarded as safe

A Group at Commemoration 1939

Showing (left to right) Canon Tapper; R. Teasdale, Esq; (afterwards Chairman of Governors); J. C. H. How, Bishop of Glasgow (afterwards Primate of Scotland); Sir Charles Wilson, M.D., President of the Royal College of Physicians, afterwards known as Lord Moran, medical adviser to Mr. Churchill; the Headmaster; Major-General J. H. Beith (Ian Hay, the novelist) and Dr. A. F. A. Fairweather, Medical Officer to the School and later Chairman of the Governors.

areas, black-out regulations brought the same worries as before, and the special constables watched like lynxes for any streak of light, while the boys had to endure curtained dormitories lit with the dimmest of *blue* light-bulbs.

Experiences of the previous war had taught the need of looking to supplies of everything from foodstuffs to notebooks. But quite a new feature loomed up with the newspaper headlines, 'Evacuation of School Children'. Within a week of our return, Hull and Sunderland were to send their train-loads into Pocklington as a Reception Area. A lightning war of heavy raids was the bogey broadcast by Hitler and Goering. Hence these tears! — tears of infant evacuees and their mothers. By previous arrangement between the authorities of the schools concerned, Pocklington was to provide the seniors of Hymers College, Hull, with classroom accommodation, and on 1 September an orderly regiment of Hymers seniors, about one hundred and sixty strong, detrained, marched to the primary schools and the chapels for lunch and patiently waited for billets. Primary school children of Sunderland and Hull followed on Saturday and Sunday. Our scouts played a great part in conducting children to billets.

It was thought advisable to recall all our own boarders at once and within four days they drifted back and resumed work on 6 September. Some curious results were that for three days there was little to do but mourn the loss of a fortnight's holiday in beautiful weather, with the swimming bath as the sole consolation; and bedtime had to be within an hour after sunset until the blackout was ready. Help was given to farmers, sandbags filled for the local authority, a trench made in Dolman field as a refuge against stray bombers during games, and a large rough tract of the Dolman field dug over to provide vegetables. The scouts also took over the A.R.P. services for the School, so that we felt safe from fire-bombs.

A new time-table solved the needs of the Hymers visitors fairly simply, Pocklington periods being reduced from six of forty-five minutes to six of thirty-five, so as to cover a lengthened morning session of 9 a.m. to 1 p.m., while Hymers opened with prayers in Hall at 1.30 p.m. and used the rooms and laboratory till 5.30. Other adjustments made games possible for both schools. One thing cramped the time-table, the loan of the chemistry laboratory to the Ministry of Health for research, but Pocklington was lucky not to suffer the fate of other schools who lost all to the demands of inconsiderate Ministries.

The building of the aerodrome in 1941 on our doorstep delighted the boys, who flocked from the games of cricket in progress at the time to see the first Wellington bomber alight on the runway. But it rather altered the view of Pocklington as a safe reception area, and alarmed the parents of boarders, whose fears seemed justified by two or three sporadic raids on and round the 'drome by single 'planes. These visits had their comic side, one happening just as the headmaster at breakfast said the usual grace, 'For what we are about to receive...'; another just as the service in Hall on Sunday started and the hymn was given, 'Lead, kindly light', whereupon a big plomp in the distance, disturbing the electric supply, left all in darkness. The culminating visit was at midnight on 21 September about 1 a.m., when a stick of anti-personnel bombs straddled the School premises, bombs falling successively *behind* Dolman House, *between* Dolman and the Sanatorium (a narrow space), *beside* the senior changing room, on the front path, and across the road, blasting slates, doors and windows, but harming no one, a providential escape, for the intervals between the bombs were not mathematically regular and two or three yards either way must have caused serious fatalities. Splinters travelled curiously to penetrate the woodwork of the Hall and make a hole in the ceiling, to hit the old Parliament clock in the dining-hall, fortunately without serious damage, and in a third instance to star the mirror over the head prefect's bed after traversing the long dormitory. The dormitories being mostly windowless, sleep for that night was resumed downstairs on camp beds and coco-matting bought in anticipation of sirens. Smaller boys finished their slumbers in Mrs. Sands' lounge. Morning service in church was attended as usual on what was appropriately being celebrated as 'Airmen's Sunday', and the afternoon was given to clearing away glass and debris from almost every room in the main block, ladies kindly bringing brooms to help in the dormitories, while the headmaster and boys swept up the classrooms and common-rooms. Meanwhile the District Council sent squads of workmen to make windows and roofs weather-proof, but the £900 worth of damage was not finally made good till the end of term.

Within a week parents were calling to press the headmaster to evacuate the School to a safer locality. But the Governors agreed that no place now was really safe and parents soon adopted a more philosophic attitude. Less than ten removed their boys, some to more dangerous places still, for aerodromes were everywhere. One happy result was that Hull parents, now that the worst blitz was over, and Pocklington less immune, began to keep their sons at home, until, in December, 1942, the remaining eighty seniors of Hymers College were taken back to join the rest in their own quarters. After three years and a term it was a great relief to have the whole School to ourselves again, with normal teaching periods restored and all rooms available at all times. How leisurely the lessons seemed at first instead of the rush of the six-period morning! How spacious the premises seemed! It was like stretching oneself after squatting for hours in a cramped position.

This is no reflection upon our guests, whose relations with Pocklington were pleasant throughout and who made a valuable contribution to the life of the town and to School society in many ways. The headmaster of Hymers sponsored a gracious gift from Hymers College in the form of prizes for mathematics and music to be called Hymers Prizes, as a memento of their occupation of our premises.

Two unforgettable sights for those who witnessed them marked the progress of the war. The first was the reddening of the sky over Hull after midnight during the savage blitz of that poor city in May, 1941, when the explosion of the land-mines floating down by parachute to devastate whole streets twenty-five miles away shook even the School doors and windows. The other was the thrilling sight of over twenty Halifaxes speeding along the runway by Wilberforce Lodge and rising, one every minute, to circle the sky higher and higher, while other planes from neighbouring aerodromes joined the rendezvous overhead, whereupon their lights quickly faded from view and left one speculating upon another thousand-plane raid over Germany. In the early dawn those who woke to hear the returning engines throbbing awaited anxiously the last arrival. Circling round before landing, short of petrol, one crashed in New Street and set the National School on fire, another in the mist came to grief at Riverhead, demolishing a house. Another, on its way out, loaded with a pair of 2,000 lb. bombs, swerved down by the beck between the School and Wilberforce Lodge, but fortunately its blaze did not ignite the bombs.

The Cadet Corps, started in 1916, still did good work under Major Whitehouse, who had resumed charge with renewed zeal on the departure of Mr. Derbyshire for the war. The scouts under the Old Boy, L. C. Sands, gave service in many ways, in fire-watching, fire-drill, and the less spectacular salvage collection. But war needs demanded a third force, the Air-training Corps, which acquired high efficiency under Mr. R. T. E. Allen. These three forces shared in many 'Marches Past' besides making contributions to the displays with which the various 'Weeks' were celebrated — 'Navy week', 'Wings for Victory week', 'War-weapons week', and 'War-savings week'. For the last R. W. Annand, V.C., was brought down as opener and delighted the crowd in Market Street by a forceful and witty oration.

Finally, in 1945, V.E. Day on 8 May brought the agony to a close in Europe, and V.J. Day on 15 August did the same in Asia. The School duly celebrated the peace with large bonfires.

This record would not be complete without reference to the patient service of the boys in the dining-hall and scullery, in blacking-out, coke-shifting, and other ways which met the shortage of labour, the loyal hard work of matrons and lady-cooks, sweepers and stokers, and the readiness of everyone to forget one's rights. To everything one got inured, except to the loss of Old Boys in the services. These shocks were not dulled by repetition, for each boy was different and had different excellences. Yet those to whom it fell to help to forge that excellence cannot conceive of it as thrown away or finished. Resurgent! They had hardly seen life yet. Now they share it in fuller measure.

IV. P.C. SANDS
(1914 to 1944)
(An appreciation by J. M. Cobban, who was a boy at the
School from 1920 to 1929 and who is now headmaster of
Abingdon School, Berks.)

The man whom the Governors appointed in November, 1914, to succeed Keeton was Percy Cooper Sands, for eight years composition master at the City of London School. At Cambridge he had won a first in both parts of the Classic Tripos, and for a treatise on, *The Client Princes of the Roman Empire*, he was awarded the Thirlwall Medal in 1907 and elected a Fellow of St. John's College. His games record was impressive too, with College colours in both cricket and football during all the four years he was up, and with 'Seniors' and 'Trials' in football and Crusaders' colours in cricket. He was thirty-one years of age; he was married and had a son and a daughter, a second daughter being born in 1919.

Perhaps the outstanding characteristics of Sands throughout his long career as headmaster of Pocklington were his versatility and his energy. The headmaster of a small public school has inevitably to be a jack-of-all-trades, but we who hold office nowadays are spoilt in comparison with our predecessors. It is true that Sands was no longer teaching thirty-two periods a week when I knew him; but he took the bulk of the work with the classical sixth and a fair cross-section of the lower school work. In an emergency, too, he would add to his timetable. Many a boy must owe his School Certificate to the extra half-hour with the Latin set book squeezed in before breakfast throughout the summer term. I still envy him the facility with which he could mark Latin or Greek verse composition. He had kept the fine edge of his scholarship unblunted and the way in which he botched and turned our own crude versions was a joy to those whose own sense of style was only just developing.

He must have had a remarkable sense of detachment to enable him to apply himself wholeheartedly to his teaching. It has been well said that a headmaster's work consists mainly of interruptions to it, and at no time of the day was he safe from distraction. Remember that at this time he had no bursar and no secretary to help him. Most of his letters were written in his own hand, though he could (and did) handle a typewriter. The telephone was not, perhaps, such a menace then as it is nowadays, but he had frequently to cope with its insistent summons. Visitors — parents, the school doctor, the clerk, the gas manager — were liable to call at all hours. In the middle of a Homer period he would glance out of the window, cast some highly technical instructions to a passing gardener, and continue his translation almost without a pause. From the last period in the morning he would hasten to the dining hall, where the hand that had just been correcting a Greek prose would soon be carving the joints for seventy odd boarders.

He was equally active on the games field. Almost every day during the summer you would see that trim purposeful figure walking across the Common towards the nets. Club matches would give him a chance to join in the game, in which he showed all-round ability as well as enormous zest and concentration. He loved cricket and gave boys any amount of individual encouragement and help. I can remember seeing him play rugger, too, though that was not his game. In fives, on the other hand, he was really good. I think the game must have appealed to his sense of order and neatness. At all events he had an eye for a ball and he could control it with almost magical efficiency.

Sunday may have been a day of refreshment for him but it was scarcely a day of rest by ordinary standards. Service at church in the morning; sometimes Sunday school in the afternoon in the town; in the evening our own service in the dining hall. How those stories of Schweitzer and other great men stick in the memory! He had a gift for vivid narrative and his Sunday evening talks certainly got home to the impressionable small boy.

And yet withal he found time to keep up, and expand, his own literary interests. His two books on the literary genius of the Bible were written during the decade when I was at the School: perhaps he would as soon be remembered by them as by anything. The first of them was launched to the favouring wind of a review by T. R. Glover in the *Daily News* and they achieved something more than a scholastic reputation. I was sleeping at the time in a small dormitory near his study and we used to hear his typewriter clicking away long before we got up.

He could only achieve so much by a strict regimen of life. His day was an ordered pattern and one felt that there was in it none of those loose ends which spoil the web for most of us. The result was that he never seemed to hurry, he never seemed to hesitate. He did everything with the ease and confidence that is born of known purpose and he combined with this sense of purpose a tremendous personal dignity. It was a dignity that was enhanced by, but not dependent on, the trappings of his office; he retained it while serving out potatoes or marking a tennis court. Above all, there was a remarkable consistency in his character. His discipline was firm but extremely just and we all knew exactly where we stood with him.

We were well aware that he kept an assortment of canes hidden away in the big cupboards outside his room — along with the sports kit and the cock-fighting bell — and we knew that he would not hesitate to use one of them: but even the most hardened — and calloused! — reprobate was never heard to suggest that he had been punished arbitrarily or in pique.

A colleague of my own once damned a highly successful fellow schoolmaster by telling him that he had all the inhuman virtues and none of the human vices: but Sands was redeemed from such a fate by an intensely human and humane streak in his character. He could quell a loutish fifth former with a glance; but he could unbend with a ten-year-old as with his own children. He was especially kind to the weak and to those who limped along in the rear of life's caravan. He understood the mind of such a one as dear old Harold, the school janitor — if I may call him by such a high-sounding name — and he could talk to his inferiors in tones of real friendship, without either losing his dignity or appearing to patronise them. He was ready to unbend too with the sixth form. 'Come on, Fatty,' I remember him saying to Leslie Marshall when the classical sixth were tittering over Homer's proleptic use of one of his own nick-names. His quiet humour shines forth in the occasional verse he wrote for the School magazine (and I hope that a selection of it is included as an appendix to his history, for much of it is worthy of a wider circulation). In more robust vein were his contributions to the House concerts, where his renderings of such comic songs as *Mother and Me* brought the house down. He had, too, considerable dramatic talent. I was not young enough to see the staff plays of the early thirties but I remember well their forerunner — a local production of *Nothing but the Truth* in which Sands portrayed the part of, I believe, a retired butter merchant.

This may seem an idealised picture but I think most Pocklingtonians of my generation would accept it as a true one. If I had to play the role of devil's advocate, I should indeed find it difficult to build up a case against him. Yet looking back, one does feel that to some extent he had the inevitable defects of his own virtues. He was, for instance, an easy and accomplished speaker; yet in his mistrust of facile emotion he did once or twice fail to rise to the occasion when the School looked for something of a clarion call from him. He did too seem strangely remote from the ordinary weaknesses of the flesh. We felt, quite illogically, that a headmaster who occasionally made a mistake would be capable of a little more sympathy with us in our minor peccadilloes! In spite of his real kindliness of heart, he did not seem to understand what the boys growing up in the twenties were thinking and feeling. Nowadays, of course, I realise that he was probably far nearer to our thoughts than we knew at the time, but I am trying for a few moments to recapture our feelings of sixty years ago.

In other ways, too, he seemed to the (then) Modern Boy to have lagged strangely behind the March of Time. Did he really refer to the Kinema (with a hard K) as though to some strange monster, or am I imagining it? He certainly stuck to the bowler hat, the wing collar, and the umbrella long after most headmasters had broken with convention. It was, I think, the coming of the golf course at Pocklington that finally broke down the barriers. The evening when Sands appeared in Hall to take House prayers in plus fours was a real turning point in the history of the School. Such things are perhaps trivial, but they mean much to the boy.

I left in 1929, but as I revisited the School during the thirties, I was impressed by the change in Sands. He retained all his old energy and grasp; but he had become so much more mellow, so much more lovable. He saw life steadily and saw it whole; and with this comprehension had come a greater sympathy and a greater tolerance. He was not only reconciled to the marvels of modern science, he took a genuine delight in the pictures (no longer the Kinema), in the theatre and in the radio. His grown-up family had introduced him to a new world and he was ready to enjoy it without losing his bearings in the old one. I rather envied the boys who had the privilege of being under him in those years.

And then came the war. Sands was one of the few headmasters who had to hold the helm during both of the wars, and he himself has lifted the curtain enough for us to see what a burden he had to bear during this second period of emergency. And finally, with quiet and self-effacing dignity, he handed over the reins, happy in the knowledge that his successor was strong enough to hold them.

★ ★ ★ ★

I am fully conscious, in reading over this brief sketch, how much I have omitted. I have, for instance, deliberately said nothing about his relations with his staff (it was only after I left that I realised how much of his success was due to his talent for choosing the right man and giving him his opportunity). Nor have I quoted statistics to show how he built up the School until it could re-apply for admission to the Headmasters' Conference. I hope, however, that I have said enough to show what Pocklingtonians of my day felt about 'Parcy'. He was indeed the *genius loci*, the focus of our existence, in a way that only the headmaster of a small and independent school can hope to be.

There are two things which remain to be mentioned. They were perhaps the two most important things in his life. The one provided the real secret of his strength and influence, and that was his simple and unassuming Christian faith. We were no more pious than any other set of healthy boys of our age and time, but we knew deep down that what he said with his lips he meant in his heart. Many a boy must have felt the influence of Sands' example of the Christian life — and not merely during his school-days.

The second factor is, of course, Mrs. Sands herself. No one but a headmaster can know how much he owes to the help and support of his wife, whose work lies so largely behind the scenes : and in Mrs. Sands he had found the ideal help-mate for his life's work. It would be presumptuous of me to speak of her graciousness in the drawing room, her kindly attentions in the sick-room, her efficiency in the kitchens: but it would be grossly unjust if some acknowledgement were not made of all that the School owes to her, as well as to P.C. Some day perhaps an enlightened Board of Governors will interview the wives of the candidates as well as their husbands. Meanwhile it is assumed, quite illogically, that a prospective headmaster will have had the good sense or the good luck to marry a wife who is capable of acting as hostess, matron or housekeeper or perhaps all three together. Strangely enough, this assumption, by a beneficent arrangement of providence, usually turns out to be justified in the event: but all honour is due to those wives who do step so valiantly into a breach which is not of their making.

★   ★   ★   ★

And lastly, if I may finish on a more personal note, I would acknowledge my own debt to Mr. and Mrs. Sands. I can never begin to repay them for their kindness to me, and subsequently to my wife. All I can do is to attempt to pass on, in another part of England, some of the lessons I learnt from them. Yet their kindness to me was not unique. All over England — and beyond these shores — there are grown men whose hearts will be stirred by the name of Sands, and I like to think that they will join me in saluting Mr. and Mrs. Sands in their retirement. May the years pass lightly in the shade of Chapel Hill, and may they find in their grandchildren a renewal of their own youth.

CHAPTER 20

ROBERT ST. JOHN PITTS-TUCKER, M.A.

(1945 — 1966)

(i)

See also Chapter 26

The new headmaster, who commenced his work in January, 1945, was Mr. R. St. J. Pitts-Tucker, M.A., former Scholar of Clare College, Cambridge. He possessed a first-class degree in both parts of the Classical Tripos and had been on the staff of Shrewsbury School. He was of the right age for dealing with the new problems that arose, and had the necessary sanguine temperament. For, though the end of the war was in sight, the effects of it were to last for some years. The demand for places in the School was more insistent than ever and not to be denied. Yet shortages of materials and the difficulty of securing building licences dictated all sorts of make-do arrangements and accommodation for the time being, to cope with this demand. The staffing problem was fortunately eased by the return of masters from war-service, but domestic labour was in shorter supply than ever.

But the most serious problem was presented by the new Education Act which became law on 1 April, 1945, the problem of maintaining the School's independence which it had enjoyed as a Direct Grant School. Schools in this category were a precious variation in the scheme of education, standing between the public schools on the one hand, which were entirely independent of State control, and the 'controlled' school on the other, that is, controlled by Local Education Authorities, receiving from the Board of Education, now to be called the Ministry of Education, a 50 per cent. grant. The Direct Grant school, though supervised and inspected by the Board, controlled largely its own finances, maintained by grants from the Board, by fees, and by a deficiency grant from the Local Education Authority, which in return nominated some of the Governors. There was thus sufficient public control and interest to eradicate or prevent scholastic abuses and sufficient independence to encourage initiative and ambition. The headmasters appointed for their ability were not subjected to the rulings of a clerk in the offices of the Local Education Authority or to the small regulations and restrictions imposed by the supposed need for uniformity.

The new Act made a significant alteration in respect of the State grant.

This in future was to be a maintenance grant of £16 for each boy of ten years or over, and to include examination fees and other costs, while all capital expenditure on buildings and repairs to premises was left to the resources of the school. Before any school could be recognised for Direct Grant, the Ministry had to be satisfied that the Governors had the means to support this burden.

And what of the Local Education Authority? Its deficiency grant was abolished in view of the increased grant from the Ministry, but it now received the right to fill 25 per cent. of the vacancies annually in the school as the result of a county examination, the school having a voice in the final selection of the pupils.

The Ministry at this time was loth to recognise schools of this type, being pressed by the advocates of universal state control to abolish them as an anomaly. Yet public opinion, strongly voiced in Parliament, recognised the value of these schools, mostly old grammar schools, which had made so long and so strong a contribution to English education and manners. A concession was therefore made, but their number sadly reduced. Pocklington was one of the favoured few. It could put up a sound claim financially. For some years it had cost little or nothing to the East Riding Authority and it had no overdraft at the bank.

The result of this new order was the raising of school fees, which now had to bear the cost of building operations, and those too at enormously increased prices. But the Governors went boldly ahead. A new boarding-house, Lyndhurst, at the foot of Chapel Hill, was acquired at a cost of £4,000 and put under the charge of Mr. R. T. E. Allen. A scheme soon followed for the erection of a separate Junior or Preparatory School adjoining Lyndhurst, which at the time of writing is well on its way to completion.

Thus the little Guild or Chantry School founded in A.D. 1514 witnesses still further expansion into a public school of three hundred pupils. Its traditions continue. Explaining the new regulations and welcoming visits from Old Boys, the new headmaster summed up the situation: 'As it is men that make a city, so it is boys that make a school, and while there is no end to the making of regulations, yet is the spirit of the place free to blow where it will. Whether we are a good school or a bad school rests with ourselves alone, in the contribution that each one of us can make to building a happy community, where cheerfulness abounds with industry.' Signs of a vigorous spirit may still be found in the chronicles of the current *Pocklingtonian*, recording the ever-increasing interests of the foundation of John Dolman.

CHAPTER 21

SCHOLARSHIP

What is a scholar? 'A learned person', we are told, 'one versed in any branch or in many branches of knowledge, a person of *thorough literary or scientific attainments*'. The boys who proceeded to become Fellows at Oxford or Cambridge in the seventeenth century were among our earliest scholar products, but the definition will cover the mathematicians of Gruggen's time or the eminent doctors in medicine mentioned below, or again the brothers Foxley of Wilkinson's time, one of whom chose architecture as the medium of his 'thorough scientific attainment'; or again, A. S. Duncan-Jones, Fellow of Caius College, who became an authority on church music, and other eminent divines, Hebrew scholars like J. C. H. How, Primate of Scotland. S. L. Brown, devoted to scholarship in the narrower acceptance of the word, specialised in theology and Hebrew as a professor of London University and Doctor of Divinity, while J. M. Cobban's researches in ancient history won him the Thirlwall Medal at Cambridge. K. A. Pyefinch, an exile on Bardsey Island, scrutinised through a microscope the weeds and growths of the ocean shores in pursuit of biological truth. The institute with the famous letters I.C.I. absorbed the scholarship of R. C. Welch and D. Whittaker, the making of a dam in Egypt occupied the expert engineering of O. L. Prowde. Edward Robson's legal acumen won him the gold medal in the Law examinations, while A. J. Bull, Doctor of Music, made and taught harmonies. The term scholar is wide and embraces a wide selection of O.P.'s besides the examples mentioned.

Once the selection was narrower. Only in the nineteenth century did science begin successfully to claim its rightful place in education, but it will be noted with pleasure that Pocklington in a humble way was in the van, when Mr. London in 1884 first applied his scholarship to electric lighting and Mr. Hutton, as already told, was keen to note the new trend, built a laboratory and appointed a first-class scientist. Better laboratories replaced the old in 1931 and the succession of good demonstrators was not neglected. An early start was made in biology. No one can complain of the narrowness of curriculum. The supply of scholars for the medical professions and for industry was as forthcoming as that for the Church, the Bar, or the Civil Service, for the Services or the schools. In one year five boys went to study medicine at five different universities, continuing the tradition which began perhaps in the eighties, when Dawson Williams (afterwards knighted) obtained the first place and gold medal in the London M.B. examination, after which Twistington Higgins became head of the Children's Hospital in Great Ormond Street, and C. M. Wilson (Lord Moran) became Principal of St. Mary's Hospital, President of the Royal College of Physicians, and medical adviser to Mr. Churchill.

But doctors, chemists and physicists may all suffer from a lack of the humanities. It is the duty of a school to forestall such a catastrophe. So side by side with laboratory instruction the religious and moral sense must be fostered and artistic and literary values taught, since the end of education is not a scientific handbook or a Latin grammar, but a man, a whole and complete man.

Still people ask, 'Why are dead languages taught?' Substitute the phrase 'the ancient cultures', the speech and ideas of those who were masters of the art of thinking and living, which have much the same effect as the Bible and Shakespeare upon those whose minds are steeped in them, and, through them, upon others.

No one would deny the effect of Shakespeare's plays upon our way of life to-day, even if 95 per cent. of the people are unconscious of it. To most, Shakespeare is an ancient, and his language, if not dead, difficult. Yet the recent film of *Hamlet* revealed how many of the sayings of that play have become popular currency, proverbs in men's thought and on men's lips, a guide in critical situations, helping them to meet, if not to solve, life's problems. The would-be suicide (and the number has been reckoned at 16,000 a year) may yet be checked by Hamlet's questionings:

> For who would bear the whips and scorns of time . . .
> But that the dread of something after death . . .
> . . . . puzzles the will,
> And makes us rather bear those ills we have
> Than fly to others that we know not of?

Science suggests that man is a pygmy, a mere cypher, because the worlds in the universe are counted by the million. Shakespeare restores our balance and self-respect:

> What a piece of work is a man! How infinite in faculties! . . . in action, how like an angel!
> in apprehension, how like a god! the beauty of the world, and the paragon of animals!

That is why the humanities, as they are rightly called, the writings of poets and thinkers, of historians and philosophers, must be part of our training, if we are to see reason, see our way through the tangle of living and retain hope and faith. In the emergencies of war-time all our top boys were bribed by State bursaries to study physics, harnessed to the struggle against German science, that we might be beforehand in the battle of wits and scientific devilries or precautions against devilries. But these were emergencies. No people could stand such a one-track training for long without going insane. Moreover, the breakaway from the spirit and discipline of the classics has resulted in such monstrosities as the licence and so-called self-expression of those impressionists who seem unable to say what they mean, who excite a gape or a gasp rather than sympathy in the beholder or reader and who obviously are reverting to the primitive.

The shortness of this chapter is, therefore, no indication of the importance attached to scholarship in relation to school games. It is merely in keeping with the habit of taking work for granted and talking sport, which our readers will expect us to do at some length.

CHAPTER 22

GAMES AND ATHLETICS

The spice of a schoolmaster's life is witnessing the evolution of some raw, often unprepossessing or sickly boy of ten years into a youth who becomes outstanding in some particular line. The junior boy's exterior so often conceals football or cricket sense, a swimmer's or a sprinter's paces, an actor's adaptability, the flair for poetry or scholarship — an urge to excellence that responds to or even anticipates training and teaching.

'Try everything once.' In 1890 the School tried lacrosse. Later it began hockey. The first venture did not last but in 1895 we find that T. F. Brewster played in most of the Cambridge University XII's matches, and in 1906 one or two O.P.'s played for their college and one, much later, for Yorkshire — D. W. A. Fleming. Hockey, after two or three seasons, made way for concentration upon rugby football. There was a time when cycling was recognised by a half-blue at Cambridge and O. L. Prowde achieved the honour the very last time that it was awarded, in 1902, winning the mile, the ten miles, and second place in the four-miles event. O.P.'s have carried their prowess at fives into the university fives court, as McLellan in 1923, and S. C. G. Bach in 1931. Our fives court, built in 1896, is on the Winchester model, the single sloping buttress on the left providing just the variety needed to redeem the game from a slogging match, which the Rugby code of fives produces.

Gymnastics. Before passing to the greater sports, all who have witnessed the display of gymnastics at Commemoration will expect from us some mention of this basic method of building a sound physique, long a school subject under the name of P.T., for work on the bars persisted when the Swedish scheme of exercises was tried in England. Then came a system more on the Danish mode, exercises on the horizontal bar being condemned, and although His Majesty's Inspector in 1930 gave much offence when he likened our agility upon it to monkey tricks, more than one cricketer, expert on that bar, has confessed that its over-development of the shoulders disabled him as a bowler by checking his action. But its fascination has caused it to reappear here and there.

One would expect good results from forty years' instruction by such a gymnast as Mason Clarke, who in 1899 became an English international,

Gymnastics at Commemoration (Mason Clarke in the background).

representing England against Sweden. In 1901 he was English gymnastic champion. In the 1890's he could walk erect under the lath over which he had just jumped and on his first day at the School his feats so enthused his pupils that after school they carried him shoulder-high to the railway station. The tradition in gymnastics triumphed over the modified code of 1936, with its emphasis upon suppleness and agility, and in two years the efforts of the new instructor, J. Lamb, satisfied the Old Boys that little had been lost, and caused Sir Arnold Wilson, visiting at Commemoration, to pronounce the display as one of the best that he had witnessed. Several O.P.'s have gained a place in their university VIII's, G. H. A. Robinson at Cambridge in 1936, A. D. Boult and T. Hartley at Leeds. The name most often on Mason Clarke's lips was that of H. M. Savery, who came eighth of fifteen competitors for the English championship in 1909, although by far the youngest competitor, and who at School amused the boys by walking on his hands from the gymnasium to the School corridor.

Football. Association, 1883-1910. It was only when the Rev. C. F. Hutton brought his reinforcements to the School that its records in games became noteworthy. During the years 1889-1910 the standard of football was high, especially when one notes that the boys numbered only about a hundred until 1896, when they had risen to one hundred and fifty. In 1892-3 the School's total of goals scored was 80 as against 20 by their opponents; three years later, 113 against 21, and only once in those first nine years was the School's score exceeded by that of their opponents, who represented much larger schools. The peak was reached in 1895-7, when the records for two seasons stood as follows: 14 games won out of 17, and 18 games won out of 25 (five being drawn), including a 19-0 victory over Hymers College. It is natural to find that a master who acted as coach was a Welsh Soccer Trial player, D. J. P. Davies. The star player was F. D. Cautley, a Cambridge Blue, while others gained places in the teams of other universities, H. Dodgson at Edinburgh, C. E. L. Burman at Durham, H. H. Anson at Leeds, or gained their 'Seniors' at Cambridge, like C. J. Snowden, or captained their college XI, as R. Brice-Smith that of St. John's. G. Kirk played for Leeds City and later Bradford City F.C. Small schools are more prone to fluctuations, as leading players are less quickly replaced, but the force of tradition comes to the rescue and after a year or two the story of the Phoenix is re-enacted.

Rugby. The rugby code, introduced in 1879-80, survived one or two seasons, but lack of numbers compelled reversion to soccer. Re-introduced in 1910-11 on the initiative of G. H. Keeton and of W. Cobby, games master of Hymers, both of them internationals, it attained remarkable success here during the seasons of 1913 and 1914, for it is remarkable when a XV drawn from sixty boys beats such large schools as Leeds Grammar School (17-0), St. Peters (35-3), Hymers (37-6), Ripon (41-0) and even a Hull and East Riding first XV. It was a quick spasm of life, reflected later in the appearance of a number of O.P.'s in good club sides, G. C. Wood playing for Headingley, J. C. Burbridge captaining the Riding, and R. J. Cobb playing in the Yorkshire Trials. Then came a slump, as numbers in the School fell still further, until about 1924, when, once more expanding and profiting by the new 'House' system, the School began to win matches again and produce players of county standard, as N. B. Bowen, who captained Durham County, J. S. Mellor, a member of the Yorkshire pack from 1928-1935, and G. F. D. Pearson of the Devon pack. The School side owed much to the Lampitt brothers — Stanley, who afterwards captained Leeds University, and Norman, scrum-half at thirteen years, who saw the School side rise from the doldrums to a very strong XV. Later he captained Middlesbrough.

The next outstanding team was in 1928. Of this XV D. M. H. Craven, after captaining Reading University, played for Berkshire, till his wanderings in the R.A.F. enabled him to play for Lancashire in its championship year, the Eastern Counties, and also Surrey, thus receiving four caps, not to mention his scoring of a great number of tries for the R.A.F. — a great left-winger! At School, partnering J. L. Wilson for three seasons, he shared in the scoring of 54 tries with him for the School. W. Madderson, a forward who scored a large number of tries, obtained two County caps, playing for Durham and later for the East Midlands, while S. L. Barkas played for Durham County. This XV, ably coached by E. B. Johnson, won nine games out of twelve and scored 181 points to 62. The flower of the side helped to make the following season nearly as successful.

A eulogy of this XV printed in *The Pocklingtonian* may be of interest to all who follow rugby and appreciate the qualities that it calls for:

THE SYNTHETIC PLAYER

(With apologies to W. S. Gilbert)

If you want an imaginary figure of fame
Which is certain to be a unique Rugger man,
Take all the best qualities known in the game
And join them all up on the following plan —

Take the kicking of Craven and also his pace,
Add a touch of the spirit and tackling of Hale,
Of Wilson's defence we add more than a trace,
And Mudd's we throw in, in case Wilson should fail;

Then the handling of Barkas, and passing of Parker,
  The 'selling the dummy' and coolness of Wright;
We must turn to the scrum, if the outlook gets darker,
  And throw in the keenness of Binns for a fight.
Take the strength of a Ludwig, the quickness of Sands,
  Sheffield's height and the hooking of Weeden, so neat,
For the line-out try Whittaker's safe pair of hands,
  And Madderson's skill when he's using his feet;
The pluck of a Peacock, and Easterby's weight,
  Hard working of Dearnley, who makes up the eight.
Oh! Take all these qualities, reader obedient,
  Cook 'em up nicely and leave 'em to cool,
And perfected you'll find by each sauce and ingredient
  A rattling good player, called Pocklington School.

O Si Sic Omnes!

Another good side was that of 1932, which defeated a Leeds XV in a game which few will forget who saw the young stand-off B. K. Lawson, aged sixteen, twice slip through the centre on a sticky ground, as if the mud were a cinder-track, to score the equalising and winning tries. Other victims of this team, known as 'Sheffield's Team' were Wakefield, Hymers, Ripon and Woodhouse Grove. The brilliant leader of the pack, W. Sheffield, later played for Leeds University, but was more famous as a swimmer. E. G. Petrie, whose stride brought many spectacular tries from the left wing (eleven against Ripon who lost to us by 97-0), after playing for the Yorkshire Schoolboys, cut short his sprinting career most tragically by enlisting through some romantic urge in the forces opposing Franco in Spain and there died of wounds. P. A. Giovetti played full-back for Bradford and won his cap for Yorkshire. His elusiveness (he seemed to move horizontally to keep his legs out of reach) and his strong kicking with either foot brought him real distinction in rugby circles. He, too, is mourned as a war-victim, one of those who did not return from an air-raid upon Germany.

Since that time Pocklington's reputation as a good nursery of the game has been maintained. In 1949 the School was the only side which supplied two players to the Yorkshire Schoolboys' XV, and in 1950 shared that honour with one other school. J. G. Allison, N. Ogle, R. Binns figured in Yorkshire Trial games; N. Banister captained Exeter College, Oxford. The Universities of Bristol, Durham and Leeds have given places to G. E. Halliday, R. E. Grayburn, G. J. Jefferson respectively, while R. Levy (Lewis) helped St. Mary's Hospital when at its strongest and A. G. I. Wood has played three times for Yorkshire straight from school. In measuring the success of the School's rugby football, it must be remembered that at no time till 1940 did the number of pupils reach two hundred, of whom about seventy were juniors. The record must bring satisfaction to all those masters who spent time and energy upon the regular coaching of the Thirties.

Cricket. In cricket two factors affect the record more than in rugby football. One is, of course, the competing of so many interests to-day in the summer term and the short time available for school cricket. An Old Boy explained how, in 1896, net practice was an everyday affair and cricket monopolised the months of May to July for every boy. There was no swimming bath to attract the juniors, trying to learn the game or to endure it, when 'out for a duck' finished their chance of improvement for the afternoon, until the signal at 4.30 p.m. cut short their boredom and sent them rushing back to swim. There was no corps or scouts to occupy one afternoon a week, no School Certificate to distract the seniors. Consequently, in the nineties and for some years after, cricket enjoyed the monopoly of the summer term and was played with great zest. Boys proceeding to the university frequently figured in the Seniors trial, four at Oxford (L.Covey, S. W. B. Holbrook, A. G. Butt and P. R. Wardroper) and two at least at Cambridge (E. D. Gilbert and F. D. Cautley, who captained his college), while others went further still and played for their counties: H. G. Sale for Worcestershire, A. K. Wardroper for Northumberland, and C. E. Anson and P. Whiting for Yorkshire, Anson acting as captain in several matches.

The other factor is suggested by the familiar adage, 'A cricketer is born, not made.' We remember George Hirst's remark about our J. H. Daniel, when he saw him at the nets at the age of twelve with a style already matured and the straightest of bats. When the over-eager coach asked Hirst what he should teach him the veteran replied, 'Let him alone, don't try to teach him,' and the young colt justified the remark by scoring 40 not out in his first School match at the age of thirteen. T. F. Smailes came to us 'ready-made', in the XI at fourteen years, useful with bat and ball, and holding one-handed slip catches.

So even when cricket ceased to be the only interest and net practices had to be curtailed, the School continued to produce cricketers of quality, as G. A. Pennington who played for Northants and T. F. Smailes just mentioned, whose all-round play was for long a factor in Yorkshire's success and finally won him a place in a Test team against Australia. To him fell all ten Derbyshire wickets in 1939.

Individual excellence has more weight in a cricket game than in football. Two players may carry the team on their back if supported by good fielding, which of course *can* be taught. This ensured that teams of later years have often rivalled the performances of the nineties. 'Those were the days' when C. C. Cooper's team claimed an unbeaten record, ten won and two drawn in

1890 against worthy opponents — St. Peter's, Hymers, Ripon, Yorkshire Gents, and Londesborough Park, and when F. D. Cautley's XI in 1897 won ten and drew four matches out of sixteen, defeating all six schools opposed to them. The years 1907-8 were also vintage years, when the Ansons helped the School to beat Durham and St. Peter's, and both first and second elevens rarely knew defeat. But to shorten the tale the teams of 1916, 1926, 1934, 1941, 1948 and 1949 were little less successful, built upon such players as Smailes, N. L. Lupton, J. H. Daniel, E. R. Peart, J. G. Watt, G. L. Wood and others too numerous to mention.

Individual feats are of the essence of cricket recordings, but only a selection can be made. A rare specimen is G. A. Pennington's effort against St. Peter's in 1916. St. Peter's were all out for 56. In reply Pennington hit 45 out of 47 while he was at the wicket, his seven successive partners contributing 2 between them, and the 'tail' scrambled home with 5 runs to spare. F. D. Cautley scored the first century made on the School ground, against Hymers in 1896, and N. L. Lupton the highest score for the School, 126, against Ripon in 1934, among the many centuries recorded in the magazine. But Wood's century against a stronger school, Leeds, in 1949, may have been a better performance. P. M. C. Bradshaw alone is credited with three centuries in one season (1946).

The rare feat of taking all ten wickets by M. I'Anson against Leeds in 1900 eclipses all the many good bowling performances of two or three generations, though 7 wickets for 7 in 8 overs by R. Harrison in 1892 and the hat trick taken by F. D. Cautley in *both* innings against Ripon in 1896 are exceptional. In that year School bowlers took six hat tricks in all. More bowling feats are credited to A. H. Anson than to anyone else — 8 for 13 against Hymers, 5 for 10 against St. Peter's, 6 for 4 against Bootham, 8 for 12 against Hymers, 7 for 17 against E. R. Clergy, 6 for 17 against Leeds, and a further 6 for 13 against Hymers during the seasons 1907-9. Yet for a single season's doings N. L. Lupton holds the palm with five batches of very cheap wickets. As for other doughty bowlers' doings are they not written in the chronicles of *The Pocklingtonian?* We cannot compete with Wisden. Let us conclude with brief acknowledgements of those masters who coached and especially of that popular figure, W. D. Featherby, who taught the finer points of batting and bowling and fielding to those who already possessed a good eye, some sense of style, and the love of the game, which alone can take the tiro to cricketing heights.

Athletics. Of the high standard of athletics at Pocklington, again it may be said, unusual for a School of less than two hundred boys until 1940, the evidence is based on several considerations: (1) the records achieved in the various events, which compare not unfavourably with those which are gained in public school contests; (2) the frequency with which good times in races and good heights and distances in jumping or putting the weight have occurred; (3) the setting up of new records today, keeping the School's progress in line with the progress made in the athletic world generally; (4) the reproduction of all-round athletes, since this English ideal is in contrast with the aim of the specialising American; and, lastly, the successes won by Old Boys after leaving School.

Under (1) examples worth noting among School records are the following (and it may be said that great care is taken in timing; also that runners suffered from the handicap of a track on grass with a circuit of only 360 yards):

100 yds.	10.2 secs.	G. F. N. Pedley	1938
120 yds.			
High Hurdles	17.2 secs.	G. F. N. Pedley	1938
220 yds.	23.1 secs.	M. A. Galtress	1949
Quarter-mile	55.2 secs.	M. A. Galtress	1949
Half-mile	2 mins. 4.5 secs.	J. L. Kitchen	1949
Mile	4 mins. 56.2 secs.	M. E. Graves	1950
Long Jump	20 ft. 10 ins.	H. M. Tapper	1893
High Jump	5 ft. 5½ ins.	G. W. Brierley	1898
Weight-putting			
(16 lb.)	41 ft. 2½ ins.	A. G. I. Wood	1949

(This would have won the Army Championship that year, or second place in the Cambridge and Oxford Sports.)

Weight-putting			
(12 lb.)	51 ft. 4 ins.	A. G. I. Wood	1949

(This put was made in the Junior English Championships and was the first official put of 50 ft. or over by a British subject with any category of weight and a new best performance in the A.A.A. Junior Championships; also a Junior British National and British All-comers' record.)

Under (2) anyone who cares to peruse old magazines may see for himself that these high levels have been frequently approached. In the 100 yds. for instance, P. Slater in 1935 registered 10.4 secs, passing E. G. Petrie's best, 10.6 secs., in 1933, and he also did the hurdles in 17.8 secs. that year; J. Leaf did a quarter-mile in 58 secs. in 1935 and D. M. H. Craven in 57 secs. in 1930. The half-mile had been done by E. H. Dodds in 2 mins 11.8 secs. in 1921 and was done in 2 mins. 10.8 secs. by E. C. Ainsworth in 1950. It took sixty years, however, to beat C. J. Snowden's time for the mile, 4 mins, 57 secs. in 1890.

Performances in the high jump tend to sag between the years, but though Brierley's record of fifty years ago still stands, J. R. N. Mossop came very near it in 1939 with a jump of 5 ft. 4 ins., and other jumps of 5 ft. 3½ ins., 5 ft. 3 ins., 5 ft. 2½ ins. and 5 ft. 2 ins. have often been recorded. In two different years, 1929 and 1950, four competitors passed the 5 ft. level in one batch of jumpers and three in another year. Long jumps of 20 ft. 3½ ins. and 20 ft. (Pedley), 20 ft. and 19 ft. (P. Slater) have been registered.

But it is in putting the weight that the School has earned special distinction and was first noticed in higher circles, when D. Waring obtained his Blue for it in 1925 and G. F. D. Pearson followed him in winning the event in the Cambridge Senior Sports after Waring had held this lesser distinction in 1923 and 1924. Waring at school made a School record in 1922 with the 16 lb. weight, but this continued to be beaten in the next decades by A. C. Robson, 31 ft. 4 ins, 1932; by B. Allison, 34 ft 1 in., 1943; and by A. G. I. Wood, 41 ft. 2½ ins., in 1949. The introduction of the 12 lb. weight in 1934 witnessed a similar progression, for N. L. Lupton's first winning put of 34 ft. 4 ins. was soon beaten by P. Slater in 1935 with a put of 37 ft. 3½ ins.; by B. Allison, 40 ft. 11 ins., 1943; and by A. G. I. Wood with puts of 48 ft. 4¾ ins. in the East Riding School Sports, and 51 ft 4 ins. as mentioned above in the Junior English Championships. Still again, in 1950, D. R. Chappell won this event in the London Athletic Club's School Challenge Cup Meeting (commonly called the Public Schools Championships) at the White City, though eighteen months under the maximum age. Thus the two major Junior Championships in the country in this event have fallen to two Pocklington Schoolboys.

This phenomenal advance in standard has much to do with the assiduity of the coach, G. F. D. Pearson,[1] who followed Waring on this particular trail. If, in the old days, Pocklington used to be known as the School where Hebrew was taught, today it might be spoken of as the School where they put the weight. At present, honours rest with Wood, who went on to win the Yorkshire County title in the men's event (16 lb. weight), establishing a record in it, and was chosen to represent Yorkshire.

(3) Evidence that there has been no falling off in standards is shown by the athletic events of 1949, when six of the eleven recognised School senior athletic records were broken, and 1950, when the sixty-years-old mile record was at last beaten and second best performances in the half-mile and the weight were recorded.

(4) It is a common occurrence in smaller schools for one boy to win many events and wise athletic committees limit the number of events for a single competitor on the same day. It is considered more important to get one or

[1]He also coached for two years at Newton College R. H. B. Edwards, President of the Cambridge University Athletics Club in 1949, who got his Blue for the weight after returning from war service.

The Swimming Bath in 1939. (Mr. T. W. Pay in charge of swimming practice).

two really good firsts than a large number of firsts and seconds at a lower standard. At the same time there is plenty of scope for a boy to become an all-rounder without spoiling his times or distances. Perhaps the best all-round performance, allowing for the high standard reached in each event, was that of P. Slater in 1934, when he did a long jump of 20 ft., a high jump of 5 ft. 2 ins. and the 100 yds. in 10.6 secs.; or again in 1935, when his long jump was 19 ft., his high jump 5 ft. 3 ins.; his 100 yds. was done in 10.4 secs. and his putting of the 12 lb. weight reached 37 ft. 3½ ins., not to mention his winning hurdles and the cricket ball throw. Such successes have often been approached in other years. Usually the sprinter contests the championship cup with the long-distance runner, each adding to his points by field events. The old temptation of 'pot-hunting' was dealt shrewd blows by the substitution of small cups or medals, or even tokens, for the valuable presents that used to be awarded, and again by the house system introduced in day-schools and smaller boarding-schools when each competitor, instead of being 'out for himself' wore a House-ribbon and gained points for his own House — points which he saw swelling the House total as it rose on the board. Runners, like cricketers, are born, not made, and sprinters owe less to coaching than weight-putters, so that D. M. H. Craven, E. G. Petrie, G. F. N. Pedley, P. Slater and many other fliers just 'came, saw, and conquered'. Long distance trophies fall to arduous training and endurance, but a good stride and a stout heart go far. One item must be mentioned: J. Leaf's winning of both Junior and Senior Cross-Country events in the same year, 1931, at the age of fourteen. Outstanding cross-country and mile performers have been Snowden and Graves, already mentioned, the three Dodds brothers, T. E. Scaife, L. C. Sands, J. L. Kitchen and others.

Lastly, the sequel, the after-doings of Old Boys, is much as in the previous account of games. Cambridge Blues were H. St. C. Tapper and D. Waring. An Old Boy named Power jumped 5 ft. 10 ins. at Blackrock College, Belfast; another W. L. Clements, in 1912 won the Victor Ludorum cup at Durham University outright as champion three successive years. In 1930 G. E. Winpenny won the 100 yds. and the furlong in the Northumberland and Durham championships. D. M. H. Craven was in the University Athletic Union's winning team in the international relay race at Paris in 1932, besides winning the R.A.F. quarter-mile championship in 1936. A. W. Slater was in the final of the high jump in the Cambridge University Sports in 1935 and 1936. C. E. Malloch became a cross-country war-time Blue at Cambridge in 1941, B. Allison put the weight for Oxford in 1945, and G. E. Halliday for Bristol University in 1944. No list can be complete and space is short. Examples given will no doubt stimulate present and future athletic aspirants to seek further laurels.

'Art is long' and arts are many, too many to review here. We have said nothing of tennis, golf, shooting and the like. The fact that golf was not taught at school (too individualistic a game for youth) did not prevent Old Boys like J. W. Kidd, W. S. Taylor, and W. E. D. Bell from excelling later. Shooting is 'neither fish nor fowl', neither game nor earnest. We are not referring to duck-shooting but to that branch which is an adjunct to the peculiar necessity that modern wars have thrust upon us, an Officers' Training Corps. In this art, however, H. A. Fosbrooke gained the honour of captaining Cambridge against Oxford, in the small-bore rifle contest.

CHAPTER 23

THE MAGAZINE AND SCHOOL LIFE

In December, 1881, under the title of *The Pocklington Grammar School Chronicle* appeared perhaps the first School magazine of bulk or note. It was issued with the rash promise that it would appear monthly. The editor's apology in four pages (!) meets the imaginary objection, 'What good will it do us?', and includes many hints in composition to contributors whom he hopes to enlist. A ballad on Sir Henry de Bohun by the headmaster, *A Run with the Holderness*, and *A Midnight Adventure in the Streets of London* were among the original articles. The second number, dated March, 1882, apologises for its lateness and again includes a very mild thriller, followed by hints on chess and an essay on *Wit and Humour*.

In 1886 a new production entitled the *Annual Register* replaced the defunct *Chronicle*. Dispensing with the small essays of its 'monthly' predecessor, it records the doings of the School more fully and in its preface hopes that 'for all who take an interest in the welfare of the School this pamphlet may possess a charm, however unattractive, to the reader'. At the same time it recalls the School's ancient history and the example of its great 'alumnus' Wilberforce. The rest of its contents may be read in the chapter on London's headmastership, on which it throws much light. New and modern features are the printing of results of cricket and football matches, and even the individual scores and the 'characters' of the XI are added. The Athletic Sports are also reported, of which an extant programme dated 25 May, 1886, describes them as the *thirteenth* Annual Athletic Sports. Room is found, too, for the publishing of the accounts of the Games Fund, a feature not revived till 1920. The second number of the *Annual Register* (and perhaps the last, for no more have survived) is no less entertaining as a record of School activities. We now pass to the era of Hutton and *The Pocklingtonian*.

The Pocklingtonian, as printed for so many years by Mr. Forth, an artist in his profession, was an attractive magazine. It never stopped to insert advertisements, for notices of a hosier's socks or tailor's suits, whatever news value they may have, should not intrude upon the sanctity of a school chronicle. Nothing reflects so accurately the culture and progress of a school as a well-edited and tasteful magazine. The Governors knew this and bore the cost of production without the aid of advertisements.

The first *Pocklingtonian* appeared in Lent, 1891, and the second number announced that the number of boys had risen to a hundred. 'Each boy,' wrote the editor, 'will be given a copy, and it will be charged to him as in larger Public Schools ... At Pocklington there is a large class of boys who consider themselves so intellectually superior to the efforts of the magazine that they decline to purchase it.' No. 4, Lent, 1892, reported the number of boys as 'the highest on record'.

Vol. 5, No. 3, an issue of great interest, included an account of the Queen's Diamond Jubilee in 1897, besides an account of a notable expedition to the Faroe Islands and Iceland and 'Advice to Continental Travellers'. But the bulk of the earlier numbers are occupied by lengthy accounts of matches. Schools do more things now and the range of interests is wider. Original contributions are fairly constant but not easy to collect.

An editor of great ability, S. D. Alldred, reigned in 1915-17, and a sample of his ingenious rhyming, worthy of Browning, should be given, especially as it hailed an invention which still commands the battlefield:

> It's getting quite time that we seriously ought to
> Consider this gasoline demon of slaughter,
> That hops over rivers and flies on the level,
> A dreadful mechanical limb of the devil;
>
> The absolute latest in practical war toys,
> A horrible, high-paced, impregnable tortoise,
> That jumps over trenches and channels with ease,
> A fire-breathing monster that kicks over trees.
>
> As to how it's propelled, we are all in a fog. We'll
> Imagine it runs on a sort of live cog-wheel;
> Containing a crew that is merry and joyful,
> Regarded by Fritz as a new brand of Teufel.
>
> Whoever invented this engine of panic?
> Has Winston the sea-dog become a mechanic?
> Or is it the work of some second Sir Hiram,
> Inventing things just when we chance to require 'em?
>
> Whoever he is, he deserves our congrats.
> To him we would willingly take off our hats.
> For him from our mud-plastered, khaki-clad ranks
> Comes a cheer, while the Frenchman politely says, 'T'anks.'

Editors then, as now, are prone to humble apologies upon entry into office and a refreshing rebuke to such in mid-summer, 1938, under a pseudonym, Longinus, set out 'Five canons to be observed by Editors', which checked the habit for a time. The fifth canon was: 'Avoid writing an editorial about editorials or about one editorial in particular.' The same contributor (C.M.H.) had once clothed his editorial in verse and followed it up by penning his Cambridge letter in the same medium:

Dear Sir,
    At Christ's in Second Court,
A pair of muddy boots betray
The way that Peacock spends his day;
From there the nearest way is short
To Malcolm Street, where Pyefinch still
Inspects the innards of a cod
In hope of finding something odd.

I cannot write in sober style
About the clothes which gild the breast
Of Mr.Slater at his best.
Instead I ask you for a while
To leave him glittering in the lab.,
And, reaching F New Court to sink
Down in a Johnian chair, and drink
A foaming beer with yours
    Cantab.

And here are lines of protest to the censor from the same pen:

Sensitive Censor, since you shrink
In horror from my pen and ink;
And mutter, 'O he's got a kink
For using words like lice and stink,'
I try to colour all I think
With epithets not red but pink,
With nouns which 'hover on the brink',
And vigorous verbs to form a link
At which a cardinal would wink,
And Eva Booth would blush and blink.
It's only you who sadly slink
And drop them down the kitchen sink.

His verse enlivened the pages of the magazine for some years.

As a reflection of school life, the magazine notices most things, even the new boy. Everybody is new once and is baffled by customs and rules such as the sanctity of the prefects' lawn, as appears from a stanza of *A New Boy's Complaint:*

When you're rushing after dinner from the Lodge,
Fearing impots that you badly want to dodge,
    And you cut across the grass,
    Then there comes, 'You silly ass,'
From the thunderous voice of mighty Mr. Hodge;
    'What's your gambit, little pawn?
    Why that cut across the lawn?
    That's the prefects' special cut;
    Don't stand grinning, little nut,
If a prefect bids you cut, then you cut.'

The last stanza recalls the invention of the First XV 'war-cry', adapted from that of colonial tourists and carefully rehearsed by the boys, which cured the spectators of their previous apathy and certainly stimulated the players:

When you're new, you're not supposed to have a voice;
A gentle 'moderato' use for choice;
    If your accent's any weaker,
    'May I lend you a loud-speaker?'
Says the master, getting snorty;
    But avoid a double 'forte',
Or you'll suffer, while the little fags rejoice.
    Don't go whistling 'Mr. Shean',
    Everywhere and in between,
    Don't forget the happy mean,
    Save to cheer the first XV.
    Then a new-boy, though a fool,
    Cannot sin against a rule.
    When you bellow for the School,
    Shake the chimney-pots of Goole.
If the fellows bellow 'School', bellow 'School.'

Leg-pulling of new boys was as natural as that of 'Freshers' at Cambridge, who were urged to go to service at the Pitt Press 'Church' because the music was so good. Freshmen have waited vainly for the doors to open and wondered, when enlightened, why a printing-house should be built so like a church. At Pocklington a common wheeze was to warn new boys of the rigours of fasting in Lent and tell them to ask for leave off. One boy, named King, approached the headmaster after prayers, and as the following ballad illustrates other school customs and personalities of the time, it is reproduced in full. Lowest in the hierarchy of authority were the house-prefects. The tuck-shop was in those days run from the prefects' Club, where O'Conor presided as head prefect. Mr. Barkley was junior master. Mr. Pay had just joined the staff and Burkitt was mathematical master. Lee at Wilberforce Lodge was 'addicted to' poultry, Kipping ran a jugglers' troupe in his room, and Healy, a pupil, shared his flair for chess problems, which the *Daily Telegraph* was publishing:

A BALLAD OF LENT

'Tis Lent,' a waggish youngster cried;
  The guileless fresher listened;
'O royal youth, ah! woe betide
  The day that thou wast christened.

'Stout, coarser folk do litle care
  For ills that fasting brings;
But thou art spare and Lenten fare
  Is not enough for kings.'

The fresher groaned. 'Leave off, then, I
  Will seek this very hour.'
'Leave off? Of course,' he made reply,
  'House-Pre.'s are men of power.'

The House-Pre. heard the naive request,
  'Leave off? Upon my honour,
That one alone can give; 'twere best
  To seek his Grace, O'Conor.'

He found him selling. Trade was hot.
  He looked upon him darkly.
'Buns I dispense,' said he, 'but not
  From fasts. Try Mr. Barkley.'

Now Mr. B., to tell the truth,
  Was bloody with a razor;
'Don't worry,' said the fleeing youth,
  'I'll go to Mr. Pay, Sir.'

But when applied to, Mr. P.
  Professed he couldn't work it;
Declined the problem Q.E.D.
  And recommended Burkitt.

Now Mr. Burkitt saw the play
  And passed along the burden;
'Describe a circle Barmby way
  With radius Mr. Verdon.'

But to the Lodge he plied his legs
  To Lee and his incubator,
Where a Sussex Light which ate its eggs
  Had suffered as a traitor.

Lee said (the hen lay pale and wan,
  His hands with gore were dripping)
'Not my department, little man;
  Try your house-master, Kipping.

'But of his study have a care
   And read the notice surely,
Lest if you enter unaware,
   You perish immaturely.'

Then climbed the stair this royal wight
   And knocked and entered slowly,
And stood transfixed before a sight
   That petrified him wholly.

For he saw a fierce eruption there
   Like that of Herculaneum;
The Juggler was in his lair,
Balls, plates, and clubs were high in air,
From either hand uprose a pair,
   Three spouted from his cranium.

And from his boots a sullen roar
   Dictated problems freely,
'Pawn to King's fifth, and mate in four,'
   For the Daily Wire and Healy.

The youth stood dumb, until a plate
   Had nearly broke his crown,
Then fled at a most unkingly rate
   Incontinently down.

But Lent was near, his heart grew chill,
   While fear his judgement warps,
Lest fasting, fainting, fading still
   Some morn he rise a corpse.

And having failed with one and all
   Of lower rank and upper
He made a last despairing call
   And sought the Head at supper.

He held him with his fishy eye,
   He could not choose but listen;
'Say must I fast, or must I die?'
   The while a tear did glisten.

'Though shalt not die, no need to beg
   A dispensation, sonny;
Some witty youth hath pulled thy leg;
   Pray, go, I'm feeling funny.'

The Master choked. They feared the worst,
   And in the diagnosis
They found his middle boiler burst,
   And called it 'igh-explosis.

References to school servants occur from time to time. To the average youth the 'boots' and the 'lady char' are often more diverting personalities than the house-tutor. A small boy finding a youth slower-witted than himself enjoys that superior feeling which prompts the spirit of comedy. ' 'Arold' from 1916 to 1946 was the joy of the Schoolhouse. His simplicity was easily beguiled. Eight dud watches were sold him by townees in his first term. A present of razor-blades lasted his royal prodigality only a week and the next week he appeared as grisly as before. He would not take his boots to be cobbled, but bought new pairs until he had a row of nine pairs all new otherwise but down at the heel. He was rarely presentable, for the overalls bought for him he soon discarded as too 'institutional'. But returning O.P.'s always welcomed the sight of him as a familiar. *The Pocklingtonian* has crystallised him for our memories:

'AROLD
(Harold J. South, 1916-1946)

Child Harold to the Schoolhouse came
    When wars were rife and labour scant;
The south supplied his birth and name,
    No dandy youth nor elegant.

Cockney adrift on northern farms,
    He came to seek the post of 'boots',
And found it at 'the Dolman Arms',
    And stayed awhile and struck his roots.

His bell awakes the morning hum,
    His scuttle bears the master's coal;
His hand revolves the groaning drum
    That peels the 'taties as they roll.

Like Charlie Chaplin in his walk,
    He takes commissions to the shops.
What if he loiters still to talk,
    While Cook requires the mutton chops?

At eve upon the Dolman stile
    He smokes, from boots and brushes free,
Or by the kitchen stove awhile,
    The latest kitten on his knee.

His age? Though growing bald, a youth,
    And worth the title 'Willing horse';
No Derby winner, but in truth
    A steady 'gee' that stays the course.

Working with him in shrill harmony, hounding him, scolding and encouraging, Polly Smith commanded more respect, but was also a mark for raillery. She died in Coronation year, 1937, and her virtues also are chronicled:

> Nigh twenty years of willing toil,
> Of muckle sweat and little spoil,
>   And Home goes Polly,
> And, 'shuffles off this mortal coil'
>   Of pain and folly.

> Dust, and more dust, and dust again
> 'twas hers to sweep and ne'er complain
>   Day in, day out,
> And scrub the stairs and wash the pane,
>   And squeeze the clout.

> No more the pot-strewn prefects' table
> To clear and render serviceable
>   Will be her chore;
> And 'Arold 'Oney mid the babel
>   She'll scold no more.

> She takes her rest and consolation
> Sure of the angels' approbation
>   Of one who toiled;
> And shares perchance the coronation
>   Of souls unsoiled.

Wonderful snapshot sketches of both teaching and cleaning staff by a gifted artist, J. H. Daniel, then only in his teens, appeared in the magazines of 1934-6. Among the rest one of 'Johnny' Metcalfe at the piano, on which reposed the well-known bowler hat, never worn quite at the straight. 'Laugh, and the world laughs with you.' Is that why memory dwells more willingly on the master who had some oddity which was a joke, than upon the flawless form master who recalled Shakespeare's aphorism, 'It is ill joking with the rock you may split on.' That same oddity warms the affection, and gentle J.M., who gave lessons in pianoforte for over twenty years till 1938, had his great moments in the old dining-hall concerts before the new hall was built:

> His fingers strayed along the keys
> His eyes the distance sought,
> As rapt by love of melodies
> To ecstasy of thought;

> His pupils banished from his mind,
>   Unwilling and unripe,
> The discords of the daily grind,
>   The murdered 'Shepherd's pipe'.
>
> Commemoration's concert most
>   His gentle spirit stirred,
> When from a glad uproarious host
>   The Harrow song was heard.
>
> Then loth to leave the lovely lilt
>   Of Auld Lang Syne's refrain,
> His famous bowler at the tilt,
>   He sought the Londesborough train.

But affection was never more signally roused than by the respected Mason Clarke, link between Hutton's days and the new régime. All boys passed through his hands (and, if laggards, felt the touch of his small drill cane) and so, when revisiting, found at least one link with the past, who spread and perpetuated good feeling in the School:

> Forty years back, when the slim, supple M.C.
>   Came in the 'nineties to Hutton's new gym.,
> Lithe as an acrobat, strong as a Dempsey,
>   Circles and arm-plants were simple to him.
> Rings, horse and parallels, rope, horizontal
>   Forty years taught he to father and son,
> Swedish and swimming, both dorsal and frontal;
>   All generations acclaim him as one.
>
> Forty years on we behold him rotunder,
>   Keen, though, as always, and brisk of command;
> Proudly recalling the past for our wonder,
>   Alldreds and all who effected 'the grand';
> 'Who was it walked on his hands for a wager?'
>   'When shall we see such a gym. team again?'
> Yet thinks the new will eclipse the old-stager,
>   Sanguine, encouraging, working amain.
>
> He with a bonhomie nothing could alter
>   Faced all the changes that gliding time brings,
> Days of depression, when ageing chiefs falter
>   (Schools have their winters as well as their springs);
> He like an evergreen always could rally,
>   Cheerful and cheering in sunshine or rain.
> How shall we part with him? say the word 'Vale'?
>   Long may his spirit amongst us remain!

The departure of so many masters to become headmasters seemed to call for a special ode. Their various contributions to the School many Old Boys may like to recall in this ode printed at length and covering almost an era:

TO ELEVEN HEADMASTERS

So 'Shorty' goes to reign beside the Trent;
Some called him 'County', tribute to his style;
Scholar and athlete he, nor yet content
Allied himself with Wisdom ere he went.

His shapely form in Scouting kit no more
We'll see; nor hear, when Latin howlers rouse
His spleen, that yell, that fierce blood-curdling roar,
When e'en the H.M. quaked and shut his door.

So passes G.F.L., and nothing stems
The flow of masters called to rule as chief,
And build scholastic New Jerusalems
From far St. Andrews to the vale of Thames.

First sought the gentle Burkitt Tamworth town,
And close upon his heels to Wednesbury
The Chemist, Kipping, went, of chess renown,
In hole-y garb arrayed, for preference brown;

But mostly noted as a juggler rare,
Who taught a troupe, the Lampitts, Bowen, Hodge,
And ever, when you ventured in his lair,
Tin plates, clubs, tennis balls whirled high in air.

And let the Major next in order come,
Wrangler and cricketer, who 'kept the sticks',
And when the Dolman hive began to hum,
Its first housemaster, ere he moved to Brum.

Hesketh and Simpson next remembered be,
Whom Hymers took and sent to headships both,
Geographers — and he who sang 'The Flea'
Mid lusty encores, popular Joe B.

What of Lathallan's Head, our J.H.N.,
Prime coach in Maths. or any other art,
But most at golf excelling common men,
As Wethered and all St. Andrews ken.

Two science men now rule on northern crags,
One built our rugby teams, 'Baron' Defoe;
While Turner brought wall-pictures, concert-rags,
And Magna Carta's freedom for the 'Fags'.

There reigns another Head on Wycombe's Hill,
Blithe eager spirit, blithe as Shelley's lark;
Fives, rugger, tennis, dancing with his Jill,
Nothing with his gay energy sorted ill,

(Save walking; oft his Essex engine's roar
From Dolman noised his minute's drive to post);
His flair for drama, taste for classic lore,
The social charms of Ronald et Uxor,

We now recall as from a time of gold.
Too soon he went, as other ten have done,
To quicken life elsewhere, build new for old,
And justify the School beneath the Wold.

'Welcome the coming, speed the parting guest,'
So sang the bard; and we, who ever stay,
Absorb their spirit, profit by their zest,
Then sadly wave them on their knightly quest.

Passing fashions are sometimes heralded. Many public schools have sported and suffered from peculiar headgear. The topper was in vogue till the first war when, production ceasing, it seemed a good opportunity to abolish an obsolete hat which parents paid for and boys kicked about. Its chief value was on 'Full-cock' Sundays, the last Sunday of term, when the boys 'processed' to church in toppers garlanded with crêpe paper and flowers, and unruly members would crash down the hat of the boy in front over his eyes. Quite naturally the prefects clung to *their* toppers and handed them down as heirlooms, nursing them to the very last. The boater, worn only in summer between school and church and useful only for wearing colours in ribands, was later abolished. As the hatless fashion came in and expenses of dress rose, parents welcomed the irreducible minimum of headgear — the cap, worn by order in town, but able to be pocketed on long walks, so that the bowler too was outmoded:

'THE PASSING OF THE THIRD SCHOOL HAT'

Let me recall (for hats are now my theme)
In older days the thin black straggling stream
   Of Schoolhouse boarders churchward bound
   In silken toppers duly crowned,
And how that pomp became a fading dream.

The topper passed. No more it felt the spurn
Of fist or foot, wherewith its wearers burn
   To spoil its glorious silky baize
   In callous sport, while 'Father pays.'
And then the useful bowler took a turn.

In summer still the 'boater' had its day,
With ribbon blue and Dolman badge all gay.
   A stupid hat, for frolic wind
   Besetting it before, behind,
Caught it aloft and whirled it far away.

The boater passed. The bowler held its own.
Side-tilted on the senior's pate, outgrown,
   Or swamping well the junior's ears
   It was a sight that moved to tears
And now its passing scarcely stirs a moan.

Yet, schooldays ending, those who loved to bruise
Straw, topper, bowler, one last joy will lose.
   No more their headgear hurled amain,
   A farewell token, from the train,
Shall grace the bosom of the River Ouse.

The magazine, of course, reviews lectures and entertainments as a prominent feature of School life, its light relief. The most sensational of shows is reported in the Michaelmas number of 1920. The nominal object of the entertainer, an O.P., the Rev. W. E. F. Rees, called at School 'Frisky Peter', and at this time Rector of Wiston, Colchester, was to expose spiritualism. But after imitating the illusions and tricks of mediums, he displayed his famous box-trick, which had been recorded by London journalists and successfully defied even Maskelynes to solve. 'Mr. Rees,' we read, 'was handcuffed by Sergeant Spriggs with a pair of regulation handcuffs and placed in a sack, securely tied by other members of the audience. The sack was then placed in a large box in full view of the audience, padlocked with two locks, and then bound endways and crossways with stout ropes by members of the audience. The box was then carried behind a curtain. Within three minutes, amidst loud cheering, Mr. Rees walked up the hall, having escaped from handcuffs, sack and box, left by the back door and returned by the front entrance.' No wonder he had to refuse offers to 'go on the halls', and it should be added that he gave the show to swell the funds of the School war memorial.

No school magazine is complete without photographs of elevens and fifteens. The School photographer is a hardy perennial:

TO THE SCHOOL PHOTOGRAPHER

Hail to thee, photographer!
    From beneath the black-cloth wrapper
Focusing the distant blur,
    Preserving likeness-snapper;
On the lawn awaiting us,
    Like the bull when tempests lower,
Patulis cum naribus
    Snuffing for a likely shower.

School elevens in a group
    Stiffen up at thy reproval,
Smooth the lock, avoid a stoop,
    Watching for the cap's removal.
No eleven's work is done
    Till it's registered its beauty;
Matches lost and matches won
    Fade beside the crowning duty.

Known to us the patient skill
    From the weary ushers' faces
Smoothing out the wrinkles, till
    Even learning has its graces.
Thou wouldst have us apt to gaze,
    Like an ocean-scanning coastguard,
Far into the distant haze,
    Posing for the frugal postcard.

Say what other haunts be thine,
    Bird of passage, what the bower
Where the rugby lamp doth shine
    O'er thy hatchings hour by hour;
Where upon the creamy plate
    Slow thy brood of shadows creeping
Darken as they incubate
    Ready for the hypo steeping.

Wheresoever thou dost lurk,
    'Tis for us to know thee only,
Heralding the end of work,
    As a vision fleeting, lonely,
With a tripod standing by,
    When the bell has rung the closure,
Waiting till the clouds roll nigh,
    Waiting for the right exposure.

The town and the church are noticed from time to time. The removal of
the church organ to the south transept in 1950 and the restoration of the
space behind it to its former use as a chapel must gratify a correspondent in

the Michaelmas number of 1927, who complained of the rubbish surrounding the monument of Thomas Dolman. A short article in the Lent number of 1921, based on Leadman's pamphlet, traced the origin of the church to A.D. 1080, after which 'the north aisle was added in the twelfth or thirteenth century, and the chancel rebuilt, a clerestory put in, and tower and new roofs added, making practically a new church in the fourteenth century. The font is described as an eleventh century work, but from a single piece of fossil limestone.' The pulpit is mentioned as designed by Temple Moore.

Governors, a somewhat remote body to the boys, occasionally attract the attention of editors, as when two of their number became guardians of empire:

> Two Yorkshire Gentles, Honourable Thegns,
> The King has sent to speak goodwill to Gandhi;
> E.F.L.W. a Vice-Roy reigns
>   From Everest to Kandy.
>
> And F.S.J. now follows to Bengal
> To keep the British peace upon the Hoogli
> And play the underhand communist ball,
>   As once he played the googly.
>
> Crab not his claim, nor doubt his power to lead,
> Because he won his laurels at the wicket;
> What else do Mussulmans and Hindus need
>   But just the laws of cricket?
>
> Their names are writ as Governors with those
> Who sway the fortunes of this place of learning;
> And from this Board of Governors who knows
>   Whom else the King discerning
>
> Will choose (they all are honourable men)
> Of county fame or status aldermanic,
> To represent to peoples alien
>   His Majesty Britannic?

Gandhi has gone, F. S. Jackson's cricketing fame is fading, but how unfortunately familiar we still are with communist bowling.

A lesser light, but well known to the School, town and county, steeped in local affairs and a shrewd chairman of the governing body for many years was Alderman Fred Smith, who died in 1938. The School's nickname was Wuff-Wuff, and notable was his frequent habit of giving a quick brush with his hand to either side of his beard. He never missed a committee and was always before time:

Six years and forty watchdog without pay
    Of County works and monies, ways and means,
To every friend it was his pride to say,
    'I was at Beverley all yesterday.'

Kingmaker in the council, but not king,
    He lobbied votes for others, not himself,
School-sites, asylums, drainage, anything
    The Riding lacked, he took beneath his wing.

And on the Bench, a patient chairman, heard
    The well-conned patter of the sleuth's report;
With lagging pen wrote down his every word
    With 'Just a minute. Did you say the third?'

The days of the Pocklington Literary Society which used to bring a
fortnightly relief from preparation to the boarders were usually presided
over during forty years by an Old Boy of Wilkinson's days and a staunch
Governor, whose gifts to the School included pictures, reading-desk,
athletic cups, and declamation prizes — Alfred Summerson, J.P.:

Still now, methinks, I see him sit
Devoted chairman of the lit.,
Who could assure us from the chair
The lecturer had the proper flair.

Vine-pruner, garden-lover he,
And on the bench a ripe J.P.,
And ever generous with the shekels;
Long may his race survive in Eccles!

His daughter married a prominent engineer of that name.

But no magazine could overlook the claims to notice in its pages of one
who might almost have boasted that he knew the boys inside and out, the
School Medical Officer. The subject of this ode is the middle one of three
successive Angus Fairweathers of Faircote, a name known therefore to
three or more generations. He, as an Old Boy, could recall days spent in the
primitive laboratory of Mr. London in the eighties and he became Chairman
of Governors before he died:

TO ANGUS FAIRWEATHER, ESQ., M.D.

Alumnus Pocklingtoniensis,
'Twas here he learned his moods and tenses,
And how the atmosphere condenses
    And other topics;
At Aberdeen his physics, lenses,
    And 'stethoscopics'.

A medicus and country gent.
He settles in his father's tent
And doses laddies to him sent
    With salve and bottle,
And with a spoon for instrument
    Inspects their throttle,

While they say 'Ah' (or 'ninety-nine'
If lungs are needing anodyne);
And epidemics, who so fine
    In bud to nip?
Or ken the scarlatina sign
    Or swab for dip?

On holiday with trusty gilly
He treads the torrent swirling chilly:
So deft his cast that willy nilly,
    The salmon strike,
Then played with skill and gaping silly
    Await the pike.

With 'Tank' or others of the breed,
The Faircote champions of the mead,
Behold him where the pheasants feed
    Blazing from cover,
With right and left as they at speed
    Come driven over.

Then o'er the wine with ready zest
He tells a story of the best;
And every man that's been his guest
    Will wish him, when he takes his rest
    By stream or heather,
Full creel and bag attend his quest
    And fairest weather.

Not easy to appraise in verse but invaluable to the Governors was the counsel of Mr.Reginald Teasdale, who retired from the chairmanship in 1950 after forty years on the Board, soon after losing his friend and fellow-Governor, the Old Boy, F. J. F.Curtis.

One incident, that of the Blitz on 19 September, 1941, was an obvious inspiration to the versifier of the magazine, and the last lines of the following ode place on record deservedly the calm reaction of the boarders to bombing:

The Nazi bomber dropped his load
And straddled Dolman's fair abode.
Thus rudely wakened, muffled forms,
Like Agag, trod the glass-strewn dorms.

At dawn they gazed and wondered still
What power had fended off the ill,
When shrapnel-studded roof and floor,
Old clock and mirror, panelled door
    Were so disfigured;
But young and old unruffled hail
The morning sun, and on the rail
Some waggish youth had summed it all:
'Scarred but not scuttled,' ran the scrawl,
    'Jarred but not jiggered.'

Very occasionally the editors have glanced beyond the railway and deigned to notice town celebrities. Many will remember the stationer and printer, John Whitehead, who at one time used to print the School magazine. When retiring he seemed loth to sell out his stock, and hours were spent in selling it by oddments in repeated sales. There was a chronic water shortage in those days and the workman employed in turning the water off and on was a rather mournful personage named Todd. The Clerk to the Urban District Council, as it was then, looked after the fire service. The fire engine required towing out by a motor vehicle hired for the purpose. Its painting did not add to its efficiency:

John Whitehead was a citizen
    Of credit and renown,
And his 'final sales' were chronic
    Before he left the town.

A monster store of envelopes
    Early Victorian note,
Sofas and horns of antelopes
    And tins of creosote,

He gave them all a home in need,
    He pitied every waif,
Two halls were filled and ran to seed,
    When he summoned Mr. Scaife.

And 'Tom' says he 'it'll knock me up
    To let these treasures go;
But mebbe I'll easier drink the cup,
    If you knock 'em down quite slow.'

So in '21, when the trees were bare,
    They were booking the Central Hall,
And all the town was gathered there
    As to Whitehead's funeral;
And in '22 they were selling with care,
    And in '23 withal.

Then the Council thought it a good idea
  As the fire-brigade was keen,
And fires were scarce from year to year,
  Since they painted the engine green;

To get a little practice like
  And set the stuff ablazing;
And in a wink the sky grew pink,
  And the roar was quite amazing.

Then up rose Captain Margeworth,
  The Warden of Chapmangate,
The High Surveyor of roads and ruts,
  And addressed his second mate:

'Go measure thy footsteps nimbly
  To the Lord Low-water Todd,
And bid him ply right cunningly
  His best divining-rod;

'For a fire there be upon us,
  And the water supply is queer;
Not enough to brew, if report says true,
  A bottle of Government beer.

'And ask Everingum Brothers
  Bring out their chara-bus,
And for better or worse their horseless hearse
  To carry the hose and us.'

Then the Captain donned his helmet,
  And he strode into the square;
And from two to four they strove to draw
  The engine from his lair.

But at five they were hard a-pumping
  And squirting upon the hall,
And the flames ran high and the pipes ran dry,
  For there was no water at all.

And the Captain's brow was sad,
  And the Captain's cheek was pale,
And darkly looked he at his hose,
  As the water began to fail.

Now it chanced that Chinese crackers
  Were embedded in the pile,
And right on top J.W. sat
  With a Casabianca smile,

Foreboding his sales were numbered,
    As the fire nearer roared,
When a spark in fun kissed a Chinese gun
    And the printer upward soared.

And his whole stock went up with him,
    And it never in Pock. came down,
But it floated on high, promiscuously,
    Till it dropped in Scarborough town.

And he's busy collecting it yonder,
    Now he's once more hearty and hale;
Believe me or not, I care not a jot,
    But I'm telling you what's the tale,
That he's advertising a most surprising
    Last, final, and closing sale.

And some think, if he goes to heaven,
    After saying his last good-night,
He'll buy up old worn harps of gold,
    And second-hand robes of white;
And he'll hold a sale of everything stale,
    For those who pass beyond the veil,
    And enter the realms of light.

The greatest function of the magazine is its linking of past and present. The Old Boy, picking up his copy exclaims, 'Just to think! That midget S——is now a prefect.' The present boy, taking up his, and recalling a once insignificant fifth-former, exclaims, 'Just to think! Old stodger B. has won the D.S.O.' The cricket and rugby games are perhaps the favourite browsing of the O.P. The present reviewer confesses that, while collecting items for this chapter, his 'prep' was wasted by wading through all the matches of the past. It could not be helped. It is only another instance of the Englishman's perverse concentration upon sport. Editors are fortunately cultured folk and do not entirely give way to this, but preserve a balance between the light and the serious. For the motto of a school magazine should be that of the old *Boys' Own Paper*, parodied from Juvenal:

Quidquid agunt pueri . . . nostri farrago libelli est,
Whatever boys do, is the hotch-potch of our book.

CHAPTER 24
OLD POCKLINGTONIANS' CLUB

That a strong Old Boys' Association is a necessity for every school that is anxious to establish and maintain its position goes without saying. But such a society is more than that. It is as natural for Old Boys to want to foregather as it is for the elders of a tribe or family. The Pocklingtonian Old Boys' Club or Society has been formed more than once, only to dissolve through the lack of a central 'caretaker'. In 1898 a gathering in the Holborn Restaurant made the first essay, the prime mover being P. R. Simner, now Sir Percy Simner, who attended the London Dinners in 1948 and 1950. The first O.P. Dinner was held in the same place in April of that year, 1898, and an O.P. cricket tour was arranged. But this effort was not sustained and a revival some years later was no more lasting till C. E. Anson took over the secretaryship and by 1915 had built up a small but more permanent membership with some funds in the bank to pay for expenses. The Club was giving two prizes to the School, one for an English essay and one for an event in the sports.

It was soon felt, however, that a joint secretary was needed to work at the School itself, and the headmaster was appointed at an annual meeting in the twenties to collaborate with C. E. Anson in extending the membership. Two principles simplified this process: a life membership fee was substituted for the annual subscription and, secondly, parents were asked to allow their sons to join the Club on leaving the School, so that recruiting became almost automatic. Two benefits resulted. The work of the Hon. Treasurer, borne by the headmaster, was reduced to a minimum, and further, the magazine, sent to all O.P.'s who notified their changes of address, maintained their interest in the School and kept them in touch. Funds thus grew and were duly invested, and so long as the costs of the magazine remained moderate the financial position of the Club was sound.

It came to be felt, however, that the magazine alone was not enough to make the Club into a Society and more social gatherings were needed. At the suggestion of C. D. Kettlewell, the headmaster nominated Mr. T. W. Pay to the secretaryship with the goodwill and approval of the members and confined his own responsibility to that of Hon. Treasurer. From that date the Club may be said to have become a Society. Assistant Hon. Secretaries were appointed in various districts of the country to foster branch gatherings in their neighbourhood, while Mr. Pay organised large gatherings in the North, which culminated in a most successful dinner-dance in the Station Hotel, York, in 1938, attended by over one hundred and fifty Old Boys and their wives. J. M. Cobban and S. G. Bach, with 'Birdie' Edwards and others, started London meetings, that of 1948 being presided over by Lord Moran (formerly Sir Charles Wilson). It is a matter of great satisfaction that the war did not damage the fortunes of the Club and that its social side is still active both in York and London as centres, with occasional gatherings too in Leeds and Hull.

Other school magazines usually confine items about Old Boys to births, deaths, marriages, and honours or awards, but the enterprise of the Hon. Secretary has built up a running commentary on the doings of Old Boys which is of great interest and justifies the arduous labours spent upon it. An Old Boy receiving his copy today has more to intrigue him than the accounts of cricket and football matches and in mind can keep in touch with other Old Boys of his generation. May this feature never be lost in some form or other, even if the editors find it difficult to find space with costs of printing so enhanced.

By 1945 the numbers of the Club had reached four hundred and twenty and its financial resources warranted the starting of a Benevolent Fund. In 1950 the membership stood at five hundred and forty-six. May the bonds of the membership never slacken!

Needless to say, memorial services were held in 1921 in the dining-hall and in 1947 in the parish church to commemorate those Old Boys who had fallen in the two great wars. The oak tablet, designed by Allen Foxley, and affixed to the wall of the dining-hall, was dedicated by the Rev. C. F. Hutton for those lost in the first war. The tangible memorial to those who fell in the second is under consideration. As in the first war a number of Old Boys won the D.S.O. and other honours, so in the second several won high distinction in the Battle of Britain, as R. F. Hamlyn, or on sea patrol, as Herbert Thompson, or in the Army, as R. W. Annand, the School's first V.C. As a tribute to them we reprint by request the address delivered by the former headmaster at the service of 22 March, 1947:

> Memorial services for those who lose their lives in war go back many centuries. A famous instance is recorded as far back as two thousand five hundred years ago, and a great speech has been preserved from that occasion, the speech of Pericles addressing the citizens of Athens. He said many noble things in that speech about the glories of Athens and its liberties (just as we might today about the glories and liberties of England) and what an honour it was to die for such a city. But when he spoke of comfort for the bereaved, how difficult he seems to have felt it! 'Honour,' he said, 'is the measure of happiness; those are most fortunate who have gained most honour, whether an honourable death or an

honourable sorrow. I know how hard it is to make you feel this,' he said. Well he might, since for them, as for him, death was the end. 'Remember,' he added, 'that your life of sorrow will not last long, and be comforted by the glories of those who are gone.'

If I believed that death was the end, and that that was 'all there is to it' I could not have accepted the invitation to speak to you to-day. But I welcomed the invitation for two reasons:

In the first place, how can one help wanting to pay tribute to those old pupils of ours? At school for thirty- six weeks in the year and for three to ten years, one has the unique privilege of watching the growth of young minds and spirits (as well as bodies) from childhood almost to manhood, till one comes to regard them almost as sons. Most of you are gardeners and watch your plants with absorbing interest, but no gardener can feel anything approaching that interest of watching human young beings grow, which makes a schoolmaster's work so engrossing.

And because of that very intense interest, there is a sad side to it, in a war like the last. Just because one had so many of these ties, almost paternal, one received shock after shock, as one heard of this brave spirit and of that brave spirit being lost to us. When they had been over to see us on leave, we felt respect for that wonderful modesty of theirs, of men losing themselves in their job, youths who threw themselves into the worst hazards again and again, into a life that was the biggest possible contrast to that happy existence they had led before the war. And the end for them, often a certainty! If ordinary human beings can be said to have offered themselves in the spirit of the Cross, what a multitude of lesser Calvaries we have witnessed!

We are apt to think, 'What a waste of excellence!' But we must be wrong to think in terms of years and age. Even Christ withdrew himself from the earth at thirty-three!

And that brings me to my second reason for welcoming this occasion of speaking to you — I want to share with you my own personal convictions in this matter, as I have often done on Sunday evenings at school.

When old people die, it is no special shock to us — they have run their course — it is natural — and we just think it may be our turn soon. But when the young die, it is a shock and a challenge to us — it raises the question at once, 'Is that the end?' If it is, what an apparent waste! What did we come on this earth for at all? If *not* the end, what comes next? What is all human life for? We cannot put aside this question.

And, of course, what you think about that makes all the difference in the world to your plans for living, even to you boys now at school: whether you adopt the slogan, 'Let us eat and drink, for to-morrow we die,' or whether you say, as St. Paul said, 'My *real* citizenship and life is in the heavenly places, the spiritual sphere — *that* is going to be my real life, life untrammelled by this body. This life is only a bit of it — it is the next stage I must prepare for. So I must not get absorbed in this much-talked-of standard of *living*, that people worry about so much at present, 'What shall I eat, what shall I wear, how many points or coupons shall I need?' but in that much more important standard of *life*. For my personality here only begins to develop. When this body is tired out and laid aside, then I shall know what life really is. Shall I spoil this spirit and personality of mine by cheating and lying and sinning here, or shall I try to make it as perfect as possible?

How careless one tended to be with an old motor car when cars were cheap and plentiful and one could get another for the ordering! But since we knew that that was the only one we should get for long enough, how carefully we looked after its engine, the thing that makes it go!

We shall not get another *personality*. We cannot scrap it and order another. If it is to be usable in the next life, it must leave our old body with as few flaws as possible, in good running order. The old body with its dints and scratches or short sight (our headlamps gone) can be sent to the scrapheap. But the spirit that makes us go must be kept clean and well-lubricated, and the lubricant is prayer and Bible-reading.

That is why, merely as a schoolmaster, I think the Christian faith in the future life the only possible solution of this problem. For look at this business of schooling itself. Suppose, when a boy left us, the headmaster had to say to him, 'Now, I am very sorry about it, but all that you have learnt here is not going to be of the slightest good to you. You won't be able to apply it. It is all done with, and of no further use. It has been amusing watching you grow and develop into such a fine fellow but, of course, you might as well not have tried. I did not warn you. Perhaps I ought to have, but education ends here, and it serves no purpose whatever. Other boys will come to take your place and I shall lead them "up the garden path" just the same, and when they leave us their schooling will go for nothing. Vanity of vanities, all is vanity!'

How could any master possibly teach if that were his belief? He would be a hypocrite indeed.

And yet there are people who think that God is capable of that very fraud, that he puts into us an instinct that we have an immortal spirit, an instinct that all this struggle here is a preparation for much greater things — refining us, educating us, making us more and more godlike, with an ideal before us of a perfect man serving a loving Father, and then — the absurdity of it — allowing this wistful struggling heroic son of man to go out like a match — a wonderful life ended by a tiny germ or a contemptible bullet? Is it likely? What *are* we putting to God's account?

I dislike those pagan symbols of death in cemeteries, the broken column, the urn (as if an urn could suggest the passing of a spirit to join its Maker); the pagan phrases we use, 'cut off in his prime' — the mourning in black. Why, even Socrates puts Christians to shame!

You remember how he was sitting in prison waiting for the gaoler to bring him the poison to drink and his friend Crito asked him, 'How shall we bury you?' 'Bury me as you wish,' said Socrates, 'if you can catch me.' And with a quiet smile he looked at his friends and said, 'I cannot persuade Crito, gentlemen, that I am this Socrates who is now talking with you, but he thinks I am the one whom he will shortly see dead, and he asks how he is to bury me. He thinks all my long argument nonsense, in which I have shown that when I have drunk the poison I shall no longer remain with you, but shall go away to some happy haunts of the blessed ones.'

I attended another memorial service in October and could not help contrasting it with the pagan service in Athens. The minister[1] was one of the most experienced in England today. I quote what he said:

'I think that life must be so wonderful that it is in the mercy of God that we are not allowed to see its detail very clearly. I have seen hundreds of people die and sometimes the passing over from this world to the other is shrouded in unconsciousness, but, when it is conscious, I have never known an exception to the rule that to cross over from this life to the other seems to be an experience of ineffable joy and happiness.'

But there is a greater authority by far. I would, as that same minister said, 'stake my faith on those words of Jesus to the thief on the cross, "Today thou shalt be with Me in Paradise." If Jesus did not know, then nobody knows. He did not say to the thief, "I think we shall meet again," but, "Today thou shalt be with Me." The last thing one would say of Christ is that he was inclined to "wishful thinking". He was a realist. Wishful thinkers do not go as far as a crucifixion!'

If only we would take these words of Jesus as our fathers used to do, so simply and so surely, as Gospel truth. Should we not then think of these young men just as friends who

[1]Rev. L. D. Weatherhead.

had received a higher appointment elsewhere and not so far away perhaps either?

The real attitude, I am convinced, is St. Paul's — hear his way of regarding death: 'I am doubtful whether to want to depart and be with Christ, which is far better, or to stay on with you, for you need me.' How very matter-of-fact and serene!

What will it be like then? Only the parables of Jesus can give us hints what that future life will be like. But they are pretty definite hints. They suggest that the things we count best in this life will be features of the next. What *do* we count 'priority' things in this life?

Surely, first, love and friendship. As loneliness is our greatest fear, so friendship is our greatest blessing. Then, secondly, work. Our second greatest fear is, surely, unemployment, and happy work is our second greatest blessing. Both these things — friendship and work — Jesus says unmistakeably will be part of the next life too. It would take too long now to give chapter and verse from His teaching. I must pass on to the third thing.

The greatest happiness of man is when he has forgotten all about himself and is lost in ecstasy of admiration, perhaps of some sublime picture or beautiful landscape or of some great man speaking, and his spirit passes into an attitude of worship. It is a curious thing that the more we can lose ourselves in admiration of someone or something outside ourselves, the more complete is our enjoyment. One of the good things in the new life will be to see something of the wonders of God Himself and to understand something of them. Jesus says that 'to see God' will be the special reward of the pure in heart. The climax of his own life was to be, He said, to ascend to His Father. That is why we Christians hold this service as a service not of mourning but of thanksgiving, knowing that those whom we commemorate are just entering into the new beginning of love and work and worship.

One last word about those whom we no longer see. The world may regard them as victims merely, heroic victims of an appalling war, and may wonder why God allows it, and their faith suffers in consequence. Let me end then with the testimony not of a bishop or a clergyman, who might be suspected of putting the best complexion on a bad business, but of a war-correspondent,[1] who followed the war through ten campaigns; he has spoken of the depressing side of the war, but his last words suggest that even in a bad war these young men and women were not forgotten by God. God seemed to lay a personal hand on them all, bringing divine spiritual good out of human physical evil. He says:

'Only one thing stood against this depressing tide ... one saw an immense change take hold of the soldier, the ordinary man or woman in the war. The clerk from Manchester and the shopkeeper from Balham seemed to me to gain tremendously in stature. You could almost watch him grow from month to month in the early days. He was suddenly projected out of a shallow and materialist world into an atmosphere where there were really possibilities of touching the heights, and here and there a man found greatness in himself. The anti-aircraft gunner in a raid and the boy on the landing-barge really did feel at moments that the thing they were doing was a clear and definite good, the best they *could* do. And at those moments there was a surpassing satisfaction, a sense of exactly and entirely fulfilling one's life, a sense even of purity ... Not all the cynicism, not all the ugliness and fatigue in the world will take that moment away from the person who experienced it ... He was for a moment of time a complete man and he had this sublimity in him.'

You can see from those words that this journalist had been observing a spiritual process at work, the grace of God uplifting and refining these young people as by fire, in readiness for the more important work to which they have been promoted — God treating the war as a kind of university with one of those 'intensive courses' allowing these young men to develop spiritually in a few months, as they never could have done in a lifetime of peace. Let us praise God for them.

[1]Alan Moorhead in *Eclipse*. (Pub. by Hamilton)

CHAPTER 25

SCHOOL BUILDINGS

The School has almost entirely existed on its present site practically since its foundation. A memorandum in the Vellum register, which has been carefully preserved by successive headmasters since its first use for admissions in 1650, provides good evidence of this. The memorandum was made by Thomas Dwyer in A.D. 1698 and is headed: 'The case of the free School of Pocklington'.

It begins with the granting of the licence by Henry VIII to John Dolman for founding a fraternity or guild and supplies the date in the margin: 'May 24 Anno sexto Regni Regis Henrici 8^{vi}.' The next paragraph runs:

> A.D. 1522. The Dean and Chapter of York under their coмon seal confirm a writing made by Mr. Christopher Wilson, then Prebendary of Barmby, to the said Dr. Dolman, dated July 10. 13 H 8, whereby is granted to the said Dr. Dolman and Guild *a parcell of Land with the edifices newly built* for the help and support of the said Guild or Fraternity together with a certain GraMer School in Pocklington founded by the said Dr. Dolman. ...

Thus, within eight years of the foundation of the School, teaching was provided for on the present site.

Passing over the next paragraph in the memorandum, which describes the founding of the Dolman Scholarships and the regulations for election to them, dated A.D. 1525, and a further section about the Guild and the School and appointment of the masters — a section referring to the first and fifth years of Edward VI — we come to the next important evidence of date, where Dwyer makes his forceful and dignified appeal for funds to rebuild the School's fabric:

> All this while (viz. till A.D. 1698) no provision was made for repairs of the buildings of the said Guild, wherin the school was settled, so that in the space of 148 years ever since the dissolution of the Guild all the said buildings and schoolhouse have been running into ruin, and had ere this fallen quite down, at least a great part thereof, if not underpropped, according to the judgment of severall as well gentlemen as artificers and others who have viewed the same.
>
> Now the annual rents for support of the master and usher being so small and the greatest and best part of the lands and tenements belonging to the said free school being held by a long lease of 81 years, of severall messuages, lands, tenements and hereditaments in Thriberg comencing Anno 13o Caroli 2di At the making whereof neither the old rent was encreased nor anything done towards repairs by the then master and usher, though the decays of the edifices were then visibly great and now can no longer be supported but must

be entirely taken down to prevent them falling, which is continually expected:

The unavoidable great charge of taking down and building up the said schoolhouse (whereof no part as it now is can be continued standing) would swallow up all the rents for many years to come and nothing bee for the maintenance of the said master and usher:

They therefore are absolutely necessitated to become humble suppliants and petitioners to all such as have been educated in the said school or are inhabitants in the parish or placed adjacent or owners of land or tenements in the said parish or may have occasion to send either children or relations thither. But especially to such eminent persons in Church and State whom Almighty God hath blessed with estates and noble charitable minds, that they would be pleased to subscribe what for the advancement of learning and promoting so necessary and charitable a work they shall think fitt to bestow, wherby, as by a fund, workmen may be treated with for the taking down and rebuilding the said schoolhouse ere it fall down of it selfe.

The appeal, it will be noticed, is to the Old Boys, local residents, prospective parents of pupils, landowners and, above all, to men with 'noble charitable minds'. A £10 gift from the Archbishop of York heads the list, and many clergy from a wide radius, extending as far as Hull and Sheffield, gave their one or two pounds apiece. The Rev. Jonathan Dryden and Mr. Francis Hillyards, it is noted, 'procured the largest subscriptions in Yorke'. Other collectors helped. The Earl of *Burlington and Corke* (a curious combination of distant ports) gave £20 and the Bench at Beverley Sessions £8, but St. John's College, Cambridge, as might be expected, was the biggest contributor, giving nearly a quarter of the amount raised, viz. £47 9s. 10d. An interesting gift is 'One oak-tree valued at and sold for £1 2s. 6d., given by the Countess Dowager of Middleton', and a note explained that 'this tree was sold to Gregory Richeson, as payment for the stoops and railes hee set down along the front of the Schoole towards the West Green'.

So the front of the School seems to have been enclosed even at that early date.

After the subscription list in full comes the audit of the account, dated 28 June, 1698:

	£	s	d
Totall suMe of contributions received by Mr Thomas Dwyer	218	14	7½
Total of Mr Thomas Dwyer's disbursements in building the new schoolhouse of Pocklington, as appears by Mr. Henry Topham's receipts and other particulars	246	9	2
Due to the said Mr Thomas Dwyer to ballance this accompt which hee is out of pocket	27	14	6½
Deducting Mr. Thomas Dwyer's own contribution mentioned in the letter D	4	13	4
Rest due still to him	£23	1	2½

This accompt drawn up, compared and examined by, and all the papers relating therto, are in the custody of   John Moore
                                                      Vicar of Pocklington

Thomas Dwyer, having like Nehemiah, completed the good work, resigned the headmastership immediately in favour of Miles Farrer. His building seems to have lasted till the end of the eighteenth century. At any rate the dearth of records leaves no hint of further building till 1818, when Thomas Shield rebuilt the Schoolhouse with a schoolroom as part of it. The account of this will be found in the chapter about his headmastership. He himself is said to have temporarily occupied a cottage.

In 1850-51 came one more rebuilding, which gave us a large part of the present School frontage. The word *instaurata* in the superscription may cover some use of a former fabric. The engraving referred to in the chapter on Gruggen and reproduced on p. 55 is a very attractive view. In 1858 Wilberforce Lodge was built and later St. John's Lodge and Dolman House. Behind Gruggen's frontage in 1879, Wilkinson added two classrooms and a dormitory above, with a corridor dividing the old and the new rooms (see p. 66).

As the aims of education expanded, more buildings were needed of new and various types and Hutton (1889-1910), eager to keep abreast of the times, did his utmost with small resources to supply the demand. The growing prominence of science, manual training and games dictated his first efforts, the erection of a gymnasium in 1891, a cricket pavilion in 1893, and a fives court in 1895. For these he had to beg from parents and friends and in each case provide a considerable balance out of his own pocket. The science laboratory, later reconstructed to form part of the physics laboratory in 1932, was another detached building raised in 1907, in order to qualify for the grant from the Government for the teaching of science. But Hutton's main addition to the School was the large dormitory with two classrooms underneath and a new bell-tower, all finished in 1898 to the design of Brierley and Rutherford, architects, of York, at a cost of £2,800. To meet this outlay the Charity Commissioners allowed the selling of Consols, on condition of replacement during a period of years.

The first major improvement after the First World War was the building of the swimming bath, projected in 1914 to commemorate the fourth centenary of the School, but in 1920 adopted as the main war memorial. It measured 75 ft. by 25 ft. and held 60,000 gallons of water. Three generous donations from T. F. Brewster, R. E. Abbott and Major P. M. Stewart swelled the fund, which was completed by a liberal contribution from the builder, Mr. P. T. Kettlewell, the father of three Pocklingtonians.

When the number of boarders began to increase rapidly in 1918-19, Wilberforce Lodge was, of course, ready to take the surplus and was reopened as a junior house under Mr. and Mrs. R. S. O. Lee. A further surplus of boarders were temporarily accommodated at the vicarage for bed and breakfast, otherwise living at the Schoolhouse. To avoid refusing boys, the headmaster bought a house in York View privately and in 1922 installed Mr. and Mrs. T. W. Watson there with six boarders. Meanwhile the Governors negotiated the purchase of Dolman House, built formerly by Dr. Gruggen, but sold to other tenants, and now easily adapted to boarding-house requirements. On the appointment of Mr. Watson to a headship in July, 1925, the younger boys from Wilberforce Lodge were transferred to Dolman House as nearer to the School, with Mr. and Mrs. Lee still in charge, while boys of eleven to fourteen years were housed at Wilberforce Lodge in the charge of Mr. and Mrs. T. W. Pay.

With Dolman House came the three-acre field which relieved the over-worked cricket field. Through the skilful work of Mark Moore, the groundsman, both this field and the one behind the School underwent extensive levelling and provided at a very small cost two full-sized football grounds. The tons of earth ejected from the site of the new buildings in 1931-32 were utilised almost on the spot in filling up the hollows of the Dolman field pasture.

The School was thus growing eastwards towards the railway, but not in a haphazard way. The Assembly Hall built in 1928 was so placed as to preserve the line of the School front and leave a square in front of the laboratory to make a small parade ground for the Corps or for physical instruction. True, old landmarks had to be sacrificed, the last four of the old elms, once called the Apostles, fast decaying stumps, being felled to clear the site. An owl, as of old, was occupying one and a striking thing happened. As this tree, the last of all, was slanting to its fall, the owl waited almost till the crash before it flew mournfully forth, leaving a solitary egg in its nest, which was found unharmed by the fall. So passed the Twelve Apostles, rendezvous of boys in the old days who wished to settle their differences by fists.

The architect of the Hall was Allen Foxley, who had designed the memorial panel in the dining-hall, and his building was much admired for its beauty and excellent acoustics. Unfortunately, its size was cut down from the original design on the ground of expense by a higher authority quite needlessly and with little faith in the future. The formal opening took place at Commemoration 1928, the veteran headmaster of 1872-84, the Rev. C. G. Wilkinson, performing the ceremony after the Ven. Archdeacon J. M. Lambert, chairman of the Governors from 1916 onwards, and also an Old Boy, had pronounced the prayer of dedication. It was the first prize-giving worthily accommodated. Previously the ceremony had to be held in one of the halls in the town, which were by no means academic.

Two years later, in 1930, the Board of Education pressed for additional accommodation, especially for more and better laboratories. The contracts for these additional buildings, when placed, were so reasonable owing to the slump in the building trade that the Governors at their meeting, which was attended by Lord Irwin (now Earl of Halifax), just returned from his Vice-royalty of India, consented to carry out the full scheme designed by the County Architect, Mr. B. B. Stamford, providing new changing-rooms, two new classrooms, an excellent art room over the new physics laboratory, and a spacious corridor to give access to these new quarters. The old changing-rooms were converted into rooms for the headmaster and the staff, who had been previously quartered, most inconveniently for interviews, in the upper regions. More rooms were also made available for common-rooms. New oak doors dignified the front entrance of the School and a new entrance to the new corridor for some months puzzled Old Boys, whom long habit caused to look for a door into what was now a small bookroom. Space was left over the new chemical laboratory for further classrooms when required.

The general effect was to complete the equipment of a well-appointed School, to make the boarding-house more comfortable for the seventy or eighty boys it contained and to separate the teaching premises from those of the Schoolhouse proper which, however, still retained three classrooms within its doors for the purpose of evening preparation.

Three years later, in 1934, a body of Scots artificers working for an Aberdeen contractor descended on the School in the long vacation to install electric light throughout. The dormitories resounded with the cries of 'Jock', with sawings through joists, and the noise of hammers, and the last of the ancient gaspipes and the smell of the 'by-passes' disappeared.

But once more the numbers increased after a temporary slump during the economic crisis of 1930-34 and boarding accommodation was again insufficient. The building of a new boarding-house did not commend itself to the Board of Education. But a way out was found which not only met the pressing need but effected a further great improvement in respect of sick-room accommodation. This had been for years inadequate and only the good health record of the School in its healthy climate and surroundings could have enabled it to suffice for so long. The Board, therefore, while rejecting a boarding-house, readily accepted the idea of a sanatorium, thus setting free various small rooms for additional boarders. The sanatorium included a house for a master and his wife, who acted as matron. Much patience and persistence had to be employed to secure the utmost usefulness of the sanatorium and so to design it as to keep running costs low. The regulations of Board and County for sanatoria, imposing at that time excessive proportions, would have made the cost prohibitive for the

School's resources. Technically it was styled a sick-bay therefore and the plans at last went through. Its chief feature was the number of small rooms separated by glass screens, which enabled different suspects to be isolated and yet not to feel too lonely and bored.

From 1942 onwards boarders had to be refused in growing numbers. It was not till 1946 that the Governors were able to acquire a new boarding-house, Lyndhurst, released at last from its war-time uses. Lastly, plans were passed in 1948 for the extension of Lyndhurst by such premises as would enable it to serve as a separate and complete Junior School. Permission was also obtained to erect extra classrooms over the chemistry laboratory, as originally prepared for in 1932. These buildings, at the time of writing, are nearing completion.

There still remains the need for a library. The need of a chapel has never been felt because the close connection of the School from its foundation with the Guild Chapel of St. Nicholas in the Parish Church has caused generations of boarders to occupy the north transept there and in particular the portion of it known as the Dolman Chapel, close to the tomb of Thomas Dolman. There are two special seats for the headmaster and the second master at least a century old. Any overflow of boys has been seated in the nave of the church. The benefits of attending the services of a Parish Church, of worshipping off the School premises away from school routine, are obvious. A school chaplain is a member of the staff and is so regarded and his ministrations can be too closely associated with school discipline in the minds of the boys. In the parish church, ranged alongside a congregation of townspeople, they have more chance of acquiring a habit of worship which it will be more natural to continue on leaving school.

SUMMARY

SCHOOL BUILDINGS

MAIN DATES AND HEADMASTERS

1522   (or just before). First buildings of the Guild and School, presumably on the present site.

THOS. DWYER:

1698   Schoolhouse rebuilt on the same site, a full memorandum making no mention of transfer.

THOS. SHIELD:

1818   Schoolhouse restored, with schoolroom as part of it.

F. J. GRUGGEN:
1850-1 Schoolhouse and new buildings erected.
1858   Wilberforce Lodge built.
1860   Dolman House and St. John's Lodge leased.
(circa)

C. G. WILKINSON:
1878   Two classrooms and dormitory above, in rear of Gruggen's classrooms, with narrow corridor between.

C. F. HUTTON:
1891   Gymnasium.
1893   Cricket Pavilion.
1896   Fives Court.
1898   Large dormitory, classrooms below, tower.
1907   Science Laboratory (absorbed later in Physics Laboratory, 1931).

P. C. SANDS:
1920   Swimming Bath.
1924   Sick bay added to Wilberforce Lodge.
        Dolman House bought and adapted as third boarding-house.
1928   School Hall built.
1932   New laboratories and three classrooms above; changing-rooms and offices.
1938   Sanatorium.

R. J. PITTS-TUCKER:
1946   Lyndhurst bought as fourth boarding-house.
1949   Junior School begun as addition to Lyndhurst.
1950   Classrooms over Chemistry Laboratory built.

In Hutton's time, 1897, the Dolman Chapel (strictly called 'the Chapel of St. Mary and St. Nicholas') was restored and the old pews in it replaced by oak seats.

PREFACE

to Chapters 26–28

I owe everyone an apology for taking so long a time over a small task. The reasons for this are my own dilatory nature and my insatiable desire to go on adding and correcting — an apparent perfectionism which I fear will not be reflected in the finished article.

Several people deserve my warmest thanks. I owe much to the patience and encouragement of the chairman of Governors, Mr. Robin Fenton, and the headmaster, Mr. A. D. Pickering. Both of those former headmasters whose régimes are dealt with here, Mr. R. St. J. Pitts-Tucker and Mr. G. L. Willatt, have given me great encouragement and unstinting help, along with valuable suggestions. I am grateful also to Mrs. Cottom for help that has invariably been both willing and prompt. Several other friends, whose knowledge of the subject-matter was either partial or virtually non-existent, have read major parts of the typescript and made very valuable suggestions — Ronald Chapman, Eric Bassett, Robert Dunsmore. But none of those most closely connected with the events has read any of what follows, with the notable exception of David Nuttall, the present second master, whose help has been too great for me to express my gratitude adequately. The time-honoured exoneration of all these from responsibility for any of my errors and misjudgements is more than usually apposite.

This account has been written far too close to the events and personalities to be anything better than an interim treatment. I hope it will offer modest help to future students, and be meanwhile not without interest to some of those who are and have been concerned with this splendidly English institution.

J. H. EGGLESHAW
1987

J. H. EGGLESHAW

A note on the author of Chapters 26–28

The three recent chapters in this History describe a renaissance of the School in terms of numbers and academic standards, an increased awareness of previously unacknowledged fields of study and a strengthening and broadening of expectations, academically and culturally.

It is inevitable that the author of these chapters should fail to portray his own significant role in the years 1939 to 1976, a period throughout which, with the exception of his war service, he was second master, head of classics and an *éminence grise* behind a wide range of activities.

James Eggleshaw, a Scholar of St. John's College, Oxford, where he took First in Greats, was a mixture of the formidable and the diffident. Incisive and witty in his scholarship, which has always remained live and searching, he could stumble endearingly over an Assembly warning on the dangers of riding bicycles on the Dolman Drive. Often alarmingly knowledgeable in others' 'specialist' fields, he could embarrass colleagues and prick bubbles of pretentiousness. How own phrase, 'lack of intolerance' (Chapter 28, page 206), expresses well his ability to work constructively alongside those with whom he disagreed, and always his concern for any boy or colleague in trouble or need was deeply compassionate and his help very practical.

Eggleshaw's excellence as a schoolmaster lay in his faith in the capacity of any boy, however hampered by previously limited experience, to be touched by the wonders of history, language, art and music. A high proportion of gifted boys gravitated to A level classics and gained distinction at universities. Many imbibed the joys of Florence which he explored with them and expounded to them indefatigably on numerous trips. Others listened to music in his home which was decorated and sound proofed with books whose variety demonstrated the richness of his scholarship.

Enhanced performance on the sports' field owed much to Eggleshaw's dedicated coaching. In winter, clad in Stanley Matthews shorts, he coached colts' rugby; in 'spring', wearing trilby and muffler, the high jump; in summer, still mufflered, cricket.

To every activity he brought the same meticulous attention to detail and he demanded the highest standards of self-discipline. He sought excellence.

To the staff, all of whom he entertained unsparingly in his home, he brought the warmth of his own *haute cuisine* and claret, even if it meant standing impassively at the kitchen stove with waistcoat ablaze in order to perfect a flambé dish. The same warmth has made Old Pocklingtonian meetings in Oxford meaningful.

These chapters in the thoroughness of their detail and in their attempt to achieve a detached perspective at such a short distance in time express Eggleshaw's selfless dedication and at the same time his uncompromising independence of spirit, both of which made his contribution to the School's history in this period so important.

D. Nuttall
Second Master
1980-

Robert St. John Pitts-Tucker, M.A.

CHAPTER 26

ROBERT ST. JOHN PITTS-TUCKER
(1945-1966)
(ii)

P. C. Sands took his account up to the year 1950, thus including Pitts-Tucker's first few years. But the beginning of the post-war era was so significant in every way for the School that it has seemed necessary to attempt a picture of the School, its virtues and its limitations, as Sands left it, and with, it is hoped, a little more perspective than he himself could have used.

If there is a hero in the history of Pocklington School it is surely P. C. Sands. To take on the headmastership in 1915 and face all the obstacles and privations of the First World War, then to maintain the School despite the apathy of local authorities and the positive attempts of Whitehall to close it down, to keep going through the slump years of the thirties when several similar schools went under, and, finally, to have to meet all the difficulties imposed by a second and still longer war — these were heroic achievements. But heroism takes its toll. The School could be kept going only by the most rigorous economies, so as to keep the fees down to a figure hardly believable to us now; in 1939 the combined boarding and tuition fees amounted to just over £70 a year. In an earlier chapter there is a charming account of the School, and of Sands as headmaster, written by his most distinguished ex-pupil. The present writer has neither the knowledge nor the wish to question a single word of what J. M. (now Sir James) Cobban wrote there. But it was written of the one period in Sands' eventful tenure when the threats to the School had relaxed enough to permit this idyllic picture. There followed the slump of the early thirties. By the end of the decade Sands was, not unnaturally, tiring and ageing, and his outlook became more and more that of a scholar who thought deeply rather than widely. To those who joined the staff then, Pocklington seemed a school that the world had largely passed by, and, if they and any outside readers had been asked to judge the account written by Sands in 1950, they might have found in it something near complacency. Perhaps only those members of the staff who stayed on and worked closely with Sands through the trials of the Second World War could recognise in him, as well as his indomitable will, a growing mellowness and humanity.

There were in those days about 140 boarders and 75 day boys, of all ages from eight to nineteen. Of the boarders all the eighty or so oldest, save a few prefects at the junior houses, lived together at the School House with the headmaster as housemaster and one young house tutor of brief tenure. The rest lived in two small houses, each under one housemaster. These houses were nearly, though not quite, parallel; generally those who entered at eight went to Dolman House, while entrants who were a little older went to Wilberforce Lodge. At twelve or thirteen, boys went up from these houses to School House. Since day boys shared games houses with boarders, the boarding divisions cut right across the four games houses. Moreover, the concentration of almost all the older boarders under one roof, with amenities that even in those days would be thought barely adequate, was unhealthy. This situation indeed lasted for most of the Pitts-Tucker years too, and the latter took a long time to change it. However, as will be seen, when a good opportunity arose he did take it, whereas Sands' account suggests that he justified it to himself.

Furthermore, at the lower end, boys from eight to eleven, boarding and day, were lumped into one 'Form I' under one teacher, often unqualified for the specialised purpose. This pupil-teacher ratio, though less inadequate than that which apparently prevailed under the redoubtable Lluellin (Chapter 8), might suggest to us now that pupils were taken on under dubious pretences. This anomaly Pitts-Tucker did reform as soon as he could.

Academically the School's performance was, judged by high standards, on the whole mediocre. To a large extent this was inevitable given the quality of the intake. Many parents had no broad conception of education, and few of them had themselves enjoyed an education of any breadth. Leaving school at sixteen from a secondary school was in those days the rule rather than the exception. In any case many boys came from farming homes where they were needed, or expected to return, by the age of sixteen. But there certainly was a narrowness and a lack of distinction in any sphere, although the School was doing a good job in and for its environment, and was, thanks to Sands' husbandry, in a position to take advantage of the expansive post-war period. It should be added that there was the beginning of a science sixth with young and capable teachers to bring it on. In the rest of the sixth, however, there was little more than sporadic activity, and below the sixth it was a one-stream school.

There was one peculiar consequence of the School's set-up that helps to explain why in these two chapters the names of the two headmasters turn up, not just frequently, but ubiquitously. Some readers may find this excessive. But there is some justification for it. On the one hand the School was almost as independent of external authority as any in the country; on the other hand there were no entrenched housemasters like those who played so large a part in the more notable public schools and, in reality though not always openly, imposed a big limitation on the powers of headmasters. This is the underlying reason why everything of importance that was done at Pocklington seems either to have come direct from the heads of the headmasters or to have grown from ideas they had endorsed and, one might almost say, made their own.

One day in 1945 one of the town's all but omniscient ladies was recounting a conversation in the market place. '....Suddenly a big untidy man came past, and I said to her, "Who's that?" and she said, "Don't you know? That's new headmaster," and I said, "Nay!"....But it was.' Pitts-Tucker was indeed a contrast with the compact, immaculate Sands; and the differences went well below the surface. Robert St. John Pitts-Tucker was at Haileybury College, whence he went up to Clare College, Cambridge. At Cambridge he won first class honours in the Classical Tripos. Before coming to Pocklington he had been House Tutor of the School House at Shrewsbury School, and a prominent member of the distinguished group of classicists teaching there. His wife was, like him, a Cambridge graduate with first class honours in classics, and the name of being a capable teacher, which she fully upheld at Pocklington when needed. He himself had played rugby in his school pack, and was a tennis player with enthusiasm and a hefty service. He was, and is, a big man with a big voice and the unmistakable accent of the southern public schools — perhaps the first product of the famous schools to be closely associated with the School, and the first to bring to bear on the School's problems the outlook of those schools.

Inevitably there was a strong East Riding element in the Governing Body, leavened though it was by representatives of various learned institutions (see Appendix D). There was enough goodwill for Pitts-Tucker to be able to enlist their backing for his policies; for this they were commended in the report of a General Inspection conducted by a group of H.M. Inspectors in 1947, a very valuable document to which reference will frequently be made in these pages. Later, imagination and expertise were added in the persons of Mr. (Later Sir William) Tweddle, one of Leeds' most prominent public men in various spheres, and Mr. Douglas Cumming, a director of Reckitt and Colman (Hull), whose financial flair and sure judgement were of enormous value. It was these two men above all, after Tweddle became chairman in 1963, who gave the School a governing body of more than ordinary quality, particularly when joined by the Vice-Chancellor of Hull University, Sir Brynmor Jones.

In 1945 the School received Direct Grant status. A good summary of what this means may be found in Sands' account in Chapter 20, with the one proviso that the word 'supervised' on page 109 exaggerates the function and powers of the Ministry of Education. To many who are not committed to complete state control, the Direct Grant seemed and still seems an imaginative solution of the problem how to combine the maximum of independence with social responsibility, and avoid excessive preoccupation with considerations of finance. It gave Pitts-Tucker the basis he needed for expanding the School. It ensured that the School continued to serve the needs of a very wide social spread; and its abolition by the government under Pitts-Tucker's successor would almost certainly have stunted the School's further growth if the efforts of both headmasters had not by then raised it to such a level that the catchment area could be extended in other ways. The part played by the local authority was crucial from the beginning, and here the School was lucky that Mr. Victor Clark, Chief Education Officer of the East Riding County Council, was a friend who, despite all the fluctuations in post-war educational policy, steadfastly maintained that the School was playing a valuable part in the education of the area. It was Clark who secured for Pitts-Tucker a seat on the East Riding Education Committee. The Direct Grant did, then, relieve the School to some extent of financial anxiety. But, even when at last money was allowed to run more freely and ambition to flower into achievement, there was always a shortage, despite the help of an enlightened bank. In 1958 the School had to resort to the expedient of an appeal, the first of a series. Later appeals, following the usual patterns, used professional fund-raisers. But the first appeal was launched without such recourse, by a committee composed of the staff, old boys and former parents; so yet another load was thrown on shoulders already carrying heavy responsibilities. It was by no means a failure. But the School had, and has, no Maecenas among its friends, and no millionaire, so far as is known, among its former pupils; the burden of giving fell mainly on those who were already paying, namely the parents of present pupils, from whom one could hardly expect much, generous though many were. Subsequent fund-raisers found exactly the same. After all, fees had been kept low precisely to attract those who could not afford more.

The report of the Inspectors in 1947 referred to the appointment of a Bursar-cum-Clerk to the Governors, expressing the opinion that this should relieve the headmaster of much routine responsibility, but stressing that the functions of the office should be clearly defined, and that the headmaster's over-riding responsibility to the Governors should not be in any way diminished; clearly they saw the possibility of clashes. And in fact the arrangement did not work long. Pitts-Tucker then took over all bursarial duties, the School's accountants providing permanent help with accounting details. This suited Pitts-Tucker's personal style, for he was a centraliser by nature. He wanted to keep a firm grip on everything that went on, and he had the qualities needed for this. He was meticulous, he enjoyed detail and was very good with it, and he was an immensely hard worker. It must be said that Sands had done the same, and that for some years the School was little bigger than in Sands' time. But this was already the beginning of the Paper Age that succeeded the Iron Age; bureaucratic demands were becoming more and more heavy. Also, Pitts-Tucker was exceptionally generous of his time, whether to boys or to members of the staff; no one asked for his help or advice in vain. And he did it all with evident gusto and enjoyment: a boy who was going to Cambridge for an examination received from the headmaster in person not only an *absit* chit but also precise details of the trains he was to take on that perilous trip to the Fens and back, and where to change, all planned on a tight schedule to get the boy back to school with the minimum of time lost. Even before the School became much bigger and more complex he had generated an intensity and put on himself a strain which was almost too much even for him, and was inevitably passed on to staff and prefects. But though small tensions abounded, and things occasionally got out of proportion, the big issues were handled in such a way that they usually turned out right in the end. His own batteries Pitts-Tucker often charged by attendance at a special interest of his, the Church Assembly, sometimes in mid-term. This did no one harm, and only provoked speculation whether he practised on those austere benches that almost Churchillian capacity for taking catnaps which he was seen to indulge in both in his drawing room and at concerts.

Centralisers or not, headmasters in the years following the 1939-45 war were in for a very frustrating time. It might be thought that, for example, if an increase in numbers made it imperative to buy more beds — especially beds of the antique boarding school variety — it would have been possible to go to the appropriate shop and buy, or at least order, them. Not so. Only gradually were oblique approaches to such problems learnt and mastered; in the case of beds, through the help and advice of His Majesty's Inspector, Mr. J. P. Lefroy, it emerged that a demarche through the Ministry of Education might pay. It did, and beds began to rain on Pocklington. But in 1947 the School was allowed to buy Lyndhurst, a large house on the Bridlington Road about half a mile from the School (efforts to find somewhere nearer were vain), and so could embark on one of the most urgently needed reforms, the constitution of a proper junior school to cope with a steady and increasing flow of entrants, boarding and day, at the age of eight, and an end to the rattling of one of Pocklington's biggest cupboard skeletons. Lyndhurst was converted into a house for junior boarders, and after another two years a block of three classrooms was built on the same site and extra staff engaged to give adequate teaching for boarders and day boys of eight to eleven in three forms. There was now a resident housemaster, R. T. E. Allen, already senior science master, while the very capable teacher of the old 'Form I', Miss P. E. Dalgliesh, became headmistress of the Junior School. The Clock Mill Field, very near Lyndhurst, was also acquired for recreation.

A big advance, certainly. It might, of course, be argued that the junior end was not an essential part of the School, and that, had it been removed instead of reformed, the Governors and headmaster could have concentrated better on more important things. But it is always difficult to abolish, whether immediately or even gradually, something that has long existed, and, as in this case, had had a new lease of life during the war, when

Lyndhurst

parents had been anxious to send children to a 'safe' area. Also, although Pitts-Tucker soon realised that the most satisfactory recruitment age for Pocklington was eleven plus, a junior school was a valuable extra way of entry; once in, a pupil was unlikely to be removed. This was good for the School. Whether it was equally good for a boy to spend up to eleven years in what is, after all, one school is less certain. Again one might ask why the opportunity was not taken of tidying things up by appointing a person with special experience of this age group to combine the posts of house master and junior school headmaster. Dolman House had been used by Sands to attract highly qualified teachers to the staff. The appointment of Allen to Lyndhurst was in part a reward for his remarkable services to the School, and could have been retrospectively justified by the 1947 Inspectors' comment that the School was too sparing in its rewards for outstanding services. A better justification was Allen's proved loyalty and uncommon efficiency which enabled him to do his job at Lyndhurst without detriment to his other contributions to the School, whether regular, like his successful direction of the science department, or occasional, like his work for school appeals. Moreover, he and his wife, by now themselves parents of a young family, soon made it clear that they would approach the pastoral side of their work in a new 'family' spirit. However, the division of authority at Lyndhurst did cause difficulties; it could hardly have been otherwise.

Yet another peculiarity of the Lyndhurst set-up was that as a boarding house it held a number of the younger boarders in the Senior School, who therefore had to pass through the town four times a day, since they took lunch, like the other boarders, at their resident house; they were also cut off in other ways from what should have been the focus of their activities. The plain fact is that in those immediate post-war days numbers were growing fast, including boarders. Dormitories had to be found for all, and new building was still hedged about with all manner of restrictions. But Lyndhurst could at a pinch house seventy-five or so and, had it been filled with junior boarders alone, would have called for two or three more classrooms in addition to the three just built; otherwise day boys would have had to be excluded, which was unthinkable.

The constitution of the new Junior School gave it three forms and a regular staff of three teachers, who could not have covered everything on their own. The discrepancy was made up partly by visiting part-time staff, but mainly by men seconded for a few periods from the Senior School. To this expedient the half-mile between the two buildings was only one of the drawbacks; another was that in no way did the two timetables correspond. But this was no one's fault. There were only two ideal solutions — either abolish the Junior School or build it into a self-contained and autonomous

168 A HISTORY OF POCKLINGTON SCHOOL

unit. The arguments against abolition have already been rehearsed. The second solution was also impracticable. The 1947 Inspectors' report had indeed envisaged as essential 'as soon as conditions permit ... a separate and self-contained junior department'; but one cannot help wondering whether they had given much thought to the feasibility of this, considering the age range involved and the small size of the School, together with the financial stringencies. In all probability only a junior school covering the ages eight to thirteen could have stood on its own legs, and then only in the context of a school twice Pocklington's size and five times as wealthy. Pitts-Tucker retained a firm overall control over the Junior School, especially its entry policy; and, although this suited his temperament, he had probably no alternative.

At this point one might ask what master-plan the headmaster and Governors had in mind. The answer is, perforce none. They did at times state what they thought the most suitable size for the School, only to find the figures passed in the next couple of years. But a master-plan strictly adhered to would have been a strait-jacket. The School had to go where the facts of the situation led it. One fact soon discovered was that the main age for recruitment was eleven plus, not thirteen plus. The H.M. Inspector already referred to, Mr. J. P. Lefroy, had quite early put to Pitts-Tucker the alternative: was Pocklington to become yet another minor public school or something *sui generis* which might roughly be described as a mainly boarding grammar school with some public school characteristics? It was the facts that decided on the latter choice. Pitts-Tucker made considerable and not unsuccessful efforts to recruit from the preparatory schools for a thirteen plus entry, but success was limited. By and large little of the best (especially in an academic sense) material from the preparatory schools came Pocklington's way, and it became almost a cliché with the staff that Common Entrance Examination results were to be regarded without illusions. The next headmaster had much greater success in this field, but some of this may be attributed to Pitts-Tucker's achievement in building Pocklington's reputation. In such matters there is a time-lag; preparatory school headmasters had to be convinced that they were not losing face by sending boys to Pocklington. So numbers grew, both boarders and day boys, without it being clear when the growth would slow down or stop, and in which of the two groups it would persist the longer. It was reasonable then to believe that the boarders would continue to be the heart of the School and would set its 'tone', whatever that elusive term might mean; but that almost certainly they would never again dominate the School as they had under Sands. To generalise a little rashly, boarders usually provided more than their due share of members of the sports teams, but day boys on the average performed better in the classroom. So it would never be right to make a firm decision to increase the one group at the expense of the other. This meant that, if ever more boarding accommodation were envisaged, it would also entail more classrooms, and vice-versa. Perhaps the most awkward crisis arose when British Rail announced their intention to close the York-Hull line on which so many day boys travelled. It seemed certain that the number of day boys would drop significantly, and that it would be necessary to augment the boarding element to ensure a full school. But the number of day boys did not in fact drop. By one device or another, parents made sure their children could continue to come, and fresh recruits came pouring in, so that classroom space was soon inadequate. This was only the most conspicuous example of the impossibility of planning ahead with confidence. An upper limit might be proposed as 'ideal', but what was it an ideal of? There was always this justification for greater numbers, that only such numbers could ensure a sixth form big enough to offer a variety of advanced courses that would satisfy widening demands. Numbers, buildings and the curriculum were matters that could not be treated separately.

In 1947 the School was, materially speaking, to be found in a series of uninspiring rooms on either side of the long corridor leading out of the dining room, and in laboratories and various huts. This meant that amenities for the boarders were barely thought of, and for the day boys as yet almost unthinkable. The needs were obvious to all, and the Inspectors of 1947 gave a broad hint that the fees were utterly inadequate to the needs. The problem, however, was very difficult. Finance permitted only small piecemeal alterations, yet the idea of building two or three classrooms of a permanent type when at least ten were needed was false husbandry. It should not be thought that nothing was done; for example, when money became available to use the space above the laboratories, use was made of it. But it all amounted to very little. Boarders had little space to relax in; for the day boys, apart from the classrooms of which they could make limited use at lunch-time and while waiting for trains and buses, there was just one double army hut, graced with a shower or two, for their ever-growing numbers to use as a changing room. This they aptly and philosophically named 'The Shack', and 'The Shack' it remained until its unlamented disappearance in the late fifties.

The report of the 1947 Inspection did not mince its words on the subject of buildings. This was good, though one might cavil at its choice of words when it roundly said: '(The School's) chief drawback is the lack of a suitably dignified environment.' The Gruggen frontage of 1851 surely deserves the epithet 'dignified'. But the Inspectors had done their work thoroughly.

They had penetrated the facade and viewed from every angle what was behind, and one must applaud what they went on to say — 'Although a good deal has been done to improve the premises during the past eighteen years, it must be realised that the task has only just begun, and that in many respects the premises fall far below the standard which it would be reasonable to expect from a school of this calibre.' A nicely calculated challenge — a potentially good school handicapped by ignoble buildings. The back of the old buildings was indeed most unprepossessing and, apart from a pleasant little Assembly Hall and some utilitarian but now inadequate laboratories, the rest was largely a mess of old army huts and an open-air swimming bath blackened by long proximity to the railway and effectively usable for about two months in the school year. With what relief would a visitor at that time extricate himself from all this, go out on to the Near Dolman field, fill his lungs with good fresh air, and take in the view looking east — the comfortable little town, the noble church tower, and the first slopes of the Wolds!

A visitor who came a few years later, say about 1960, looking at the long new building that now faces the Near Dolman, might well have asked, 'Where *was* the School?' and his guide would have been hard put to it to answer.

There were three major building operations in Pitts-Tuckers's time, apart from Lyndhurst: the big increase in laboratory space in 1958; the new classroom block followed by and connected with the new gymnasium and the three classrooms built over it, together with much improved changing accommodation, also in 1958; and the moving of Wilberforce House to where the old Sanatorium had been, and the extensions on that site which increased and improved the accommodation of both Wilberforce and Dolman Houses, in 1965. For the extension of the science wing a possible source of financial help was found in the 'Industrial Fund for the Advancement of Science Education in Schools'. The School was not so successful as it had hoped in tapping this source, for the Fund, financed as it was by hard-headed though imaginative industrialists, required that in order to get help from it a school must meet certain requirements, for example in size of science sixth. To this end it employed an ex-H.M. Inspector whose eagle eye missed nothing. As yet the School hardly met the Fund's specifications; but there was recognition that the future was bright. So some help did come, though less than had been hoped. Thus, after various changes, extensions and adjustments, the foresight of those who in the thirties had built the laboratories solid enough to carry more rooms was justified, and at last the School possessed a self-contained science wing, to be completed in due course when an adequate biology laboratory was added.

Next, and probably most important, came the building of classrooms on a long frontage facing the Near Dolman, housing a set of rooms in two storeys. These new rooms were deliberately designed to hold no more than twenty-five pupils, except for the two at the west end, which were larger as befitted the practical nature of the subjects taught there, art and geography. Needless to say, it proved impossible to stick to this 'ideal' figure, and soon classrooms were accommodating sets of thirty-two and over. In the same operation the old School House changing rooms which now linked the old buildings to the new classroom block were given to the day boys. Over them was built a new set of changing rooms for School House boarders, together with, at the Near Dolman end, some seminar rooms which could also be used by sixth form day boys to keep their books, and, at the School House end, a few sixth form studies — this last the small beginning of a most important development. It would be an exaggeration to say that with one bound Pocklington School was free. But it would be fair to say that in a very few years the School emerged from its Middle Ages, lessons could be taught in an agreeable environment, sixth form teaching in mathematics and on the arts side emerged from holes in corners and beneath staircases, and The Shack became a part of East Riding folklore. The huts between the new block and the old buildings were pulled down, flower-beds took their place, and the St Nicholas Court was born — though some did wonder why, in order to obtain a raised cloister effect, it was necessary to drop the ground below the step and so create a small lake in bad weather.

After another two years came the splendid new gymnasium, with the classrooms above it. Chapter 22 makes it clear that gymnastics had played a larger part at Pocklington than at most schools. The present (written in 1984) Library was the old gymnasium, and it is hard to conceive how so much good work was done in so small a space; part of the answer must be that as much as possible was done out of doors. The great Mason Clark had had a capable successor, but the demands of the armed services during the war deprived the boys of skilled instruction, and at the time of the 1947 Inspection the teaching was still shared out among willing but not specialist members of the staff. Naturally the Inspectors recommended that a suitably qualified physical education instructor be appointed. The actual selection might have turned out one of those unsatisfactory compromises to which a small school is subject: R.S.M. Watt was appointed to combine two jobs, P.E. instructor and drill instructor to the Cadet Corps. Rarely has a compromise proved so beneficial. 'Jock' Watt combined his two functions with enthusiasm and skill. The boys loved him and his work, and responded to his enthusiasm with equal warmth. He was an excellent disciplinarian, yet as far removed as could be from the conventional picture of a sergeant major. He could produce good gymnastic displays in the old Mason Clark tradition, but his great achievement was the building of strength and stamina. He was prepared to embrace in his work new ideas like weight and circuit training; and in many a school rugby match one saw a Pocklington pack, less skilled maybe than its opponents, but wearing them down in the end by virtue of hard training in the gym.

'Out of the strong came forth sweetness'; or at any rate literacy. The old gymnasium was converted into a library which met very pleasantly for several years one of the School's most desperate needs. The handsome room that emerged was given a special significance because it bore on its walls portraits of William Wilberforce and previous headmasters, and the three primary documents of the School's origins: the foundation charter of John Dolman, the re-foundation charter of Thomas Dolman, and the 'Inspeximus'. These documents had been repaired and handsomely remounted by the Public Record Office.

As for the third big achievement, the 'new' Dolman and Wilberforce buildings, an account of its genesis has already been given. But it would be unfair to leave it like that, as an error of judgement that luckily turned out well. Both Dolman and Wilberforce Houses were very short of amenities, and a big improvement was overdue. Moreover, Wilberforce had been very isolated half a mile down the road from the main buildings, and an arrangement which brought it in next to Dolman and sent the Sanatorium to the former Wilberforce site was bound to be an advance. But, best of all, the move made it possible at last to bring games houses into line with boarding houses. Boarders in Dolman and Wilberforce games houses henceforth remained in their houses for the whole of their senior school career, while all Gruggen and Hutton boys now went to School House, which was divided between them. No longer were almost all the senior boarders herded into one house, with the chance of promotion to positions of responsibility open to very few. There was now far more chance of becoming a prefect, especially with the numbers in each boarding house now much closer to the figure of fifty or so which had long been found suitable in other schools. Some anomalies remained. Lyndhurst continued to house boarders who were in the Senior (i.e. eleven plus) School. The headmaster remained housemaster of Gruggen and Hutton, with a resident house tutor for each house, whereas Dolman and Wilberforce each had a resident housemaster and house tutor. But, taken as a whole, this was a most valuable development, and probably no other single change had a better effect on the morale of the School. The day boys continued to be divided between the four games houses, but now joined their boarding counterparts for the midday meal. Before long, the new house buildings began to look less blatantly new, for supervision of the garden beds round the houses was put into the experienced hands of J. H. Derbyshire, housemaster of Dolman and senior physics master as well as Officer in Charge of the Cadets.

The housemasters, although their position and emoluments were altered to bring them into line with modern notions, continued to control domestic staff in their houses and were responsible for the condition of their premises and, most important, the feeding of their boys and their domestic staff. Ideally there was much to be said for each house continuing to feed its own, but it was an extravagant system, as most even of the oldest public schools have found, so it was reasonable that in the new Dolman-and-Wilberforce the two houses should pool their catering and the houses take turns for meals. Thus began the process which ended (if it has ended) in the remarkable new dining hall built by the Dolman Drive, which is outside the scope of these chapters.

The problems of catering had always added to the strain already endured by headmasters and housemasters and their wives. Experiments were made with the employment of catering firms. But the main contribution of these firms was in purchasing. True, they supplied kitchen supervisors. But if one of these was missing for any reason it was impossible for the firm to make an immediate substitution, and it was the housemaster's wife who almost invariably stepped in. She would also have to act as peacemaker whenever there was trouble between caterer and locally enlisted domestic labour, who not unnaturally preferred the angel they knew. These responsibilities were loyally and cheerfully undertaken by the ladies. But the strains imposed were such that they were barely compensated by the satisfaction of a necessary job done. After all, Latin lessons and cricket matches can be postponed; the troops have to be fed.

With the day boys things stayed for the most part as before. They remained divided into the four games houses, but for games only. It was obvious that they needed a housemaster to give them pastoral care as well as a measure of administration. Pitts-Tucker had long ago chosen C. V. Winsor for this task. His good judgement and kindly firmness soon won him the respect of boys and parents. However, numbers grew, and the burden on him was almost intolerable, splendidly though he bore it. As day boys began to be counted in their hundreds, younger members of the staff were assigned to help Winsor, but delegation was not easy, and did not work well. A more drastic solution might have been found, but possibly Pitts-Tucker did not want to spoil the excellent rapport he had with Winsor, and maybe also he felt that it was a problem best left to his successor to solve. It was in fact one of the first things Willatt tackled when he had got the feel of things.

It is high time to discuss teaching and learning — which many will regard
as the true business of a school; but it is notable how often it is elbowed out
by other considerations, as this account shows all too clearly. Pitts-Tucker
took over the School when the country was still at war. The requirements of
war and the lack of funds had left a school inadequately staffed, though
perhaps no more so than most; and this remained the case for a year or two.
Apart from geography, only chemistry and physics were well manned;
mathematics teaching could be described as only promising; biology hardly
existed and had no laboratory. So the science side meant the time-honoured
combination of mathematics, physics and chemistry, with biology teaching
confined to part of a general sciences course in the lower forms, which could
be covered adequately by anyone with a science degree. If an occasional
sixth former was determined to pursue a medical career, a visiting teacher
was engaged to offer a few periods of biology when he could. It was the
chemistry and the physics, with the mathematics getting stronger all the
time, that were at the core of a science department which a later group of
H.M. Inspectors (1957) described as the strength of the School, and which
remained so for at least half of Pitts-Tucker's years; indeed, encouraged by
the increase in and improvement of laboratories, it did not decline even
when the arts subjects began to catch up. Much was due to the organisation
of R. T. E. Allen (senior science and senior chemistry) and J. H. Derbyshire
as the head of physics. For biology, however, although a full-time teacher
was appointed in 1951, half a hut had to suffice for years until at last, in
1958, a laboratory emerged from the increased science buildings. Even so,
and despite the recommendations of Inspectors as far back as 1947, it
remained a Cinderella subject all Pitts-Tucker's time and well beyond. This
was of set policy, a seemingly harsh decision which illustrates the difficulties
an ambitious school of moderate size has to face. Such schools must decide,
for their sixth forms, which baskets they are going to put their limited
number of eggs into. In all except the biggest schools, some subjects must
be either sacrificed or held down so that the others may flourish. As will be
shown, geography suffered similarly. Incidentally it was one of the School's
earlier biology masters, Michael Ball, later Brother Michael of the
Community of the Glorious Ascension and now Bishop of Jarrow, one of the
famous episcopal twins (the other being Peter of Lewes), who left as a
remembrance of his stay at Pocklington the striking wall plaque of St.
Nicholas which dignifies the approach to the court of that name from the
Near Dolman.

   In other subjects there was not enough well-qualified teaching. In history
and English the dominant figure had been the housemaster of Wilberforce
House, T. W. Pay, a most experienced and trenchant school-master who

deservedly enjoyed the respect and affection of generations of boys; but it could not be said that he was abreast of modern developments in the teaching of these subjects. It was only when he relinquished control, first of history and then, on his official retirement, (though he stayed on some years as a part-timer and gave great help) of English, that specialists began to be recruited who brought the teaching up to date. In modern languages there was for a long time only one well-qualified teacher. The 1947 Inspectors criticised shortcomings in art, music and physical education. The last of these has been dealt with in connexion with the gymnasium, and music may be left to a later chapter. As for art, the retirement of yet another personality from a former age, W. E. Whitehouse, allowed the appointment of R. E. Brown, the first of a young and vigorous line of teachers who eventually brought nation-wide repute to the art of the School. But this too is better left to a later chapter.

In classics it was some time before the second master, who was the head of department in addition to his other commitments, received extra help. However, the enthusiastic support of the headmaster made a big difference; Pitts-Tucker was determined that the traditional course should be kept up, and was even reluctant to concede that a fair proportion of boys would never get anywhere in Latin and would be better employed doing something else. Geography deserves sympathetic mention. Rigorously taught by that legendary Old Pocklingtonian, G.F.D. Pearson, around whom so many anecdotes clustered, it became a Cinderella subject like biology, and for similar reasons. There were also at the time considerations of academic prestige. In the late forties geography had, especially at the two old universities, less prestige than most subjects. As a headmaster determined that the School should win more and more recognition in those exalted spheres, Pitts-Tucker made the decision that he must choose between history and geography. Inevitably he chose history, and geography was crowded out of the sixth form. At one moment the policy appeared sensationally justified when, soon after the arrival of a forceful history teacher, A. J. Maltby, later headmaster of Trent College, a clutch of able modern historians from the School made their mark at Cambridge. This notable success was not repeated, though it was far from a flash in the pan, and history has continued to be a strong subject at Pocklington. Future, or even present, thinkers may frown at this apparent preoccupation with Oxbridge, though it still seems natural to the present writer, convinced as he is that in some metaphysical way the rarest flights of pure mathematics at Cambridge help to keep up the standards of arithmetic in Form IIBY.

The structure of the curriculum and its evolution are too complex to be dealt with here; many experiments were made during these years. Those who do not know much about the inner workings of a rapidly developing school may be surprised to learn that an entirely new timetable had to be constructed every year without exception to meet the needs of these experiments as well as the changes in staff personnel. First a two-stream system was brought in, then three streams for the last two years before School Certificate, which roughly corresponded with the later Ordinary Level. Then a fast stream was launched of abler boys who would reach O level in four instead of the usual five years. Pitts-Tucker was very conscious of his own experience as a boy of having been held back in his earlier teens, and was anxious not to inflict the same frustration on brighter boys. But the scheme did not last. As the percipient 1947 Inspectors saw, there were rarely enough bright boys to justify it. Besides, 'brightness' in some things meant immaturity in others. It is a striking discovery of the last thirty years that seven, or even six, terms in the sixth forms are sufficient preparation for a stiff university course provided the foundations up to O level are adequately laid.

Eventually a timetable was devised which ensured that no boy need make an irrevocable choice between the arts and the sciences sides for the purpose of sixth form specialisation until he had reached the sixth form. To those who dislike the English tradition of sixth form specialisation, and find far more to admire in what is done at equivalent levels abroad, above all in Western Germany, this may not seem a matter for much pride. Nevertheless it put the School in this respect ahead of many other more famous schools in the land.

In another enlightened but more controversial step Pitts-Tucker whole-heartedly embraced a movement called Agreement to Broaden the Curriculum (inevitably 'ABC'). By accepting its principles the School undertook to devote no more than three-fifths of its sixth form periods to specialist (i.e. A level) subjects, leaving the rest available for non-specialist activities, varying from modern languages for non-linguists and religious studies for all to, for example, archaeology or elementary economics (at a time when economics played no part in the 'official' timetable). There were objections to this: choice of subjects was arbitrary, depending on who on the staff was willing to offer what, and it did unduly, as it was thought, restrict the number of periods available for specialist subjects; moreover it was found that those who benefited most were losing all their valuable periods of private study, while those who gained least were getting too many. The scheme did not long outlast Pitts-Tucker, but is mentioned here as yet another indication that the School's outlook was by no means blinkered.

As has already been said, Pitts-Tucker soon found that the most likely age for entry was eleven plus. Recruiting at eleven meant a study of primary schools over a wide area, and some of the better of these schools became as important to the School as any preparatory school. There was, as stipulated under the Direct Grant scheme, an entrance examination at eleven plus, but this may well have been a better test than most eleven plus tests, for there was at Pocklington less emphasis on the I.Q.Test and more on arithmetic, English and interview. The result is that many boys were taken who would have failed local authorities' tests, but hardly any of these failed to obtain several O level passes, while many did well at A level too. It has been one of the School's best justified reasons for pride that the (academically speaking) average or even less than average boy regularly does better in his schooling than could possibly have been expected. Higher up the School, standards were raised by the decision in 1953 to abandon the Northern Universities Joint Board and take the Oxford and Cambridge for external examinations. The change gave the School quite a shock at first, for the papers set by the latter Board turned out less straightforward and less easy to teach for. But methods were altered accordingly, and it was not long before results at both levels were better than ever. The change also helped the academically gifted to tackle the demands of Oxbridge entrance. In 1960 pupils of the School actually won seven Oxbridge open awards, and in a variety of subjects.

It might not be out of place to list here those pupils of the Pitts-Tucker epoch who have won academic fame at a still higher level. The list may well be incomplete, and the writer would like to forestall criticism by getting his apology in first. A list of distinguished chemists reflects the strength of the science side: Professor Robert Cundall of Nottingham University, and Mark Child and Alan Creighton, lecturers at Oxford and Kent respectively. David Fleeman, English tutor at Oxford, Christopher Dent, until 1984 Chaplain of New College, Oxford, and author of *Protestant Reformers in Elizabethan Oxford*, Michael Wadsworth, former Chaplain at Sidney Sussex, Cambridge, David French, who became Director of the British School of Archaeology at Ankara, and Peter Dickens, tutor in Architecture at Cambridge, are products of the School's arts side. The first internationally famous O.P. since Wilberforce, Tom Stoppard, did not go through the full academic routine; it is the mark of genius not to do the obvious. Two distinguished names from the Sands era may also be cited: the scientist Colin Adamson, sometime Rector of the Polytechnic of Central London, and the poet and literature scholar, Robin Skelton.

Chapter 17 shows how a shrewd headmaster saw in the study of Hebrew another way of getting boys into the older universities. Only recently has that generation of Oxbridge dons died out who, whenever Pocklington was mentioned to them, immediately asked if they still 'did Hebrew' there. A headmaster as firmly committed to his religion and religious studies as Pitts-

Tucker was bound to hanker after a revival of the subject. One Speech Day the Archbishop of York, Michael Ramsey, was chief guest, and when the matter was mentioned to him he promptly replied: 'I'll find you a teacher', and he was as good as his word. More than one boy benefited, especially at Jesus College, Oxford, where a forgotten endowment for a closed award by an O.P., S. W. Holbrooke, shared with Wadham College, was given a timely revival. Hebrew teaching did not long outlive Pitts-Tucker at Pocklington, but it was a pleasant echo of the past, and not without its uses too. Fortunately now Oxbridge dons have other reasons for recognising the name of Pocklington.

The School's grounds are among its chief glories, and are probably surpassed by those of very few in the north of England. For those who rejoice in them now it is not easy to picture their appearance at the end of the last war. On the Near Dolman, Sands had been growing the grass long for a hay crop. Diagonally across it was an old right of way. When the field was recovered for games, matches were only rarely played on it, which was just as well because in the middle of a fierce rugby practice you could have seen some citizen sturdily asserting his rights by walking right through the melée, miraculously protected, as one might have said, by St. Nicholas, had the plaque been up then; for no 'incident' ever occurred, only defiance on one side and irritation on the other. This nuisance was only removed years later — one of several special services done for the School by Mr. L. C. Sands, son of P. C., when he assumed the post of Clerk to the Governors. The Far Dolman was not so broad as it is now. A long narrow field beyond it, belonging to St. John's Lodge, was bought later in Pitts-Tucker's time and greatly improved it. Between the Far Dolman and the Common were allotments, some with huts and, more alarmingly, greenhouses, vulnerable to rugby touch-finding on the Far Dolman. An Old Pocklingtonians' War Memorial Fund, opened after the First World War, had lagged badly, and even after the Second World War was still meagre, until the prospect of acquiring this allotment field for a cricket ground fired imaginations, and money began to roll in. The ground, and the fine pavilion, were ceremonially opened by Sir Percy Simner, a distinguished O.P. who had been one of Hutton's and Stewart's Hebrew scholars, in 1955. It is matter for debate whether at the outset enough was done, or even could have been done (shortage of money being once again an obstacle) to ensure that a wicket was laid down worthy of its surroundings. Of the beauty of the ground itself, with the three great chestnut trees between it and the Common, there can be no doubt. There was still the Big Field, so distant from the School, where nevertheless first eleven cricket matches were regularly played, and sometimes first fifteen rugby too, and at the far corner of which were the 'Spinney' and the 'Bather', amenities of a bygone age. Not much could be done with this field. The Luftwaffe had not helped by creating an enormous bomb-crater near the Spinney. The drainage under the wicket was regularly blocked, so that the pitches never had any life in them. However, the field remained and remains useful, in view of the great growth of the School. As for the historic pavilion, successive coats of paint had not saved it from becoming by 1955 a most unpicturesque semi-ruin, its rotting floor a trap for unwary ankles. Eventually, what could be salvaged of it was moved to the Near Dolman to augment some outbuildings already there and help to house groundsman's equipment. To round the territory off, a six-acre field on the way to the Big Field was acquired but deliberately left rough for use by the Cadets for exercises as well as for housing their huts and rifle range.

The more the grounds grew the more work was needed on them, above all when a new cricket ground was created. A good groundsman is of incalculable value, but the virtues required of him are almost impossibly varied. However, before very long the School struck gold with the appointment of Mr. P. Giles. He was not primarily a cricket ground expert though he knew a great deal and learned more. His strengths were above all his capacity for unselfish hard work, his cheerful enthusiasm and pride in his work, and his flair for maintaining machinery; what he saved the School merely on this last count cannot be estimated. Although it is out of place, it is convenient to mention here a similar, though far less conspicuous, contribution made to the care of the School buildings by Mr. C. Broadhead, another servant of the School who did not count the hours he put in, and that though he often suffered poor health. Here too a place may be found for one more name, that of Miss Mary Forth, the headmaster's capable and devoted secretary for several years.

A headmaster as sincerely and deeply religious as Pitts-Tucker might be expected to have left a mark on the School's religious life. But in fact the chief outward changes of worship in his years were largely made inevitable by the School's growth. Even if any previous headmaster at Pocklington had ever contemplated building a school chapel, the cost must always have made it an impossible dream. Besides, it seemed historically appropriate to worship in the parish church of which it was a part when founded. Well into Pitts-Tucker's period the boarders continued the tradition of attending Sunday parish matins, the headmaster and second master gowned and enthroned at the back of the Dolman Chapel, the sixth form sitting in front of them, the rest mostly in the north transept, joining lustily and not too unmusically in the hymns, but still noting the more eccentric soloists in the parish congregation, especially a certain basso profondo and an elderly high soprano. They also, when they could, whiled away the time between the end of the service and the headmaster's sign of dismissal by gently humming or stamping accompaniment to the organist's voluntary, especially if it happened to be *Land of Hope and Glory*. All of which did not prevent many finding these services to be among the more memorable experiences of their School career. Although the increase in numbers was probably the main reason for change, another was undoubtedly a campaign, in which some younger members of the staff played a vital part, which urged that in a rapidly changing age conventional parish services were diverging more and more from what young people both wanted and needed. So it was decided that there should be School matins in a shorter form, varied by a shorter service of Holy Communion, before the main parish morning service every Sunday. Pitts-Tucker also inaugurated a custom of holding Thursday morning Prayers in the church instead of in the Assembly Hall. Those who were there will not forget one Thursday when the brief service was attended by two Russian headmasters who were staying at the School for a few days. They were accompanied to the church, they conformed outwardly with proper decency, and they afterwards declared themselves impressed by the dignity of the occasion.

The second innovation was the appointment of a School chaplain. Again increased numbers were a large factor in this. Up to a point an enthusiastic headmaster, with some necessary help from the vicar, could do what was needed (the heaviest task being that of preparing boys for Confirmation). But no longer. The first choice for the post was a sparkling one. The Rev. J. N. (Noel) Duckworth, historian, Cambridge and British Olympic cox, prisoner of war whose heroic fortitude in Japanese camps had won him the respect and love of many who shared that fearful experience, missionary on the Gold Coast (now Ghana), and protagonist (or is it victim?) of a *This is Your Life* television programme, he brought back colour to the East Riding of which he was, surprisingly, a native. It would be unfair to other equally devoted Pocklington figures to describe his deeds at length here. One would like to be able to add: 'Are they not written in ...?' Perhaps they will be some day, somewhere. Of course the headmaster continued to play a great part, and he, Duckworth and R. F. Kirk, School House tutor and son of a former Bishop of Oxford, made a formidable teaching team for the lower sixth at OA level divinity; the pass rate was phenomenal. The elusive Duckworth did most of his teaching in his lodgings in the evening, with suitable bribes for attendance — 'Pork Pies and Prophets'.

In the fifteen or so years after the war, the problem of how to entertain the boarders on a Saturday night and keep them out of mischief was resolved by a series of films, the choice of which was in part left to the boys, alternating with visits from outside lecturers and musical recitals (in those days the fees of quite distinguished classical musicians were miserable enough for the School to be able to afford them). By the mid-sixties this had changed. Senior boys were allowed to go to the local cinema, and all could pass the evening, in varying degrees of discomfort but at least as they wanted, listening to record player or radio or watching television (which had by now stepped over enough dead bodies of educationists to be respectable), although what they heard and saw would be regarded by their elders as rubbish. This is a slight example of what was happening in that rapidly changing period. The emphasis was less and less on 'what's good for them' and more and more on how 'they' would like to spend their leisure hours. These changes in the attitudes of youth, and of their elders towards youth, were both cause and effect of the explosive years around 1968. Pitts-Tucker retired a few years before the most difficult period and, given his fairly traditional outlook, was probably lucky to have done so. But he deserves credit for recognising and encouraging developments in the boarding house towards a régime in which more attention than ever before was paid to the needs, especially the individual needs, of the boys. Hitherto Pocklington had been staffed mainly by young men, few of whom came from the more famous public schools and who, partly because they had so many other duties to perform besides those of supervising boarders, and partly because they were mostly transient, tended to accept and apply a 'traditional' discipline which, though by no means as unfeeling as some have suggested, held that in the nature of things handling children in large numbers was bound to be a completely different thing from dealing with them in a 'family' unit. It was under Pitts-Tucker that, probably for the first time, young men from the more famous public schools were appointed. Paradoxically these schools, largely because they were manned by people who knew the defects as well as the virtues of their system, were already moving towards more modern ideas; and when their products came to teach in schools like Pocklington they brought this spirit with them. In the acceptance of this spirit there was, it must be admitted, prudence as well as idealism. Boys who saw the progressive 'liberalising' of home and day school discipline were already chafing at boarding school restrictions; they were learning to use those convenient Aunt Sally terms of abuse, 'establishment' and 'system', and some of them were already pressing their parents either to take them away or at least send them as day boys. Only a measure of 'liberalising' in the boarding house could stem this tendency. One wise move was accomplished with remarkably little fuss. Hitherto boys had worn their traditional dark suits all day except when changed for sport. Sober subfusc persisted even when hideously frayed at the cuffs by innocent horseplay and caked with mud on the trouser legs by 'small games'. Now they were allowed to put on the most informal clothing once their official commitments were over. Again, Pitts-Tucker accepted in 1965 a suggestion from some of the younger staff that boys in their second year in the Sixth who wished might opt out of Cadets or Scouts to do some approved form of social service — the origin of the Community Service Unit. These and other changes went some way towards stealing the thunder of the rebels.

The reader who knows his facts may object at this point that these problems, and the measures taken to meet them, would have been more appropriately discussed in the next chapter. Undoubtedly they did become much more pressing for some years after 1966, and the steps Willatt took to meet them then were far more comprehensive; in fact Willatt's achievements in this sphere were far more important than Pitts-Tucker's, and an attempt will be made in the next chapter to make this clear. However, the difficulties were already confronting the School in Pitts-Tucker's last years there, and it seems helpful to discuss them at some length at the point in the story where they first arose.

One particular aspect of this change was a gradual, but finally complete, change in the attitude of, and towards, prefects. It may be said of the old-style prefects that their position allowed them great influence for good or ill, and that control over their powers was probably less complete than Sands' account suggests. At some time in Pitts-Tucker's epoch caning by prefects disappeared, largely because prefects no longer wanted to cane, and no longer felt self-important, though at the same time they became, most of them, less responsible. One might say that in these later years they were rarely as good as the best of their predecessors, and never as bad as the worst. Certainly the old and often absurd sense of hierarchy disappeared, and was supplanted by, at the worst indifference, but more often a friendly tolerance and a readiness to help the weaker.

A later chapter will deal in more detail with out-of-classroom activities in the 1945-80 period, such as sport. Here it is enough to say that, the school Pitts-Tucker took over being a very small one, it seemed natural to concentrate on the leading activities and do them well, and not greatly to encourage 'minor' sports. Rugby football was succeeded by cross-country (for the whole senior school) in February, and then track and field athletics in March, very much in the old Oxbridge style. The chief departure from this was probably the extension of track and field athletics into the summer term to allow the sport to flourish in the weather best suited to it. This led to some great successes, of which perhaps those dearest to Pitts-Tucker were the six successive victories in annual triangular matches over two schools of similar status and constitution, Stamford and Abingdon. Rugby had varying success in his time, but in the celebration year of 1963-4 there was a first fifteen that managed to win all its matches. In cricket, on the other hand, the arrival in 1955 of an enthusiastic and gifted coach in M. H. Stevenson soon brought a great advance in standards, a bigger and better fixture list, and the beginnings of what can already be called a remarkable tradition. Pitts-Tucker himself, despite all his other commitments, usually found time to watch matches and tour the grounds on ordinary games days. Both music and drama flourished, and these activities also will be described at greater length later. Here one may single out the fine series of combined choral operations under the Director of Music, F. A. Sefton Cottom, when the School's tenors and basses joined successfully with the choirs of several girls' schools; and M. H. Stevenson added to his cricket triumphs a series of play productions which were always good and sometimes brilliant.

Anything that brings a school into closer contact with the outside world is usually desirable, so the School's connexion with the English Speaking Union deserves a paragraph. This connexion took two forms: one a series of visits by lecturers from the U.S.A., culminating in 1965 in a 'teach-in' when we were favoured with a posse of three American speakers on life in America and its place in the world, who kept a large group of sixth formers busy for two days. American boys, too, came to us from some of their most famous schools for a year and Pocklington boys went to U.S. schools also for a year. Close contacts between the nations have been known to do harm; this, so far as the writer knows, did nothing but good.

In 1964 the School celebrated its four hundred and fiftieth anniversary. Should the School have waited until the five hundredth to celebrate? There was a fair as well as an obvious answer to this: the year fitly marked the climax of the greatest period of growth the School had known or was ever likely to know. The summer of 1964 was filled with various events, but by far the most spectacular of these was the Commemoration Service held in York Minster on 23 May. There are schools of ancient foundation up and down the country who hold annual services in cathedrals with which they are traditionally linked. But to Pocklington, thirteen miles away, this was a special occasion requiring special organisation. The difficulties of controlling the crowds of visitors and particularly of transporting the whole School and timing its arrival were overcome, if barely so (and in this case 'barely' means 'perfectly'). The prefects did the marshalling admirably, the School Choir rose to the occasion, and the Archbishop of York gave a most impressive address. Pitts-Tucker did not retire for two years more, but it is likely that this was the happiest day of his headmastership.

He retired in the summer of 1966, a few years earlier than had been expected, to become, first, assistant to the Secretary of both the

Headmasters' Conference (the Public Schools) and the Incorporated Society of Headmasters, and to take on the senior posts after a year or two. The school he bequeathed to his successor was about two and a half times bigger than the one he had inherited twenty-one years before. Of course the times had been ripe in almost every way for such an expansion, but even so the figures speak for themselves. In the preceding pages an attempt has been made to describe this growth, its mechanics and its progress. But the way it was achieved calls for a deeper analysis for, however favourable the circumstances, the progress could not have been sustained over so long a period if it had not been clear to the outside world (or whatever part of it was interested) that what was being built so quickly was also being built on sure foundations. It was claimed for the Emperor Augustus that he found a Rome of brick and left a Rome of marble. Historians now hold that this is to be interpreted metaphorically; and it implies no adverse criticism of the School's architects and builders in the literal sense to concentrate, as here, on other less material aspects of Pitts-Tucker's achievement.

Firstly, he succeeded throughout his tenure in enlisting a teaching staff prepared to a man (and woman) to put in far more effort than the minimum that was professionally required of them. Even those young men who, unused to the demands of the older sort of public and grammar schools, came with some misgivings about taking posts in a school in a remote corner of the country which demanded six, sometimes seven, working days a week, found themselves before long accepting with enthusiasm the claims made on them. When they left, many did so with genuine regret. They had been fired by Pitts-Tucker's own example and uninhibited enthusiasm, far though most of them probably were from sharing his outlook on the world in general. Secondly, he succeeded in winning for the School the reputation for caring for all of its pupils, but particularly those of only average or even less than average promise. This of course grew out of his success in assembling the staff he wanted, but it was also due in part to his own intense interest in each pupil.

Pitts-Tucker's own personal attitude to the swiftly changing world was traditional without being in the least ostrich-like. When it was clear that some contact with girls was becoming desirable for the older boarders, he wisely encouraged combined choral operations with neighbouring girls' boarding schools, but, when dances together with these were first mooted, it was like him to insist that they should be 'given' by him and attended by some members of the staff and all prefects, with dinner jackets the rule — this at a time when in the world outside all those conventions were being enthusiastically abandoned, and only Moss Bros. were happy to pick up the crumbs. Of course he did this and other such things out of a desire to show senior boys 'how these things should be done'; and probably something of this sense of occasion rubbed off on them, however much some of them chafed at the time; and, having penetrated, is surfacing now in the more circumspect eighties. The best example of this side of Pitts-Tucker's feelings for propriety and social responsibility was shown in his generous entertainment of almost every lecturer or performer who ever came to the School. In this and in many other spheres both he and the School owed an incalculable debt to his wife who, herself a scholar who probably did not regard herself as one of nature's caterers and organisers, set a magnificent example of loyalty and self-sacrifice as well as efficiency which helped to bring out similar qualities in others, at the same time as she was also bringing up a family of four.

This chapter, with its emphasis on the achievement of one man, will win little approval from the school of historians who would have preferred a comparative study of, say, the relative costs of making your own chipped potatoes and buying them ready-made. But the plain fact is that, for reasons and in ways already indicated, Pitts-Tucker stamped his impress on most aspects of the School's life; although it would be preposterous to imply that there were not plenty of initiatives from other quarters, accepted by him with various degrees of enthusiasm. Everything he was and did, his judgements and decisions, were shaped by or in the light of his religious convictions, and the latter were of a kind that generates heat as well as light. It would be wrong to suggest that in all this he always carried others with him — the times were not propitious, and younger people with convictions of their own felt things differently; but simply by aiming so high he ensured the continuance of some traditional values. He probably would have wished that the School and everyone connected with it could form one family, with himself the benevolent paterfamilias; and this too did not fit the more sceptical, independent and pragmatic views of the majority. But it was not an ignoble ideal. Of the magnitude of his achievement there can be no doubt. The old judgement on Augustus has been quoted; one might also have cited Wren's epitaph in St. Paul's. It remains to add that at the moment of writing (April 1985) Pitts-Tucker is very much alive and almost as active as ever in public service.

CHAPTER 27

GUY LONGFIELD WILLATT
(1966 to 1980)

This chapter will be shorter than the previous one, but only because Willatt's tenure of the headmastership was shorter than Pitts-Tucker's, fourteen years as opposed to twenty-one. If the story of the years from 1966 to 1980 appears less spectacular than that of the previous two decades (and even that may be questioned), it was just as significant, and during its course the School's outer and inner aspects were almost as fundamentally changed. This change was by no means entirely the result of external pressures, for the new headmaster's qualities and outlook played a positive role.

G. L. Willatt is an Old Reptonian. No one, especially if he still reads *Ranji's Book of Cricket,* can doubt that Repton is one of the 'great public schools'. But it is also a 'great public school' in the North Midlands. So Willatt, who comes of a respected Nottingham family (his father had actually been a school friend of P. C. Sands) was by breeding and schooling a North Midlander, that is, closer to the North than to the South. He had finished his schooling before the Second World War, and once, much later, at Pocklington in a staff meeting, drew a picture of himself as a right prig of a pre-war public school prefect (his staff were not completely convinced). But he was essentially a post-1945 man in his outlook. He had read both history and English in the Tripos at Cambridge and achieved a second class in both. He also won Blues at association football and cricket. After Cambridge he taught at both his old school and Edinburgh Academy, and captained Derbyshire at cricket — an experience that must have taught him much about man-management or more likely developed his innate flair for it. In 1955 he was appointed headmaster of Heversham Grammar School in Westmorland, a small and until his arrival not very significant school, which seemed to the local education authority to have very little future; in fact it looked as if he had been appointed to it as a sort of executor if not undertaker. Not unnaturally he jibbed at this role, and proceeded with great success to build up the moribund institution until it gained, locally at any rate, considerable respect in many fields, especially rugby. He did all this, in part, by exploring ways of increasing the existing small boarding side, above all by attracting the attention of parents who for various reasons lived abroad — an experience which helped him greatly when he came to Pocklington in 1966.

In person and personality Willatt was quite remarkably different from his predecessor. Almost his first remark to the writer was that he supposed he was the first non-scholar to be appointed headmaster at Pocklington. This was typical of his modesty. He hated any sort of pretentiousness, and was quick to disclaim knowledge or expertise in any field where he was not quite sure of himself. Some might say he carried this to a fault; but it was part of his nature, and it did not prevent him from being the right man for Pocklington in the critical late sixties. Just as one respects the inspiration behind many of his predecessor's ideas, so one must admire Willatt's appreciation of Pocklington as an essentially down-to-earth school, and sympathise with his reluctance to let it attempt things beyond its capacities. Which is not in the least to suggest that he lacked imagination; what follows will adequately refute that. A photograph may convey his unpretentious modesty, but cannot conceal both his refinement and his strength.

A man with his experience was not likely to make startling innovations in his first year at a successful school. One change, however, was soon remarked, and it was in more than one way symbolical. Willatt allowed nothing to stop him from beginning morning assembly strictly on time, and from conducting it with quiet dispatch. It was an efficient, low-key beginning to the day's work, and by no means indicated that the new headmaster was going to undervalue the religious side of school life. But equally he did not mean to use the daily event as a medium through which to stamp his impress on the place. What he did imply was that punctuality gave a good start to the day; and this was generally welcomed. The short Thursday morning services in the parish church were soon discontinued. Something was missed thereby, chiefly perhaps the brief involvement of the day boys in school worship; but public transport, the police and conscientious teachers of the attenuated first period will have been pleased. Sunday worship by the boarders continued as before in the church with a service separate from parish matins, and a succession of chaplains developed an admirable custom of consulting with those boys who were interested about new forms of services to meet the needs of rapidly changing times. A large number of visiting preachers came, but Willatt maintained an old tradition by preaching himself, usually twice a term, and his addresses were always worth hearing for their sincerity and common-sense. Later he decided that attendance was optional for those in their last year at School, but reasonably he required that prefects should take turns to attend and control.

The first big change Willatt made was one many thought long overdue.

Guy L. Willatt

The Day Boy 'house', now enormous, with over 200 boys and quite unmanageable despite C. V. Winsor's exertions, was broken up into four. The new houses comprised those who had been attached to each of the four old games houses, and they kept the old names, Dolman Day, Gruggen Day, etc. This had the advantage that they could operate independently, as indeed they had to do for pastoral purposes (their problems being quite different from those of boarding houses) but could still combine with their boarding counterparts where desirable, especially in team games. This was particularly convenient for rugby: competitions at three age-levels between large houses were far more satisfactory than matches between very small houses where each team would embrace a vast age-range with fourteen-year-olds trying to battle against young men of eighteen. Winsor retained one of the four houses, and his experience and advice were available to housemasters newly appointed. So one of the biggest defects of the older School was finally (in so far as the dangerous word can ever be used) put right.

Pitts-Tucker had inherited from Sands a very small school which was independent for most practical purposes, and also had to be run in the most economical manner possible. These facts made it natural and even necessary for every aspect of school life to be directly controlled by the headmaster. Both Sands and Pitts-Tucker were good and meticulous administrators. But the difficulties this concentration caused were great. Willatt was determined to alter this. However, the most important step took six years to come. In 1972 Colonel James Hamilton was appointed bursar, with an office in one of the small rooms flanking the entrance to the Assembly Hall. Mr. Eric Crabtree, who had for years been devoting much of his time to the School's accounts, though still employed by the School's accountants in York, moved to do largely the same work, but as the School's direct employee, in an office in the old School building. Both required part-time clerical assistance. Thus the administrative staff was greatly increased, though no more than was needed to bring Pocklington into line with similar schools. It is unlikely that Willatt either could or would have undertaken as much detailed work of this kind as his predecessor. But by freeing himself from it he could make himself easily available, formally and otherwise, to staff and boys. In this he was helped by his own thoroughly empirical approach to problems, and also to his almost Attleeian capacity for applying the guillotine whenever endless discussion threatened, along with a gift, which was all his own, for gently but firmly ignoring anything he thought unworthy of his interest and attention.

Together with this went decentralisation in other forms. The result of it, however, was not so much a succession of new departures, (for Willatt insisted on being informed of any initiatives taken), as a general feeling of tension relaxed and a greater freedom of action. Whether this would have been equally suited to an earlier period of the School's development may be queried. But it is beyond doubt that it served the School well as it moved, along with the nation and the whole of western society, into a period when all forms of discipline and authority were fiercely challenged. Along with decentralisation went an increase in consultation. Meetings of the whole staff were not much more frequent than before, but the housemasters' meetings inaugurated by Pitts-Tucker continued, only now of course there were more housemasters to attend. In addition there were meetings of heads of departments, with the term 'head of department' interpreted broadly; for example, not merely the senior science master attended, but also the senior chemistry, senior physics and senior biology masters, so that the total membership of the 'committee' amounted to about half the full staff. One institution, however, which at the time was gaining favour in many schools, and not only the new ones, namely the 'School Council', in which boys representing various age groups met along with a selection of teachers, Willatt did not so much resist as contrive to avoid its being seriously mooted.

His attitude to the prefect system was another reflexion of his dislike of pretentiousness and self-importance. Although he made good use of his senior prefects for occasional probings into the current state of morals and morale, he was happy to accept the big change in the status, powers, prestige and importance of prefects in general that we have seen coming about under his predecessor. The whole spirit of the age and the reaction to long-standing traditions did its work without much need of a push by headmasters. On the whole, prefects continued under Willatt much as they were already becoming when he arrived, the best of them admirably attuned to the need of younger boys for help, advice and friendliness, and the worst no worse than indifferent.

Yet here too Willatt showed his insight into, and sympathy with, changing values. He saw that no longer did every senior yearn after prefectorial status. (Probably they never had done, but it had not been considered policy to admit that, for fear of devaluing the office and subverting the organisation). He put his insight into practice by making, out of the old Sanatorium in Wilberforce Lodge, a unit where sixth form boarders who preferred not to be prefects, or were not thought to be suited to the position, could lead a somewhat freer life than they could have done had they remained members of a boarding house. There was even a bar provided! The 'Unit' (another of those elliptical Pocklingtonisms) was a daring and imaginative step, and it was not surprising that it ran into trouble

in the early stages. But the appointment of D. Nuttall to supervise it
brought the right sort of balance, and the experiment persisted until after
Willatt's retirement. Whether or no it deserved permanence, it was an
example of the headmaster's breadth of outlook. He was himself a product
of an old public school, and in addition a double Blue, with a strong belief
in the traditional team games and the values attached thereto; yet he was
eminently capable of sympathising with, or at least respecting, the views
and attitudes of those very unlike himself. The bar, by the way, attracted
the brief attention of the national press, temporarily short of material.

From the preceding pages the reader will already have got a hint that the
'crisis of the late sixties', when it did arrive, never quite reached the
dimensions of a crisis at Pocklington. Nonetheless, it was a worrying time.
The writer has no intention of adding to an already long list of socio-
psychological analyses; but it may be of value to point out some factors
which made the period particularly difficult for boarding schools. Full
employment and good pay for the young made it easy for older school
children to make money by weekend jobs. Young people by and large had
more money to spare, and manufacturers of things from clothes to
gramophone records were after that money. Also, whether fortuitously or
not, young people now had, far more than ever before, heroes of their own,
like the Beatles, and martyrs, like Che Guevara. It was natural that older
children would find boarding more than a little irksome and stifling. Public
school boys (more, probably, than girls) who had been proud of their
schools, were now ashamed of them. There was much talk abroad about
'elitism', a concept which may be held to engender more heat than light; so
also with 'the System' and 'the Establishment', notions too often used with
a convenient vagueness.

As usual with times of change, much good emerged. Class snobbery
suffered a blow from which it will probably never recover. The young were
now more reluctant to obey orders 'because I say so' or accept rules 'because
they are good for you'; they wanted to know why. This forced teachers to
ask themselves why. But it was hard at the time to sort out the wood from
the trees. Take the vexed (comically vexed, it seems now) question of long
hair. To what extent was it part of the secular see-saw of fashion between
austerity and self-display? How much of it was due to the inordinate rise in
the cost of a haircut? What seems in retrospect ridiculous is that it was often
taken to be an outward and visible sign of rebellion, though in fact those
who taught through the period came to realise that it was usually nothing of
the sort. Willatt found himself bound to explain the School's policy to both
parents and Old Boys, both of which categories perhaps expected him to
take up a stern and inflexible attitude, which they neither could nor would

assume themselves. He liked to expound what he called his 'dialogue with society' (when he used portentous expressions there was usually irony just around the corner); by this he meant a strategy of alternately giving ground and fighting back from previously prepared positions. In fact he simply applied common-sense to each situation as it arose, and his only dogma, if it can be called that, was that one should never deliver an ultimatum and drive a boy into a corner from which he could not escape without complete humiliation.

Of course authority's best answer was to relax, provided that relaxation did not involve surrendering essentials. Boys of an age permitted by law were allowed to visit at weekends a public house in the town which was nominated by the headmaster. This was a limited but sensible recognition of facts, though to some lively young minds what is permitted becomes for that very reason less attractive. But on smoking Willatt remained firm and refused to follow some schools in giving limited permission. Hair was allowed to become longer and, since boys are usually in a hurry, longer meant untidier. But again there were limits, and boys could still be packed off to the barber's. Informal dress, as worn by the boys once their official duties were over, became ever more informal and even at times spectacular; but there was no weakening in the decision to keep the dark suit for wear in school hours. Permission was given at times to go to the local cinema on Saturday nights, and boys were allowed to see their parents or other visitors much more often than before. Leave to go home, even before the term ended if there was a strong case for it, was given more generously. But on the issue of Saturday morning school there was no weakening, and it was gratifying to see how loyally parents of day boys accepted something which may often have been a nuisance to them. All these matters affected boarders more than day boys; but of course they did affect day boys as well, and this was particularly important because the numbers of day boys were from now on to increase steadily vis-à-vis boarders.

During this period of stress there were possibilities of things taking an uglier turn. Pocklington was lucky to be out in the country instead of being in or very near a sizeable town. Certain university student groups were anxious to draw older school children into their subversive activities. But, though they put out feelers, the School did not suffer from them so far as is known. There was, however, some trouble with drugs. Typically Willatt refrained from holding up his hands in horror and throwing out all who had been affected. He drew a clear line between boys who made one or two experiments with drugs and those who introduced them to others. In the case of the former he regarded exposure as sufficient deterrent; but the latter had no place in a boarding school. So far as is known, the danger soon faded.

The introduction of girls into the sixth form caused remarkably little flutter, especially among the boys. One reason for this may be that it happened so gradually, with at first just one girl who was the daughter of a local bank manager; and the next year just two, one of whom was the daughter of the then chaplain, the Rev. J. M. Macnaughton, who had succeeded Duckworth. Their numbers grew slowly. There was, and there remained for a long time, no question of girl boarders, because no special accommodation could have been provided for them without an expenditure the School was not prepared to incur. If they were not residents of Pocklington or somewhere very near, rooms had to be found for them locally. Gradually the girls found ways of making valuable contributions. One obvious way was to act in School plays. A less obvious way was found by Emma Baker, daughter of the senior geography master, A. M. Baker; she became an expert cricket scorer. One of the strongest arguments against girls in boys' schools, and one naturally used by headmistresses, is that they miss the opportunities for sport which they would have enjoyed in schools of their sex. But the advance of tennis and hockey at Pocklington answered that, at least in part. *The Daily Telegraph* conducted an investigation into this phenomenon in the late seventies, and in the course of it one Pocklington girl (who had in fact already left, so unworthy suspicions of pressure can be discounted) declared that her two years at the School had been the making of her, and had even offered her opportunities she would never have found in her former school. If one said there were no untoward incidents as a result of their admission one would not be believed. But on the whole the most remarkable thing about the admission of girls is that it caused so little remark. The chief disappointment, perhaps, was that it was some time before any of them reached academic distinction. Some may still ask why they were admitted at all. It had not quite the glamour of a pioneering move; several public schools had already plunged. The plain fact was that Pocklington, like most schools, had room for extra pupils in most sixth form sets; therefore the girls brought financial gain. But the School would not have begun to admit them had it not seemed probable that, at the sixth form stage, their capacity to contribute would far outweigh any disturbing effect they might produce.

R. N. Billington, the senior art master, had for years been sending out a stream of pupils to excel in the arts and architecture, and in his very first year Willatt had been discussing with him a project of major importance. This was to develop, alongside the flourishing art department, workshops with machinery, electronic and other equipment, and to bring the whole under one roof in a building where there would be opportunity for developing imaginative and creative design, and also where every pupil in

The Design Centre

At work in the Design Centre

the first three years of the senior school could have a course in the basic techniques and ideas pursued there. The conception grew in the next few years, and a building was completed and equipped ready for use in 1970. The site was the Near Dolman just beyond the headmaster's garden. In this the School could not claim to be pioneer absolute. Sevenoaks was ahead of us, though in a less developed way; and the notion of workshops for all goes back, in a different form, to Sanderson at Oundle in the first quarter of the century. But the Pocklington School Design and Creation Centre not only became the most notable feature of the School to outside eyes but achieved nation-wide fame. Both Billington and J. R. Jeffery, who was appointed to take charge of the technical side, were for some years much in demand all over the country as expositors of something fresh and exciting in education. The Centre continued to develop and diversify its activities, and even a fire in 1974, though it did some damage, failed seriously to interrupt work there for long. There was a splendid conclusion to the first chapter, as it were, of the Centre's history when, in 1976, a team of four members of the sixth form (Andrew Blacker, Nicholas Pollard, David Quarton and Nigel Ramsden) won the B.B.C. T.V.'s 'Young Scientist of the Year' competition. It may be added here that, by an ingenious use of space, the Centre was made to include a lecture room where at a pinch and in fairly spartan conditions 80 or 90 boys might be seated. This was something the School had lacked, and many societies and other types of gathering made use of it. Since the Senior School had now outgrown the Assembly Hall, some of the forms had to be taken out of the morning assembly, and this room was a good place for them to have their own assembly.

The opening of the Centre set in motion some big changes in the organisation of the School — changes that might have come about in any case, but now were given impetus. The layout of the school week was overhauled, partly to make it possible for the first three years in the Senior School (roughly ages 11 to 14) to go through training in the Centre, and partly to make time outside school hours for boys to pursue individual projects there — a complicated task which involved much juggling with the timetable. This meant the scrapping of the former week of three games afternoons (Tuesday, Thursday, Saturday). It was in any case felt that two full games afternoons were adequate. This allowed an earlier end to afternoon school, which was good for the younger day boys and, as previously said, made time for individual work in the Centre besides giving some more time for most of the year for team practices.

But the Centre was not the only reason for making changes in the curriculum and timetable. Another was the vast increase in the numbers in the sixth form. If a boy, however mediocre his academic ability seemed to be, obtained a certain number of goodish passes at O level in the G.C.E. (four was the usual requisite), it seemed wrong to deny him two years in the sixth form if that was what he wanted — and nearly all did. However, there were not enough sixth form subjects for them all, nor masters to teach them; nor were some of the new sixth formers suited to all the more traditional subjects. Willatt felt it was time to broaden the curriculum, not on the lines of the ABC of Pitts-Tucker's time for non-examination subjects, but for G.C.E. purposes. So economics was introduced, and rapidly became so popular that the master newly appointed to teach it was soon forced to cope with two large sets in both years in the sixth, which filled his entire week! Biology had for long been taught in the sixth form but had been regarded only as an alternative to mathematics for those intent on a medical or veterinary career. This view of the subject, reasonable in a small school where something had to suffer, was much less tenable by the 1970s, with careers for biologists opening up in various spheres, and the old standard mathematics — physics — chemistry course for all scientists coming to seem less *de rigueur*. To use a modish but vivid phrase, in science as elsewhere, 'the frontiers were becoming blurred'. To accommodate all this a much more elaborate yet quite flexible system of options was devised for the sixth, and indeed something similar was needed for lower forms too. Shortly after J. H. Eggleshaw's return from war service in 1946 Pitts-Tucker handed over the still fairly simple timetable to him. From then onwards, because of the rapid growth of the School, it was necessary to make a new timetable *ab initio* every year. But by taking a couple of days off just before the end of the school year he could usually bring next year's timetable to the point where all his colleagues could be informed of their commitments next year before breaking up. The task became very much harder in Willatt's time. With typical consideration and wisdom Willatt had lightened Eggleshaw's burden as second master by appointing W. G. Beer as Administrative Officer. Beer not only gave invaluable help in the later stages of timetable construction, as in so many other sides of School life, but, as it became ever more complicated, enlisted, in a flash of inspiration, D. J. Stanton, then teaching chemistry and now (1986) senior science master. Stanton revealed a notable flair for systematising the jig-saw.

The new timetable filled up the week for the sixth form to such an extent that there was no longer room for the expansive treatment of non-examination subjects hitherto prevailing. A neater system took its place in which Wednesday afternoons were set aside for sixth formers to take a variety of subjects, each in a course lasting one term only. No single topic could now be treated as thoroughly as a few had been under ABC, but the choice offered was now far richer, and the system ensured that every sixth former did at least have a grounding in a fair number (usually five) of non-specialist topics. The number of these and their significance depended on what members of the staff were willing and able to offer; but the new system was taken seriously by the staff, and under the able organisation of T. W. Hardaker proved a success.

Several new building operations, and improvements to buildings already up — improvements we call minor only in relation to the two great visible creations of the Willatt régime — may be mentioned here. The baths were at last adapted to make them usable all the year. A new biology laboratory, made necessary by the great expansion of the subject in the School, was built on the Near Dolman to the west of the Design Centre. On the Far Dolman the new 'pavilion', which had been ingeniously made out of the remains of the old farm buildings and the *disiecta membra* of the ancient Big Field pavilion, was connected up to the new squash courts and showers installed, a development appreciated not only by members of the School but also by the town squash club. The row of cottages standing back from the road, and facing the entrance to the Dolman Drive, picturesque but dilapidated, was adapted to make a most valuable set of teaching and seminar rooms for the arts sixth — so at last, one hopes, putting an end to the long period during which most arts subjects' in the sixth had to be taught in rooms that were either too big or too small for the purpose. One might almost say that the 'holes under the stairs' at last reverted to their proper task of housing mops, buckets and fuse-boxes. The two last-mentioned building achievements were largely the work of Mr. J. Jones and his staff. Jones, the first long-service occupant of his position after the retirement of Broadhead, had finally raised that office from that of a glorified school caretaker to one of a highly skilled and imaginative craftsman whose contribution cannot be sufficiently praised.

Pocklington's monumental railway station (it is in fact a scheduled building) must have surprised countless travellers and visitors. Why so splendid an edifice, covered too, like a miniature York, to serve what was really a very small population centre, call it town (correctly) or village (as most of the ignorant did)? The explanation is probably to be found in the deference which the mid-nineteenth century considered due to the landed magnates of the East Riding. Ever since the closing of the line in the Beeching reorganisation of 1965 it had been idle. For some time in the earlier seventies all over the country enterprising local authorities and independent schools had been planning and building 'sports centres', large buildings which could provide sheltered space for unorganised recreation in bad weather together with special facilities for playing and training for a variety of games during the winter. Willatt saw marvellous possibilities in

Pocklington School Sports Hall, formerly the Railway Station.

the old station and the connected buildings. The fact that a big building, and one that was largely a sound one, was already there and ideally near the School, would mean a huge saving in costs. Three big jobs had to be done on it : the roof had to be made weather-proof, the flooring brought up to the level of the platforms, and the two ends closed in. Arthur Quarmby, an Old Pocklingtonian architect with already a number of original ideas and achievements to his credit and a nationwide reputation, was enlisted, to our great advantage. But the necessary support from outside would not have been won if the School had not been ready to share the amenities of the place with the clubs of the surrounding area. It was commonsense that the School should allow clubs from outside to use the Centre at times when it could not itself do so. A grant was thereby obtained from the Central Council for Physical Recreation. The work was begun with a will, and completed in 1974. The opening ceremony was performed in February, 1974, and graced by the presence of one of the most notable figures in English sport, Mr. Walter Winterbottom, then Secretary to the Sports Council, and formerly manager and coach to the England association football team. In its way the Sports Hall formed the perfect complement to the Design and Creation Centre. Moreover it seemed most appropriate that a fine building which had served the School since it was built in 1847 (in so far as there was a school to serve at that period) and had seen the comings and goings of so many boarders, and the antics of the legendary Hutton[1], should come so fittingly into the School's hands.

Undoubtedly the most spectacular increase in the School's size was in Pitts-Tucker's time. But it was in a way every bit as remarkable that numbers should have continued to rise during Willatt's time, which was much less of a boom period on the whole. There seemed no need to make any special moves to attract day boys. But, with the fees inevitably rising as steadily as the numbers, keeping up the boarding houses was a harder task. It was in his tireless approaches to preparatory schools that Willatt gained some of his greatest successes. In this field he ranged, as he had to, much more widely than Pitts-Tucker had, convinced as he was by his success at Heversham that he could make Pocklington look very attractive to the many British citizens who were working abroad, and to some aliens as well. It was as well this rift was mined so thoroughly, for it helped to compensate in some measure for the blow suffered when the Direct Grant was abolished.

It had long been clear that a Labour government was likely to put an end to the Direct Grant scheme, so when the blow did fall the School was not unprepared for it. For centuries the English grammar schools (and Pocklington was historically speaking a grammar school) had served all the social classes, and not just some of them. But it would be idle to deny that, more and more as time went on, schools like ours were becoming the preserve of the middle classes; and the extent to which they made room for the children of the poorer classes depended on the efficiency of the machinery for admitting them and the goodwill and co-operation of the local educational authorities. In these respects Pocklington had probably been doing rather better than most. But now a society was developing where everyone knew how everyone else was faring in the social field, and where

[1]See page 74

it was no longer possible, even if it had been reasonable, to expect schools under state control gracefully to accept a position of inferiority, with many of the pupils they had hoped to retain so as to leaven the lump being creamed off into schools which kept their independence without losing their extensive state support. Partisans of the grammar schools, and of Direct Grant schools in general, argued that their system, or something like it, had for centuries functioned to the advantage of the whole community, and that the independence of a school was in itself desirable. Unofficially they were not slow to point to the weak discipline in many (by no means all) of the schools in the state sector, as contrasted with their own schools, where a combination of tradition, devoted service by the teaching staff, and middle-class parental concern, made for much better discipline and results. To this their opponents retorted partly by denying charges of a falling off in discipline, more cogently by arguing that such a falling off was inevitable so long as the social split was perpetuated by the prevailing system. So the argument went on. It may be that the historians of the future will judge, with or without regret, that the Direct Grant had already become an anachronism through the force of changed circumstances, rather than through any inherent weakness. But Pocklington, like many other schools, could not be expected to surrender its cherished independence without a struggle, and accept control by those whom they suspected of being, whether through political partisanship or mere ignorance, incapable of governing them.

There were of course circumstances peculiar to each Direct Grant school which might affect their decisions on this issue or even their power to make such decisions. Some were undoubtedly helped by the fact that their state sector rivals in the area were inefficient. This was not the case with Pocklington. The recently established Woldgate comprehensive school was well-run and successful, and Pocklington could only claim that, for the time being at any rate, it offered a bigger selection of sixth form courses for the benefit of abler pupils. In any case, comparisons in this area can be odious; Woldgate has, more recently, won several places at Oxford. It was more to the point that Pocklington had so benefited from careful husbandry and development over the last generation that it was in a position to offer all-round educational facilities comparable with that of many more famous schools and much more cheaply. Its prospects of surviving, and indeed prospering, if it went independent were therefore bright.

When the time for decisions came the Governors were very ready to find out what the local authority (Humberside) could offer. Discussions went very amicably. The Humberside committee found much to admire in what the School was doing, and was prepared to go on doing, for children from a wide variety of homes (and not just the comfortable middle class). The Governors for their part were gratified by Humberside's appreciation and welcomed their goodwill and anxiety to come to an agreement. But chances of a mutually beneficial settlement foundered, in their opinion, on several grounds. The School's academic standards had been rising all the time, but there was no guarantee that this could be maintained if it entered into a state scheme. Moreover, it would have been prevented from recruiting outside the County's boundaries, and that would have changed decisively the whole character of the School as it was developing. In particular, such limitations would have antagonised the Old Boys. Pitts-Tucker had risked this in his drive to raise academic standards; but things were different now, and it was not as inconsistent as it seemed to feel that the School would now be wise to put some reliance on Old Pocklingtonian support. Above all, the freedom of the Governors to evolve a policy of their own would sooner or later have been infringed. It is not unfair to say that the goodwill of the local authority was cribbed by national policy. At the back of all these discussions was something the Governors could not forget: the cordial and balanced relationship they could have built up with the then local committee would not have survived a swerve to the left in the Humberside authority; and against that there would have been no redress, and almost certainly no recovery. So the steadfastness of the Governors and the conciliatory but canny diplomacy of Willatt both led to the same end — Independence, formally assumed on 18 December 1975.

Of the School's achievements in sport and other activities outside the classroom in Willatt's time more will be said in the following chapter. Only a few outstanding features will be touched on here. Willatt's first year at Pocklington corresponded with Stevenson's last year in charge of the cricket. A new coach for the Eleven was then needed, and a fall in standards seemed likely. But Willatt had already observed that he had on his staff in D. Nuttall a coach of outstanding promise. He chose him and gave him his fullest support and confidence, advice too if it was sought; though with his customary wisdom he refrained from imposing his own views. Perhaps even Willatt could not have foreseen how successful his choice would be. Under Nuttall, and despite the absence of stars like those who had given lustre to many of Stevenson's teams, the eleven proceeded to do even better than before, and that though the fixture list was further strengthened so that it included some of the best cricketing schools in the country. It must have been particularly gratifying to Willatt that in a series of matches against his old school, Repton, always played at Repton, the School usually, though not always, held its own. In rugby, for several years after Willatt's arrival, the teams, at the top level at any rate, failed to distinguish themselves. This greatly disappointed him, especially since his previous school, Heversham, had won a formidable reputation in the north-west. Gradually they improved, partly because the fixture list, though never so illustrious as that of the cricketers, was becoming stronger. It was most satisfying that Willatt's last term was adorned by a first fifteen that won all its matches.

It may be said that it was in Willatt's time that the School finally realised that it was a medium-sized school and no longer a small one. Willatt's own sporting interests in a very narrow sense were concentrated on the rugby and the cricket, whereas his predecessor was interested in tennis as well and enjoyed seeing the track and field athletics flourish. But Willatt could also distinguish between private enthusiasms and public duty. He saw clearly that both the increasing size of the School and the more open, tolerant and 'classless' attitude now prevailing in schools towards sport required that a far greater variety of activities be not only allowed but encouraged, and more and more money spent on them. This accorded with the wishes of the staff who, in the modern fashion, were less inclined to accept the narrower and intenser old attitude than to offer their own personal and varied skills and enthusiasms. It was pleasing to see that this diffusion of effort did nothing to impair the success of the traditional sports — quite the contrary, in fact. Throughout his headmastership Willatt assiduously watched everything from first team matches to the most junior practices, and let nothing keep him from this except illness or the calls of headmasterly duty elsewhere — and one had the impression that he bitterly resented the latter.

The death in February, 1971, of the School doctor, Angus Fairweather, robbed the School of a very loyal friend. There had been Fairweathers practising in Pocklington for a long time, and they had been closely connected with the School. Doctor Angus's father, A. M. A. Fairweather, had actually been Chairman of the Governors as well as school doctor. Angus himself was a true country doctor, intimately wrapped up in the life of the area and devoted to the countryman's sports. He was genuinely liked and respected for an interest in the School that far outran his obligations and made his advice valuable in many spheres. Professionally his judgement was sound and modest, he was never reluctant to seek further advice, and he never jumped to ill-based diagnoses which, in a locality so far from hospitals, might even have been dangerous to life. After his death, and with the development of the Pocklington Medical Centre, his responsibilities were split up.

Changes in housemasters are conveniently recorded here. J. H. Derbyshire left Dolman after a long and fruitful tenure, and was succeeded by R. N. Billington, who handed over to C. J. Solomon in 1978. A. J. Maltby left Wilberforce in 1967 to become headmaster of Trent College, and was followed by D. G. Whilesmith. R. T. E. Allen's memorable tenure of Lyndhurst ended at the same time as Pitts-Tucker's headmastership, and he was succeeded by an Old Boy, T. G. Currey. On the latter's departure he was followed by D. Nuttall, who in his turn gave way to A. M. Baker. But Miss Dalgliesh remained in control of the teaching in the Junior School for many years, despite a very serious and long illness. After Eggleshaw retired in 1976 the work he and Beer had covered was taken over by C. E. Martin and Beer, both now sharing the title of second master. This apparently odd arrangement proved a success, not only because of the way the two worked together, but also because Willatt trusted them to work together. Throughout Willatt's headmastership Mrs. Cottom remained his secretary, bringing all her great experience and devotion to bear on an increasingly complex task.

That doughty hero of the First World War, Lord Birdwood, was once describing in a drawing room at home an experience of his at Gallipoli, when he was inspecting the Anzac lines. 'There was a momentary lull, and I popped my head above ground level. The Turkish sniping started up again. I heard a shout: "Duck yer bloody 'ead, Birdy!" ' His audience was shocked. 'Disgraceful! What did you do?' 'I ducked my bloody 'ead, of course.' Willatt had much in common with both characters in that exchange, the Australian with his concern and lack of reverence, the Field Marshal with his humility, humour and commonsense. Willatt showed plenty of reverence for humanity and the achievements of human genius (aesthetically he was certainly no iconoclast), but none whatever for institutions or authority in the abstract. For him they had to justify themselves. Things had to be taken as they came or as they were, not as part of some mysterious cosmic pattern. Not that he was incapable of seeing the wood for the trees. 'There's a sermon in that, somewhere,' was a favourite comment of his, accompanied by a wry smile. But when he said: 'I am not a scholar', you could fairly infer, first that he was a truthful person, second that he was a modest person, third that he had a proper respect for scholarship, and last (though it would be far from his intention to imply this) that there were times when scholarship did not matter.

Asked once what he would like to be remembered for, he replied: 'For my efforts to help the ordinary boy' — a typically flat, modest and inadequate statement yet one which contains much truth. He once told the present writer that he would often 'go round the dormitories and talk to boys about their favourite football teams'. To put this more pretentiously than he ever would, he knew just how to establish communication with a shy boy. Allied to that skill was his understanding of human weaknesses. He was quite prepared to punish severely and in the old-fashioned way. But he could never accept that a boy who lied should therefore be branded a liar, or a boy who stole labelled a thief. With much tenderness and understanding, though without the slightest softness, or cynicism either, he would have sympathised with the legendary schoolboy who once wrote that a lie was 'a dreadful sin and a very present help in time of trouble'. It was good, though not surprising, to find that in return he won the affectionate regard of all, including boys who were anything but 'ordinary'. The writer once heard a young Old Pocklingtonian, who was just on the point of scoring a First at Oxford, say of him without any prompting: 'He was a marvellous headmaster'.

In his charming and affectionate tribute to Willatt in *The Pocklingtonian*, a tribute that might well have been printed here in its entirety instead of these paragraphs, his second master, D. Nuttall, wrote that 'he had the knack of giving boys and staff licence to follow their own special interests with the minimum of interference'. Herein, as much as in anything else, he showed himself the right man for his times. There was poetic justice as well as good luck in the coincidence of fourteen Oxbridge places, excellent O and A level results and unprecedentedly successful Rugby XVs and Cricket XIs in his last year.

Throughout those years Willatt had the benefit of his wife's unstinting support. Mrs. Willatt is by preference a very private person who much dislikes the limelight. But she gave her husband what he most needed, disinterested and well-informed advice, firm support as the mother of his children, and above all the warmth of a home to come back to each evening.

Willatt was the third in a succession of three headmasters each of whom, in his different way and in different circumstances, steered the School's fortunes very surely. The writer is proud, and thinks himself lucky, to have served under all three.

CHAPTER 28

EXTRA-CURRICULAR

This is in fact a bad title for a chapter dealing largely with activities which either do, or deserve to, play a part in the curriculum nowadays. But a suitable title is hard to find: 'Miscellany' sounds contemptuous, 'Sporting and Dramatic' frivolous as well as uncomprehensive. 'Extra-curricular' does mean something to those familiar with the curriculum of an old-fashioned school at the time when the author of these chapters was a schoolboy. It will have to serve. The text does at times degenerate into a mass of facts and names; but for this the writer makes no apology. In it an attempt is made to treat in more detail the more important out-of-classroom activities of the School; reference has been made to these in the two preceding chapters only when they throw a special light on the two headmasterships. Even more than those earlier chapters it will be open to criticism for omission and faulty emphasis. Again, no apology is offered; but the reader should be warned that the order in which topics are dealt with has nothing to do with their relative importance.

In the period following 1945 the School was still old-fashioned and 'public-and-grammar-school' in its attitude to sport; that is, it followed, at a distance, the pattern set by the older universities. There were but few opportunities for games like fives, played occasionally in a rare form of the game, or tennis on a couple of courts in front of the old buildings. Otherwise the year was filled by the familiar cycle of rugby football until about three weeks into the Lent term; then cross-country (practised compulsorily and in the mass, as an inter-house competition) followed by track and field athletics in what remained of the term; then cricket in the summer, with some swimming. A rigorous application of this routine could not possibly be justified nowadays, and may have been unjustified even in, say, 1950. At best it seems defensible on two main grounds: firstly the School was very small and poor, with no financial resources to gratify individual choices, so that it could have seemed better to concentrate on a few things and try to do them well; and secondly that, when the School did achieve something notable in any of these limited fields, one felt a general glow and rise in morale which even the less active seemed to share. But perhaps this too was an illusion. There were few ways in which those less gifted in team sports could make their feelings known, at any rate while they were still at school; yet things were changing to the extent that a gifted boy might come right through to be Head of the School even though his gifts were unrelated to the playing fields. When the changes did come, they came at least partly through the initiative of younger members of the staff who brought fresh ideas and interests. Of their elder colleagues it might be said that they at least showed a certain lack of intolerance.

Rugby football has been the School's winter game for a long time. In Pitts-Tuckers's years the standard reached by the first fifteen was rarely more than modest, although in 1948 a strong but inconsistent team had big wins over Leeds and Wakefield. Gradually a reputation was built up of a side with a pack conspicuous for strength and stamina; but the backs rarely won praise for anything more than a brave defence. It is odd, therefore, that there was a moment in the sixties when there were three O.P. England trialists, and two of these were backs. These were the late David Bell, an indomitable full back who won a 'Trial' when on National Service, but was subsequently out of the game for a couple of seasons because of what seemed a ruined knee, and yet came back to captain a successful Yorkshire side and get another Trial; and Patrick Briggs, who won a Blue at Cambridge as fly-half, though he lost his place in the following season, surely without dishonour, to the greatest of all post-war rugby backs, C. H. Gibson, and who later, while teaching at Bedford School, became a coach at national level after being a renowned tactician and captain of the Bedford and East Midland sides for years. The forward trialist was Gordon Garside, in his day a magnificent prop. Only the 1963-4 side, appropriately since it coincided with the School's 450th anniversary, won all its matches, if only just. It was a very small, light team of great character, with a captain of courage and wit, the fly-half Jeremy Shaw, and a defence that was ferocious and of great depth, with a fine goal-kicker in Richard Allen. During most of those years, however, the record of some junior sides was better than that of the first fifteen; this may have been due partly to the many changes in first team coach (although D. G. Whilesmith must be mentioned as coach of the 1963-4 side). But the main reason was probably that at a junior level Pocklington coaching was as a rule technically better and more devoted than that of most of our opponents. Improvement at the top came, as it often does, when the fixture list was extended and improved. In 1980 probably the best rugby vintage the School has seen rose to the top, and, although it had for various reasons lost most of its most gifted backs en route up the School, showed itself decisively better as a first fifteen than all its opponents. A little earlier, David Rose had played for England senior boys at No. 8, and he in 1980 was followed to those heights by the late Nigel Castleton in the same position. In these latter years the fifteen has gained something like the confidence the cricketers had long since acquired.

Cricket was, for most of the period under review, much more clearly a success at Pocklington. The first years after the war, however, were not auspicious. The first eleven still played its matches on the old Big Field where years of neglect and misfortune had caused blockage in the drainage, so that the square had become a sort of pudding, which gave little encouragement to either batsman or bowler. All the more credit therefore to Malcolm Bradshaw and Gerry Wood, both of whom contrived to make hundreds on it; also to Gordon Watt, an attacking bowler of great and varied resource. G. N. Thornton took over the team for four seasons before going to Dulwich to do likewise, and in two of them the side was unbeaten. M. H. Stevenson's arrival to succeed him in 1955 coincided with the inauguration of the new War Memorial ground. It is a fine field in a lovely setting, with those three great chestnut trees in the background; but the square has never been entirely satisfactory, partly perhaps because not enough money was available for it in the first stages. However, for serious cricket, conditions had now become immeasurably better than before. Stevenson, a Cambridge Blue and county player, not only had the fixture list improved, but himself dispensed with professional help and worked with great energy and enthusiasm at the nets, raising standards remarkably. Without neglecting those of moderate ability — indeed several, who normally would have been regarded as merely filling up the eleven, achieved an average of about 40 with the bat — he concentrated on certain boys with exceptional gifts. He was lucky in that during his twelve seasons he had some outstanding players: Michael Rose, who made a great impression at Lords in a Schools Trial and won his Blue at Cambridge, the remarkable all-rounders Patrick Briggs and Tim Hughes, Colin Johnson, who played many times for Yorkshire, and that most gifted left hand batsman, Paul Jackson.

The arrival of Willatt brought the still greater encouragement of a former county cricket captain as headmaster. But it was during Pitts-Tucker's last term, while Willatt was briefly visiting the school he was shortly to take over, that Pocklington cricket scored its weirdest triumph. Leeds Grammar School, batting first on their own ground, were put out for 4 (Roy Flitton 5 for 0, Michael Lewis 5 for 1), and then Colin Johnson hit his first ball for a single and Paul Jackson the next for six.

Under D. Nuttall, who took over in 1968, the School's cricket became healthier still. The fixture list, with the headmaster's help, became much stronger: rival Yorkshire schools like Ampleforth and St. Peter's were at last added, and quite often beaten. Willatt even brought Repton into the catchment area; this fixture, always played at Repton, has provided an excellent series of games in which the School has usually, though not always, held its own. The difficulties inherent in cricket's having to compete with the usual English summer weather followed by examinations, were largely overcome by dividing the season roughly into three parts: May with its more traditional school fixtures in spartan conditions courageously borne; June relaxed and mainly devoted to clubs enjoying the title of Gentlemen, but including the M.C.C.; and July a great flurry of matches with a series of very strong opponents, both home and away, often quite distant — Sedbergh, Edinburgh Academy, and even, once, Haileybury (we won, a story that would have graced the *Magnet*). There was probably no one in these sides of Nuttall's as gifted as several in Stevenson's, except Jeffrey Guillen from Trinidad, a grand forcing bat. But any amount of good cricket was played, many games were won, and there were several outstanding captains: Alistair Woodhead, Alistair Shanks and, perhaps best of all, Alistair Brumfield, a rare blend of aggression and sportsmanship. Nuttall's greatest achievement has probably been to get his side to see that risking defeat is always worthwhile when there is the slightest chance of victory.

Accounts of school cricket such as these naturally tend to dwell on leading figures and highlights. But much good cricket was played all the way down the School. The very fast-drying San Square gave under-15 and under-14 sides an excellent stage; and a new wicket, and new nets, on the furthest Far Dolman allowed the under-13 to develop sides several of which in the seventies were unbeaten. The third eleven had a country-house style all of its own. The headmaster found plenty of cricket to watch, and no one could accuse him of not taking advantage of these riches. The encouragement his mere presence gave cannot be over-estimated.

The Pixies Club, founded by M. H. Stevenson, must not be forgotten. Almost, though not exclusively, manned by past and present members of the School, its chief annual function was and is to run a summer cricket week in Sussex and Kent. But one memorable year it actually reached the final of the Cricketer National Knock-out Competition.

The old Oxbridge pattern followed for so many years put track and field athletics in a position that was favourable in that at least for one part of the year it was the School's principal sporting activity, but unfavourable because it had to be practised in what were often most disagreeable weather conditions. However, a further justification for it was found in the fact, if it was a fact, that rugby was beginning to pall by then. Also the grounds were deemed unfit for hockey. So rugby fixtures and house matches ended after about three weeks in the Lent term, followed by some weeks of concentrated cross-country training for all, culminating in the inter-house races in which everyone who was not medically unfit had to run. The old course to the west of the Big Field was abandoned when the airfield was built, and after the war a new course was devised which included a strenuous crossing of Chapel Hill, hitherto dear in the eyes of Pocklingtonians because of its toboggan track. After cross-country came track and field athletics, occasionally blessed by a precociously mild spring.

Inspiration came above all from an O.P. member of the staff, G. F. D. Pearson, whose theoretical knowledge and coaching expertise were recognised nationally; indeed, for some years the best one-volume English book on the sport, with chapters written by a galaxy of experts, was still more expertly edited by him. His enthusiasm was enormous, but his relentless perfectionism led him, much though he gloried in the School's achievements as a team, to concentrate on a small number of picked performers, most of whom distinguished themselves nationally, like: Gerry Wood in the shot, Gordon Ewen in the sprints and Robert Cross (an Oxford Blue) at the middle distances.

For the School in general the four week 'season' embraced a Standards competition as well as the more conventional house championships. Then matches were introduced, first with Bootham School, then with Barnard Castle. Not very long after the war, East Riding Schools' Championships in the summer began, and boys from the School were allowed to compete so long as they did not neglect their other commitments; some got so far as to represent Yorkshire in the All-England Championships and did well at that level. The most spectacular development after this was the one already referred to, the series of six triangular matches against Abingdon and Stamford in the Whitsun break, held at each school in turn. The then headmaster of Abingdon, now Sir James Cobban, achieved a *coup de théâtre* in securing the Iffley Road track for venue when Abingdon were hosts. But even such gamesmanship failed to prevent us from winning every match decisively; the thrill of performing where the present Master of Pembroke College ran the first four minute mile only spurred our athletes on. Gradually athletics became established in the summer for a number of specialists, and matches were arranged then, of which the most memorable was probably the first with Ampleforth College in 1963, a fine victory remarkable above all for the performances of Ralph Buckton, probably the most versatile athlete we have ever had, excelling not only at high jump but also long jump, triple jump, sprints and hurdles. He and Cross, who at mile and half-mile was even more unassailable, formed a terrifying double obstacle to any opposing school. The early and middle sixties were a remarkable period for athletics at Pocklington under A. J. Maltby, himself a Cambridge Discus Blue, who organised the sport as capably as he did everything else he touched, and his successor, S. Whitehouse.

As a more modern pattern for the sport of the School emerged, the inter-house competition was moved into the summer. For some time athletics was less successful, as the world understands success, than it had been. But in the late seventies, under the very able direction of W. G. Beer, it regained much of its former glory, with a longish fixture list and much success at three age levels. The switch to metric distances meant that, for a time at any rate, it was pointless to talk about records on the track; but David Rose was a most formidable performer on the track in the middle distances, while there is no doubt that Walter Nisbet beat Buckton's high jump record. By the end of the seventies the teams were at least holding their own with every northern school they met.

The sport which has made most progress since the School's activities were diversified is certainly tennis. A. J. Maltby, who did so much for athletics, applied similar authority and enthusiasm to tennis, and after him C. J. Solomon and T. W. Hardaker watched over the development of the game and the improvement of its facilities. As regards the latter, the crucial development was the creation of a line of grass courts along the Dolman Drive and slightly encroaching on the Near Dolman. Hard work by the School's ground staff and sensible use by the School have brought these courts to a surprising excellence. Although, a little after the period strictly covered by these chapters, some of the courts were surrendered for the building of the new dining hall, the School remains one of the few in the North still equipped to play grass-court matches. Two hard courts were built as early as 1965, but the main development belongs to the eighties. The Sports Hall also offers the chance of some indoor practice all the year round.

In the earlier half of our period the licence to opt for tennis in the summer was given only to some seniors; but before long, exceptions were being granted to some juniors also. What had in the mid-sixties been a small fixture list reserved for seniors only had by 1980 become quite a long list with several matches arranged for juniors as well as seniors, and the total number of boys taking tennis as their chief summer sport approaching 100. By then there were also enough girls in the sixth to undertake matches with girls' schools. Whether quantity preceded quality or not, already in the seventies the First VI several times reached the final of the Yorkshire section of the Glanvill Cup (the national schools knock-out competition) and in 1982 won it under the captaincy of Robert Neal.

Swimming has played its part at the School since before the war, but its development has been much handicapped by the shortcomings of the School bath. No doubt in the pre-1939 period the School had, by contrast with some of its rivals, something to boast about in the possession of a bath at all. But its value was strictly limited in two ways: it was entirely open-air and without any changing accommodation, and it was within a few feet of a railway line and a number of trees. Hence, the East Riding weather being what it was, and is, it offered no attractions to any but the hardiest until at least the month of May was out; and even then it was usually dirty and full of coal dust and leaves. Not long after the war 'Jock' Watt arrived, and his enthusiasm could not fail to awaken a response and improve standards. Throughout our period there were fixtures with other schools; but, although the teams were rarely overwhelmed, they suffered badly for lack of facilities when most of their opponents by now had either good baths of their own or local facilities for swimming all the year round. Our performances improved as the bath did. But, even when a roof, heating and a cleaning system were installed, for a long time it was deemed too expensive to keep it going except for the summer term and the first few weeks of the Michaelmas term. The inter-house swimming sports continued with their finals held as the very last event of the last day of the School year. For some good swimmers and their parents this made a splendid finale, but others were perhaps in too much of a hurry to get away.

Fives too had been a Pocklington School activity for a long time, but only in the exotic form of the Winchester game, and in an unprepossessing court stowed away at the back of the laboratories. It was played by very few, and indeed in the post-war period was kept alive, or rather resuscitated, only for the annual inter-house competition, and then only by the enthusiasm of that quintessential O.P. traditionalist, G. F. D. Pearson. Eventually a more workaday use was found for the court. The story of squash at the School is more inspiring. Its inauguration came with the opening of courts in 1966, and its promotion was yet another contribution by A. J. Maltby at the end of his fruitful sojourn at Pocklington, before he went to be headmaster of Trent College. From then on a small number of fixtures with other schools has been played, with a steady improvement in standards, as supervision was taken over, first by C. J. Solomon, then by M. W. Woodruff and P. S. Thornley. Probably the best opportunity of improving standards by competition has been offered by the York and District Squash League. Some good players have already emerged, with Stephen Mulligan, who represented Yorkshire at junior county level, outstanding.

Earlier it was suggested that hockey at the School was ruled out because adequate pitches could not be found. Perhaps it would be truer to say that, in a small and very economically run school, it was never seriously considered until recently. It came in eventually, partly inspired by young members of the staff, T. Riseborough and later S. J. Bosworth, partly when the number of girls in the sixth began to give the game a claim it had not enjoyed till then. Where there is a will ... It was found that part of the War Memorial cricket ground outfield was level enough to make hockey possible without undue danger. Fixtures were soon arranged, and before long we had a side able to hold its own with schools which had been playing the game for years.

This account of the School's sport inevitably leaves gaps. No reference has been made to boxing, in which 'Jock' Watt made yet another contribution; nor to fencing, which has been encouraged by R. N. Billington and has produced some good performers on occasion. Shooting, where the School had its moments of glory on a national level, is mentioned under C.C.F., for at Pocklington it could only have developed under the patronage of the latter.

★   ★   ★   ★

Drama at the School in our period falls into three chronological sections: the Winsor period, the Stevenson years, and lastly a period not dominated by any one producer. For about ten years C. V. Winsor, ably abetted by his wife, gave us a series of productions marked by the variety of plays selected. Indeed, though all the casts that performed under him learned much about acting and gave much pleasure, perhaps the most notable of the lessons they learned and taught others was the ecumenical nature of drama. Shakespeare we had, naturally, and also Shaw and, an English nineteenth-century rarity only recently exhumed, Boucicault's *London Assurance;* but also Molière (twice: here Winsor's interest in and knowledge of French culture helped), Goldoni and Gogol. Some performances stood out, of which the writer, arbitrarily maybe, selects two, Brian Worthy's Tartuffe and Eric Roseberry's Mark Antony.

M. H. Stevenson had not been long with us before he showed that his merits as producer equalled his virtues as a cricket coach. He was extremely demanding, but the results appeared to justify all his demands. Under him décor, though not neglected, still played a limited part; sheer acting and dramatic tensions, humorous or serious, dominated. Though some might criticise his interpretations, while others felt that his productions were to an excessive degree producer's *tours de force,* his critics always risked the charge of sour grapes, so successful were his results. The writer can only say from his experience that no other school productions he has ever seen anywhere else were so consistently good; despite the limitations imposed upon him, there were never any conspicuous weaknesses. Therefore it is hard to select any particular production or individual performance for special praise. However, Ted Maidment's Bottom and the late Andrew Hutton's Willy

Loman are memorable, and, among the productions taken as wholes, *Death of a Salesman*. The School Pageant which Stevenson both wrote and put on in 1964 as part of the celebrations, though not so completely successful, was remarkable for the imaginative use he made of the meagre historical material and his manipulation of large forces.

It is to the credit of J. B. Birch that he broke the 'sex barrier'. The first girl in a School play was Stephanie Danby of Woldgate School, in 1968. Shortly after, girls began to arrive in the sixth form and made their own regular and valuable contribution, though this did not reach an exceptional level until after 1980 with Amanda Jeffery's admirable Juliet in a fine production by Martin Allison, O.P. and member of the staff. During this period there were good productions by T. W. Hardaker and C. E. Martin as well as Birch; outstanding among these was probably Martin's *Taming of the Shrew;* but the years were notable for the development of drama as an important activity throughout the School and not merely a 'first fifteen dramatic'. This came about in more than one way: there were the junior productions, in which field M. D. Aubrey in his brief sojourn on the staff showed a special flair; and there was also the promotion of drama as part of the annual House Arts Festival which began in 1967. All in all, this was a thoroughly healthy development, and one more way in which Pocklington was emerging from its Middle Ages.

Among those O.P.s who have become known to a much wider public are Dudley Foster, a favourite television actor in crime plays, Alec Sabin, Colin Hamilton, whose reputation was made on the U.S. stage and maintained in television there, and much more recently Adrian Edmondson, a School Hamlet in 1974 and now a hero of the younger generation. Martin Crimp has won commendation for some one-act plays written for radio. However none of these is as yet an internationally renowned figure as Tom Stoppard undoubtedly is. At school in the early fifties, he declined to jump through the usual academical hoops but went into journalism; it was while he was still a journalist that he began to write plays for the radio and develop his particular style. His first great stage success, *Rosenkrantz and Guildenstern are Dead*, has been played, and studied, all over the world — including Pocklington, for it was the 1969 School play. Since then his writings have steadily broadened, and deepened. Many O.P.s who are not regular theatre-goers will have seen his television play, *Professional Foul*, and been thrilled by its rare blend of wit and compassion, word-play and moral commitment.

The musical activities of the School were almost too insignificant to be noticed until in 1948 Pitts-Tucker appointed W. M. Ross as a Director of Music. Although Ross stayed only for a short time, his work on the Choir at least gave a hint of what should and could be attempted; a performance of Bach's *Sleepers Wake!* cantata will be remembered by some who took part in it. F. A. Sefton Cottom was appointed in his place.

It was difficult in those days to create a strong musical side in a small school in a comparatively remote and sparsely populated area, especially since the day boys (so rapidly becoming a large part of the School) often had long distances to travel. In such circumstances progress, particularly on orchestral lines, could only be made with any ease if there was a nucleus of musicians on the staff or at any rate in the locality; but no such resources were then available. Therefore it was unreasonable to expect that Pocklington could play a great part in that marvellous metamorphosis of England in the post-war period from the *Land ohne Musik* into a great nest of singing, and playing, birds. Vocally, the most important thing at first seemed the Choir which led the singing at Sunday services. For several years it actually rehearsed in school hours, an advantageous but questionable arrangement since a fast growing part of the School had no part in these services, except at Commemoration.

However, there was much progress under Sefton Cottom, on two fronts. At the 'top' the School did at one time achieve a remarkable series of choral awards at Cambridge — successes due to Cottom's own scholarship and musicianship, but perhaps as much to the vocal training of a visiting teacher from York, the late E. Meadows. But Cottom also evolved liaisons with three Yorkshire girls' boarding schools for the purpose of mounting choral works in which the girls supplied treble and alto lines. It was in a way unfortunate that our younger boys were left out of this, but it was inevitable. Besides, it has always been hard to secure their voluntary co-operation in large numbers, whereas in all probability the girls loved it. Moreover it made a valuable breach in the monastic, and no doubt the conventual, ramparts. One should add that it was always possible for the occasional boy to take music as part of his regular timetable, even though he was no great singer. The younger boys did of course have their opportunity in the Choir, which had its moment of glory at the Commemoration Service in York Minster in 1964.

It has already been mentioned that in Pitts-Tucker's time arrangements were regularly made for the entertainment of boarders on Saturday nights. During those days some notable artistes came. There were two chamber opera groups, including the then famous Intimate Opera, also once a small chamber orchestra, and a number of celebrated instrumentalists such as Evelyn Rothwell (Lady Barbirolli), the eminent oboist, and Archie Camden, the greatest bassoonist of his day. Perhaps the most popular of all these visitors in the realm of serious music was James Blades with his famous demonstration lecture on percussion instruments of every size and type; they filled our stage. There were also in those days inter-house music competitions, to which some notable musicians were invited to adjudicate. The earlier years of Willatt's tenure were less notable, until S. J. Dodsworth, who had been appointed assistant on the permanent staff to Cottom, backed by the now growing number of musical enthusiasts, and performers, on the staff, started a new series of annual performances of choral works, beginning most auspiciously with Haydn's *Nelson Mass* in 1974. These were done with a choir drawn entirely from School resources, but Dodsworth showed himself adept at finding soloists and raising an adequate orchestra from the hinterland.

During this period the School also produced a series of pianists capable of solo performances as well as the exacting and indispensable job of accompanist at choral rehearsals. Of these probably H. G. Southern was outstanding; he continued to do very well at Cambridge. Also, the House Arts Festival was all the time giving the opportunity to aspiring musicians to take the plunge of public performance.

This summary account can hardly find a place for the visual arts. For most of the period here reviewed, even before the Design and Creation Centre went up, R. N. Billington had been inspiring some splendid and original work which could be appreciated at annual exhibitions, and sending up to the colleges a number of very promising artists, architects and designers.

The pre-war Cadets had during the Second World War swollen into a large contingent with both army and air force sections. When the war ended the latter section ceased. W. E. (Major) Whitehouse remained in charge of the army cadets until he was superseded in 1947 by J. H. (Major, later Lieut. Colonel) Derbyshire, about the same time as the contingent changed its name to Combined Cadet Force (C.C.F.). Soon the arrival of 'Jock' Watt as R.S.M. as well as gym instructor helped to raise the standards of drill, turn-out and discipline. The earliest of the camps in summer was attended by just nine members of the School contingent, but these were worthy pioneers, and included Keith Appelbee, now a Governor of the School, and James Hall, who eventually left the Royal Navy with the rank of Commander. A series of successful and well-attended summer camps followed, in which our contingent, it may be claimed, made a most favourable impression and in various operations more than held its own with those from much more famous schools. Camps were held first at sites in Britain, but later in Northern Ireland and Western Germany. In a still later development there were under C.C.F. auspices several 'arduous training' ventures in tough conditions and difficult country at less congenial times of the year.

'At home' the C.C.F. got much benefit from acquiring in 1959 the rough six-acre field between the Far Dolman and Big Field. It was kept rough, to provide good opportunities for exercises of all sorts in the modern military manner, and obstacle courses ideal for inter-house competitions on Inspection Day. Activities widened through enlightened Army policy and imaginative use by the contingent of the new opportunities offered; there were chances of learning about driving and vehicle maintenance, signalling and radio, among much else. The Annual Inspection by high-ranking officers of Northern Command, formerly a matter of parade drill, guard-mounting and manoeuvres by the Band, became a far more varied and sophisticated affair.

In 1967, after 20 successful years, Colonel Derbyshire handed over the command to Major D. G. Whilesmith, though he continued to give more modest but valuable service supervising the R.E.M.E. section. It gave him, both then and later, satisfaction and entertainment as well to watch the career of his eldest son Christopher in the Army. C.J. has been C.O. of the R.E.M.E. Depot at Arborfield, one of the senior lecturers at the R.E.M.E. 'university' of Shrivenham, and more recently Senior Army Colonel with Commando Forces, Royal Marines.

Para-military training in schools naturally attracts much criticism nowadays, and not only from pacifists, although paradoxically it was easier to justify it once National Service had ended than previously. This criticism, which there is no point in discussing here, was in part met by Willatt when he decided to reorganise the position of the C.C.F. in the structure of the School by making it normally obligatory (there were exceptions, as for instance Scouts) to enter it in the fourth year of the senior school (i.e. roughly at 14 plus) and stay in it three years, after which it became entirely voluntary. This settlement, which had the virtue of simplicity, may have pleased no one entirely, but it was very understandable and convenient.

Apart from Christopher Derbyshire the School has produced a good number of officers for the Armed Forces, some of whom have distinguished themselves in very unpleasant conditions, such as Aden some years ago, and, of course, Northern Ireland.

Along with the six-acre field in 1959 the contingent acquired a shooting range. After this the standard of shooting rose considerably, and for a while it was found worthwhile to compete at Bisley. In 1965 the School VIII, led by Peter Haynes, actually scored more points than any other school at the Bisley competitions; they won the Public Schools' Snap and the Public Schools' Aggregate Trophy.

The Scout (formerly 'Boy Scout') movement had its part in the life of the

School, both for its intrinsic merits, and because conservative views of adolescence about 1945 set great store by Isaac Watt's contention that idle hands give Satan opportunities for promoting mischief. In the tightly-controlled timetable its inevitable purpose was to occupy boys too young for the C.C.F. at the same time as the latter paraded. It was, however, conceded throughout our period that some boys should, for various reasons (which included their own enthusiasm for scouting or their parents' objection to para-military activities), be allowed to remain in the movement right through their school careers. Hence the progression from Cubs (formerly Wolf Cubs) through Scouts to the Corps. It should be added, however, that the sort of general obligation there was to join the C.C.F. was never applied rigorously to all the younger boys; and, for much of our period, this latitude was given to boarders as much as to day boys.

Scouting, with its ideal of freer discipline, lent itself less well to the aim of profitably and creatively filling a fixed hour or two per week than the C.C.F. Therefore, although much of value was done in these fixed periods (former Scouts still recall the construction, use and dismantling of an aerial ropeway capable of getting a patrol across a 30 ft. ravine), probably the School Troop's most memorable achievements were at holiday camps both at Easter and in the summer. Easter camps were mainly for Venture Scouts (an improved development from the old Senior Scouts) and some were real adventures, like the one in Borrowdale which came to an abrupt end when a flash flood caused the camp to be broken up in the middle of the night.

By 1970 the numbers in the Scouts had risen to about 150, which required much devoted work by adults and older boys. Among so many helpers it is invidious to select. For much of our period A. G. Howe was in his modest way an indispensable leader, and those who had only known him as senior modern languages master were delighted to discover his breadth of interests, friendliness and wry sense of humour. T. G. Currey also gave good service, inspiration and leadership both as boy and later as master. Among several outstanding boy leaders perhaps Stephen English stands out for his drive and initiative, which inspired even more than they exhausted his fellow scouts. Never was a Scouter more 'prepared'. Alastair Lauckner was a lively young Scout who died by accident while doing a valuable Scout's job. The marquee which his parents presented to the Troop in a moving response to their bereavement proved most valuable. Miss Dalgliesh, accepting that it was her duty as head of the Junior School to run the Cubs, tackled her job with the same fierce enthusiasm and meticulous devotion as she gave to her other services to the School.

Pocklington, like the East Riding in general, has always been in danger of being cut off from the rest of the world or, what is worse, behaving as though it were, and a small, mainly boarding school in that area was particularly open to that charge. Although the Second World War and all the changes that followed it had much to do with breaking down or at any rate breaching this isolation, it was all too easy in so confined an environment to be obsessed by little local issues and forget that there was a world outside where misfortunes and injustices were on an utterly different scale. Occasionally some good cause in a far-off land impinged on the Pocklington consciousness: In 1961, for example, the plight of refugee children in Algeria came home to us; and a prefect of imagination and energy, John Foxcroft, organised in 48 hours, first the assemblage of numerous wheelbarrows, and then their filling with all sorts of offerings collected from the surrounding area. On a more regular basis Pitts-Tucker insisted that the various houses should collect two or three times each term for some charity, preferably of their own choosing. It was perhaps inevitable that juniors gave more generously than seniors; the youngsters were, to their credit, much more unthinkingly altruistic than their seniors, apart from understanding less well the value of money. But the idea was a good one, and perhaps it is a pity it did not outlast Pitts-Tucker's period. However, a little before the latter retired, a junior member of the staff, A. Lee, subsequently second master of Rugby School and now headmaster of Solihull, suggested that some seniors who found the C.C.F. irksome might in their last year at School be released to form a social service unit. It is said he was told that the idea would be accepted if he undertook the formation himself. This he gladly did, and, when he left, C. J. Solomon took over what is now the School's Community Service Unit — one of the first such in English schools. Its expansion of interests has been remarkable and admirable, embracing work with handicapped children at Kingsmill Special School, Driffield, and with under-privileged London children on holiday in the East Riding, and even work in the remoter hinterland of Kenya, where the contributions of Tim Dowling deserve special mention.

The School magazine (*The Pocklingtonian*) calls for a brief though maybe contentious paragraph, particularly because of its value to the researcher. Perhaps nothing in the life of English schools in the last thirty or forty years more aptly symbolises the changes that have taken place therein than the magazines. About the time the Second World War finished Pocklington was doubtless typical in this respect. Under the supervision, first of G. F. D. Pearson, geography master and unofficial O.P. archivist, and later of J. H. Eggleshaw, when he could find the time, the magazine remained above all a record of what happened, regularly published three times a year; it always contained 'School Notes' contributed by the headmaster, an editorial usually written by a boy editor on faintly *Times*-Fourth-Leader lines, a ragbag of miscellaneous doings gathered under the time-honoured and, fortunately, false title of *De Omnibus Rebus,* and records of the School's sporting and other activities, if possible written by boys and painfully extracted from them at a time when their minds were chiefly concentrated on the approaching holidays. It is not surprising that to newcomers to the staff who were interested in creative writing it all seemed irredeemably dull. The writer, who has tried, however unsuccessfully, in these pages to obscure his own opinions, believes that a compromise was at one stage achieved which was, in theory at any rate, ideal, with *The Pocklingtonian* continuing substantially as it was, but accompanied by a fairly extensive Literary Supplement (a notion borrowed from Merchant Taylors' School, London, of which an O.P. English master, the late D. J. Coulson, afterwards headmaster of three schools in succession, was the begetter), offering plenty of scope for original writing in prose and verse. Unfortunately it became harder and harder, in the face of all the competition and criticism, to obtain willing and lively co-operation from the boys for the more conventional part, though it could be achieved with distinction, as was shown by a longish article written about the two-day U.S.A. 'school' for the sixth formers in 1965. (The writer, Christopher Hird, has later achieved fame, first in student journalism, then with the *New Statesman,* more recently as a television investigator). The magazine in its present form is distinguished for other things than the impossibility of placing it on any normal bookshelf. It is very lively, much more so than its forerunners, and often well-written, and its contributions more often than not show genuine imagination. At the same time it is undeniably a record in its own fashion of the opinions and feelings of the writers, and as such will or should be of interest to readers even in the distant future. But its rare and irregular appearances have made it, *experto credite,* not easy for an historian to use. To be fair, it was not intended to be.

If these chapters are read at all, it will be mainly by former pupils of the School. So it would seem appropriate to end this chapter with a few lines about the Old Pocklingtonians' Club. Its oldest members will always remember Tom Pay with gratitude; he knew them all and he took the warmest interest in their careers. He was succeeded in the secretaryship by Eric Eldred, an O.P. himself as well as a member of the School staff: this latter qualification has proved hitherto almost an obligatory one for the post, and, though it may not continue to be so as the number of day boys continues to pass that of the boarders, it will remain valuable if only because it affords easy contact with the headmaster and his secretariat. By his devotion to his tasks Eldred won the affection of many. After he retired from the post on leaving the district, J. H. Derbyshire took over, and made a contribution to the larger community comparable with his achievements as a teacher and with the C.C.F. Under him there was a big development of regional meetings. These were now no longer confined to London, Oxford and Cambridge (in fact the Oxford meetings had ceased when Derbyshire took over), but extended at times to the North-East, Lancashire-and-Cheshire, Malton, Leeds, Hull, Nottingham, the South-West and a revived Oxford gathering. Derbyshire himself was assiduous in promoting these and attending himself. On his sadly early death, another O.P. member of the staff, M. G. Milne, took over. The Club is as lively as ever under the relaxed guidance and co-ordination of Malcolm Milne.

ANTHONY DERWENT PICKERING
(1981-)

In the eighties the School has undergone distinctive changes to accommodate and contain a new social climate under the headmastership of Anthony D. Pickering, M.A. (Christ Church, Oxford), who had previously been a housemaster, head of department and 1st XV rugby coach at Wellington College, Berkshire.

Tentative expansion into timbered classrooms adjacent to the enlarged biology area was consolidated by a more confident return to bricks and mortar with the building of a new dining hall on the Dolman Drive. Not only is the building aesthetically pleasing, especially in comparison with the functional extensions of recent years, but the introduction of a canteen system led to a better range and quality of food. At the same time the grass tennis courts were replaced with an all-weather surface on the C.C.F. site.

Empty kitchen and dining space in the senior Houses was then used mainly to create study/bedrooms for sixth formers, for whom spartan communal boarding conditions are no longer acceptable. The purchase of 'Faircote' from the Fairweather family in 1984 has enabled the School to take up to 20 girls as boarders. The Lodge, formerly Wilberforce Lodge, was sold to cover the costs of buying and converting 'Faircote'. At the same time the headmaster ceased to be housemaster in School House and accommodation for a housemaster and his family was created at the front of the School.

The number of young boarders has been steadily eroded but the demand for day places, especially in the sixth form, has increased. Day boys and girls in the sixth form now have common rooms in the new day block situated between the gymnasium and the tuck shop. Overall numbers reached 740 in 1987.

Academic standards have remained consistent and the School benefits from the provision of approximately 135 Assisted Places under the scheme introduced by the Government in 1981 to help families with limited incomes to take advantage of independent education. Also, the School awards £75,000 annually in scholarships and bursaries. In 1983 there was a rare peak of achievement when 14 boys gained places at Oxford and Cambridge, eight of them with scholarships or exhibitions.

The introduction of G.C.S.E. coincided with a spontaneous shift in the

The Dining Hall

Inside the Dining Hall

academic programme. Demand for Design Centre courses grew naturally and they now share with music their rightful position in the balance of G.C.S.E. subjects. A computer centre was created at the top of the day block and in the plans connected with the 1985 Appeal there will shortly be a new electronics laboratory and three classrooms between the old laboratories and the swimming pool. In 1989, the Library will move to the former Schoolhouse dining room to make way for a new science lecture theatre and this, it is hoped, will be a fitting way to celebrate the School's 475th birthday!

The School Chapel

APPENDIX A
SOURCES FOR THE EARLIER HISTORY OF THE SCHOOL
(1514 to 1754)

1. *5th Educational Report of the Charity Commissioners*, 1818 (pp.482-3).
2. *Report No. XIX of the Charity Commissioners*, 1828 (p. 541 and Appendix, p. 619).
3. An article by A. F. Leach on 'The Foundation and Re-foundation of Pocklington School' in the *East Riding Antiquarian Society's Transactions*, 1897.
4. *Victoria County History of Yorkshire* (Vol. I, pp. 463-6).
5. An article on 'Pocklington School and Pocklington Church' by A. D. H. Leadman in the *Yorkshire Archaeological Journal*, Vol. XIV. (But this contains several inaccuracies and should be read in conjunction with Leach's article, No. 3 above.)
6. The License for the foundation of Guild and School (24 May, 1514) may be seen in the Public Record Office. Exemplars of the deed granting scholarships and of the deed of 1551 re-founding the School are kept in St. John's College Muniment Room and by the Governors of the School.
7. A typed extract of entries in the St. John's College Register of Admissions of Scholars and Fellows, kindly supplied by Mr. F. P. White, Fellow of the College. It is now in the possession of the Governors.
8. The 'Vellum Book', a manuscript register of the School under Lluellin's mastership, with occasional entries by later headmasters; and a printed copy of the admission entries in this register with notes and additions by the Rev. Henry Lawrance, M.A., reprinted from the *Yorkshire Archaeological Journal*, Vol. XXV.
9. Correspondence transcribed by Sir Robert Forsyth Scott from papers in the College Muniment Room and published in *The Eagle*, Vols. XIX and XXI.
10. 'Admissions to the College of St. John the Evangelist, Cambridge', Vols. 1-3 (1629/30 to 1767).
    Biographical Register of Gonville and Caius College (Venn).
    Admissions to Peterhouse College.
    Alumni Cantab:
    Athenae Cantab:
    Other University and College Registers.
11. *History of St. John's College*, Thomas Baker. (Ed. Mayor.)
12. Foster's *Yorkshire Pedigrees* (for history of Dowman family).
13. For Shield and Gruggen, letters in St. John's College Muniment Room.

APPENDIX B
SCHEDULE OF PROPERTY
As at 31 December, 1910

Description	Extent or Amount			Tenant, Person liable, or Persons in whose Name invested	Gross Yearly Income		
	A.	R.	P.		£	s.	d.
School site and buildings at Pocklington	10	0	0	In hand	—		
West Green Villa, Pocklington	0	2	0	Do.	—		
East Acklam Farm	199	1	12	Frederick Smith	157	3	0
Toft House Farm, Pocklington (of which a small portion is copyhold)	159	3	4	George Barnes	152	15	6
Greenland Farm, Barmby Moor	182	2	21	Executors of Josiah Richardson	207	3	6
Newland Farm, Barmby Moor	54	0	29				
Field House Farm, Barmby Moor	146	0	0	Elisha John Richardson	194	10	0
Barrow Flats, Pocklington	32	1	15	James Thirsk and Son	56	2	8
Land at Pocklington	8	0	16		11	0	0
Do. do.	6	1	4	Thomas Spruce Thirsk & David Thirsk	23	7	6
Do. do.	12	2	20	James Thompson	6	0	0
Land, Barmby Road, Pocklington	5	1	5	Robert Todd	1	16	8
Oxgang at Wetwang	4	1	0	Sir Tatton Sykes	0	11	3
Right of road, Barrow Flats	0	1	5	Pocklington Urban District Council			
	£	s.	d.				
Consols	154	11	4	The Official Trustees of Charitable Funds	3	17	0
Do. Investment Accounts under Orders of the Charity Commissioners of—							
28 May, 1895	115	4	0	do.	Accummulating		
18 March, 1898	153	7	8	do.	Do.		
10 Feb., 1891 and 18 Mar., 1898	587	8	0	do.	Do.		
20 Nov., 1891 and 18 Mar., 1898	200	1	5	do.	Do.		
				Total	£814	7	1

APPENDIX C

P. M. STEWART

The career of this master[1], whose teaching so contributed to the prestige of the School, was a signal instance of 'casting bread upon the waters', for it was Hutton who first taught him Hebrew at the age of twelve at Daventry, and the pupil repaid him later by helping to make his school at Pocklington famous for him. After a distinguished course at Cambridge, Stewart brought his learning to Pocklington at Hutton's request, and only resigned his post for the distinction of a lectureship at Trinity College, Cambridge. On returning to Pocklington for the sake of his wife's health he wrote three well-known travel books based on his extensive tours abroad, including the popular *Round the World with Rod and Rifle*. He also cultivated water-lilies on such a scale and in such variety that no finer display of the kind is known in Europe. An ardent sportsman, he delighted to teach boys fishing, and Old Boys may remember the days when he followed the hounds, and once appeared in class in hunting-pink under his gown, so as to be in time for 'the meet'.

His gifts to the School have been many and generous.

[1]See p. 74

APPENDIX D
THE GOVERNING BODY

The membership of the Governing Body, and the principal changes that took place in it between 1945 and 1980, are perhaps most conveniently shown in the following table. The changes revealed in the 1977 list were caused chiefly by the School's becoming independent, and also the recent changes in the local government boundaries.

1947

EX OFFICIO:
M.P. for the Constituency
Chairman of the East Riding Quarter Sessions

REPRESENTATIVES OF:
Archbishop of York (1)
St. John's College, Cambridge (2)
Leeds University (1)
Pocklington Rural District Council (1)
Pocklington Parish Council (2)
East Riding County Council (6)

CO-OPTED: (to include at least 1 Old Boy) 2

1957

EX OFFICIO:
M.P. for the Constituency
Lord Lieutenant of the East Riding of Yorkshire
Vicar of Pocklington

REPRESENTATIVES OF:
Archbishop of York (1)
St. John's College, Cambridge (2)
Leeds University (1)
Hull University (1)
East Riding County Council (7)
Pocklington Rural District Council (1)
Pocklington Parish Council (2)

CO-OPTED: (to include at least 1 Old Boy) 3

1977

EX OFFICIO:
M.P. for the Constituency
Lord Lieutenant of Humberside
Vicar of Pocklington

REPRESENTATIVES OF:
Archbishop of York (1)
St. John's College, Cambridge (2)
Leeds University (1)
Hull University (1)
York University (1)
Humberside County Council (2)
North Wolds District Council (1)
Pocklington Town Council (2)

CO-OPTED: (to include at least 2 Old Boys) 6

CHAIRMEN OF GOVERNORS
R. Teasdale — Retired
L. Sampson, J.P. — 1950
C.E. Anson, J.P. — 1953
W. Tweddle, O.B.E., T.D., Ll.M. — 1963
(Sir William) (Died 1982)

APPENDIX E
STAFF APPOINTMENTS

Name	Dates	University	Subject(s)
R.St.J.Pitts-Tucker	1945-1966	Clare College, Cambridge	Classics
J.P.Fogarty	1945-1946	University College, Cork	Classics
K.F.Ireland	1946(1 term)	Jesus College, Cambridge	History
C.W.Monk	1947-1955	Lincoln College, Oxford	History
D.G.Harwood	1947-1959	Magdalene College, Cambridge	Mathematics
J.L.Smith	1947-1948	Magdalen College, Oxford	Mathematics
A.F.Edwards	1948-1952	Sidney Sussex College, Cambridge	Mathematics
W.M.Ross	1948-1950	Balliol College, Oxford	Music
I.M.Farley-Hills (Miss)	1948-1951	Clapham & Streatham Hill Froebel College	Junior School
R.N.Heaton	1949-1951	Balliol College, Oxford	History
W.A.Simpson	1949-1952	St. John's College, Cambridge	English
J.W.Cook	1950-1953	Emmanuel College, Cambridge	Classics
R.R.Watt	1950-1979	Army	P.E.
G.N.Thornton	1951-1955	King's College, Cambridge	English/French
T.C.Walters	1951-1955	Fitzwilliam House, Cambridge	Biology
E.N.Butterworth (Miss)	1951-1954	Froebel Educational Institute, Roehampton	Junior School
M.L.Edwards (Mrs.)	1951-1952	Whitelands Training College	Junior School
P.R.Buckland	1952-1962	Emmanuel College, Cambridge	Mathematics
M.F.D.Cripps	1952-1955	Christ Church College, Oxford	History
A.M.Griffiths (Miss)	1952-1955	Froebel Educational Institute, Roehampton	Junior School
R.E.Brown	1953-1956	St. John's College, York	Art
M.C.Monk (Mrs.)	1953-1955	Lady Margaret Hall, Oxford	Junior School
A.T.Combridge	1953-1957	St. John's College, Cambridge	Classics
M.A.Moore (Miss)	1954-1956	Maria Grey Training College, London	Junior School
E.H.O.Martin	1955(1 term)	King's College, Cambridge	Biology
M.H.Charles (Miss)	1955-1957	Froebel Educational Institute, Roehampton	Junior School
S.S.Speight (Miss)	1955-1956	Maria Grey Training College, London	Junior School
M.O.Hickman	1955-1956	Gonville & Caius College, Cambridge	History
M.T.Ball	1955-1959	Queens' College, Cambridge	General Science
M.H.Stevenson	1955-1967	Christ's College, Cambridge	English
R.Potter	1956(1 term)	University of Melbourne	Classics
D.C.Bevis	1956-1958	West of England College of Art, Bristol	Art
R.M.Curtis	1956-1959	Bede College, Durham	Junior School
G.O.Gill	1956-1959	Hull University	Chemistry
R.D.Harris	1956-1961	Queens' College, Cambridge	History
T.J.G.Rogers	1956-1964	King's College, Cambridge	English

Name	Dates	University	Subjects(s)
F.A.S.Cottom	1956-	Durham University & R.C.O.	Music
I.J.Loney	1957-	St. John's College, York	Junior School
C.G.Prideaux	1957-1959	Selwyn College, Cambridge	Junior School
D.H.Wright	1957-1962	Oriel College, Oxford	Classics
J.N.Duckworth (Rev.)	1958-1961	Jesus College, Cambridge	Religious Studies
R.N.Billington	1958-1988	Regional College of Art, Manchester	Art
A.J.Maltby	1958-1968	St. John's College, Cambridge	History
J.H.Cox	1959-1972	Manchester University	Mathematics
T.G.Currey	1959-1972	St. John's College, Cambridge	Biology
D.Maccoll	1959-1961	London University	Mathematics
I.S.Spaul	1959-1960	St. John's College, York	Junior School
D.G.Whilesmith	1959-	The Queen's College, Oxford	Classics
S.Whitehouse	1959-1968	Brasenose College, Oxford	Chemistry
J.W.Maltby (Mrs.)	1959(1 term)		Junior School
A.Bridgewater	1960-1986	City of Leeds Training College and Open University	Mathematics
B.Crawshaw	1960-1969	Fitzwilliam House, Cambridge	Modern Languages
D.W.Norman	1960-1968	Trinity Hall, Cambridge	Physics
R.F.Kirk	1961-1965	St. John's College, Oxford	Classics/Religious Studies
A.Lee	1961-1964	Queens' College, Cambridge	History
J.M.Macnaughton (Rev.)	1961-1972	Sidney Sussex College, Cambridge	Religious Studies
J.W.Wood	1961-1962	Merton College, Oxford	Mathematics
D.J.Barnes	1962-1966	The Queen's College, Oxford	Classics
W.G.Beer	1962-1985	Hull University	Chemistry
T.K.Herring	1962-1971	Manchester University	Mathematics
A.R.Barnard (Rev.)	1962-1979	St. Catharine's College, Cambridge	Mathematics
D.Nuttall	1963-	St. Peter's College, Oxford	Modern Languages
T.W.Hardaker	1964-	Durham University	English
A.Midgley	1964-1968	Worcester College, Oxford	History
J.B.Birch	1965-1971	London University	English
E.J.M.Williams	1965-1971	St. Edmund Hall, Oxford	History
G.L.Willatt	1966-1980	St. Catharine's College, Cambridge	English/History
J.G.Fairclough	1966-1967	St. John's College, Oxford	Classics
S.J.Dodsworth	1966-1988	St. John's College, York	Music
G.H.Sumner	1967(1 term)	Nottingham University	Geography
M.D.Aubrey	1967-1971	Clare College, Cambridge	English
A.M.Baker	1967-	Worcester College, Oxford	Geography
R.T.Gilbert	1967-1968	Balliol College, Oxford	Classics
B.Norval	1968(1 term)	King's College, Cambridge	Classics
C.J.Solomon	1968-	Corpus Christi College, Oxford	History
D.V.Rumbelow	1968-	St. Edmund Hall, Oxford	History
G.B.Brown	1968-1972	Caius College, Cambridge	Modern Languages
K.Robinson	1968-	Leeds University	Physics
A.C.Tydeman	1968-1971	London University	Mathematics
D.I.Spivey	1969(2 terms)	Nottingham University	Chemistry
C.J.L.Davies	1969-1982	University College of Wales, Aberystwyth	Geography

Name	Dates	University	Subjects(s)
J.R.Jeffery	1969-1984	Southampton University	Design Centre
T.A.Riseborough	1969-1974	Keble College, Oxford	Modern Languages
D.J.Stanton	1969-	St. Andrews University	Chemistry
D.C.Ferrier	1969-1971	University of Sydney, Australia	English/History
P.C.Harris	1971(1 term)	Leicester University	English
G.N.Harvey (Rev.)	1971-1972	University of Western Australia	English
C.E.Martin	1971-1980	Selwyn College, Cambridge	English
I.A.Macdonald	1971-1977	Leeds University	English
M.E.Young	1971-1977	St. Edmund Hall, Oxford	History
M.G.Milne	1971-	City of Worcester Training College	Geography (Junior and Senior Schools)
G.A.Sutton	1971-	Selwyn College, Cambridge	Mathematics
P.R.Walwyn	1972-1973	King's College, Cambridge	Chemistry
R.J.Peel	1972-	Merton College, Oxford	Biology
P.S.Chambers	1972-	St. Catherine's College, Oxford	Modern Languages
M.W.Woodruff	1972-	Bede College, Durham	English
G.Scott (Rev.)	1972-1974	Manchester University	French/Religious Studies
T.A.Eadon	1973-1984	York University	Mathematics
D.J.Parsons	1973-	St. John's College, York	Physical Education
P.N.Hackney	1974-1980	University of Manchester Institute of Science and Technology	Chemistry
M.T.Jones	1974-1975	St. Catharine's College, Cambridge	Modern Languages
M.G.Smith (Rev.)	1974-1982	University College, Oxford	Religious Studies
P.M.Wright	1974-1980	St. John's College, York	Art
I.C.Brown	1974-1978	York University	Mathematics
J.W.Bratton	1975-1977	York University	Mathematics
S.J.Bosworth	1975-	Trinity College, Oxford	Modern Languages
M.Stones	1975-1981	Birmingham University	French
P.G.Highley	1976-	Lincoln College, Oxford	Classics
A.W.Ramsden	1976-	Birmingham University	Physics
S.M.Mullen	1977-1980	London University	History
R.Smith	1977-	Birmingham University	Mathematics
R.M.Jones	1977-1979	Durham University	English/French/Latin
P.R.Summersgill	1978-1984	Pembroke College, Oxford	Physics
K.J.Riley	1978-1981	University College of Wales, Aberystwyth	English
N.Owen	1978-1986	Newcastle University	Geography
P.V.Hampson	1978-1982	Bristol University	Mathematics
D.A.Stork	1979-1980	Queen's College, Cambridge	Modern Languages
P.S.Thornley	1979-1987	Trinity Hall, Cambridge	Mathematics
M.J.Butcher	1979-	Nottingham University	Biology
R.E.Blows	1979-1982	University College of Swansea	English
J.Walsh (Mrs.)	1979-1988	College of Ripon & York St. John	Junior School
J.C.Driver	1980-1984	Sheffield University	Chemistry
J.L.Peel	1980-	London University/Leeds University	Russian/History
I.M.Allison	1980-1984	St. John's College, Cambridge	English

Name	Dates	University	Subjects(s)
P. Edwards	1980-	Wolverhampton Polytechnic/ Royal College of Art	Ceramics & Design
A. Hughes (Mrs.)	1980-1988	Trinity College, Dublin	Junior School
E.C. de Corte	1980-1981	City & Guilds Woodwork/Metalwork	Design Centre